The Perturbed Self

By comparison of late nineteenth-century ghost stories between China and Britain, this monograph traces the entangled dynamics between ghost story writing, history-making, and the moulding of a gendered self.

Associated with times of anxiety, groups under marginalisation, and tensions with orthodox narratives, ghost stories from two distinguished literary traditions are explored through the writings and lives of four innovative writers of this period, namely Xuan Ding (宣鼎) and Wang Tao (王韜) in China and Vernon Lee and E. Nesbit in Britain. Through this cross-cultural investigation, the book illuminates how a gendered self is constructed in each culture and what cultural baggage and assets are brought into this construction. It also ventures to sketch a common poetics underlying a "literature of the anomaly" that can be both destabilising and constructive, subversive, and coercive.

This book will be welcomed by the Gothic studies community, as well as scholars working in the fields of women's writing, nineteenth-century British literature, and Chinese literature.

Mengxing Fu is a lecturer at Shanghai International Studies University, China. Her research interests include nineteenth-century British literature, comparative literature, fantasy, and women's writing. Her recent articles on ghost literature have appeared in *Neohelicon*, *Metacritic Journal for Comparative Studies and Theory*, etc.

Routledge Studies in Chinese Comparative Literature and Culture

Series Editors:
Daniel Fried, the University of Alberta, Canada and Yanyu Zeng, Hunan Normal University, China

Routledge Studies in Chinese Comparative Literature and Culture publishes monographs, edited volumes and small-scale reference works within the established field of Chinese and Comparative Literature. For a field dedicated to the study of China's engagement with the world's various literary systems, scholarship is still often misunderstood and mischaracterized outside of its context. This series therefore works to connect Sinophone and Anglophone scholarly communities around issues of China's global literary and cultural exchanges by fostering disciplinary debate between scholars based in China, and those based in the rest of the world.

The Perturbed Self
Gender and History in Late Nineteenth-Century Ghost Stories in China and Britain
Mengxing Fu

For a full list of titles in this series, visit https://www.routledge.com/Routledge-Studies-in-Chinese-Comparative-Literature-and-Culture/book-series/CCLC

The Perturbed Self

Gender and History in Late
Nineteenth-Century Ghost Stories
in China and Britain

Mengxing Fu

LONDON AND NEW YORK

First published 2022
by Routledge
2 Park Square, Milton Park, Abingdon, Oxon OX14 4RN

and by Routledge
605 Third Avenue, New York, NY 10158

Routledge is an imprint of the Taylor & Francis Group, an informa business

© 2022 Mengxing Fu

The right of Mengxing Fu to be identified as author of this work has been asserted by her in accordance with sections 77 and 78 of the Copyright, Designs and Patents Act 1988.

All rights reserved. No part of this book may be reprinted or reproduced or utilised in any form or by any electronic, mechanical, or other means, now known or hereafter invented, including photocopying and recording, or in any information storage or retrieval system, without permission in writing from the publishers.

Trademark notice: Product or corporate names may be trademarks or registered trademarks, and are used only for identification and explanation without intent to infringe.

British Library Cataloguing in Publication Data
A catalogue record for this book is available from the British Library

Library of Congress Cataloging in Publication Data
A catalog record for this book has been requested

ISBN: 978-1-032-03615-1 (hbk)
ISBN: 978-1-032-03617-5 (pbk)
ISBN: 978-1-003-18822-3 (ebk)

Typeset in Times New Roman
by Deanta Global Publishing Services, Chennai, India

For my parents, and Zhuangzhuang.

Contents

	Acknowledgements	viii
	List of abbreviations	ix
	Explanatory notes on romanisation and Chinese sources	x
1	Introduction	1
2	"Among dark woods and black fortresses": Xuan Ding's mythologisation of national history	25
3	"These are what Westerners refuse to believe": Wang Tao's uncanny history	50
4	Two ways to conjure up a ghost: Vernon Lee's history versus fiction	77
5	The dead woman returning: E. Nesbit's Female Gothic myth	104
	Conclusion	131
	References	138
	Index	149

Acknowledgements

The origin of this research dates back to my early twenties when I was doing a Master's thesis on Pu Songling and the Gothic at University College London, and numerous people had given me crucial help on this long, perilous, and fascinating ghost-seeking journey spanning London, Hong Kong, and Shanghai.

I have met with amazing mentors on my journey. My foremost gratitude goes to my PhD supervisor Professor Klaudia Lee at the City University of Hong Kong, without whose acute criticism and encouragement this current project would not have been possible. I also thank my first PhD supervisor Dr Colin Cavendish-Jones; his trust in me was indispensable in helping me start this project. I am indebted to Professor Susanne Kord at University College London and Professor Mingjian Zha at Shanghai International Studies University, my earliest mentors who planted the seed of a comparatist in me.

I would like to thank my friends Xianliang Dong and Wei Yi at the Department of Chinese and History, City University of Hong Kong who helped to ensure the accuracy and professionalism of my Chinese references; and my friend Zexi Zhang, who as a professional translator generously reviewed all my translations of Chinese texts.

I must thank the Routledge editorial team, especially Feichi Gao and Zixu Fan who patiently shepherded the book across its various stages. I am indebted to Professor Daniel Fried, general editor of this Routledge series for giving me invaluable advice on tailoring this book and its themes. An earlier version of Chapter 3 has been published on *Ming Qing Studies* 2017 and some parts of Chapter 4 have been developed from arguments in my article published on *Neohelicon* 47.2. I am grateful to the editors of these two journals for granting me permission to reuse these materials in the book. My special thanks go to Professor Paolo Santangelo, editor of *Ming Qing Studies*, for his inspiring comment on my earlier arguments on late-Qing *zhiguai*.

This project is funded by China Postdoctoral Science Foundation and the "Chenguang Programme" supported by Shanghai Education Development Foundation and Shanghai Municipal Education Commission and I thank the institutions for their support.

Finally, my deepest thanks go to my parents and my husband. Your trust, devotion, and constant emotional support are the greatest drives behind my research.

Abbreviations

The following abbreviations are used in this book. Full bibliographical information for these works can be found in the references.

The Classic	*Shanhai jing* 山海經 (*The Classic of Mountains and Seas*)
Liaozhai or *LZ*	Pu Songling, *Liaozhai zhiyi* 聊齋誌異 (*Strange Tales from a Chinese Studio*).
YYQD	Xuan Ding, *Yeyu qiudeng lu* 夜雨秋燈錄 (*Records of Rainy Nights under the Autumn Lamp*)
DKLY	Wang Tao, *Dunku lanyan* 遁窟讕言 (*Unverified Words from the Cave of Retreat*)
SYML	Wang Tao, *Songyin manlu* 淞隱漫錄 (*Random Words by the Song River*)
SBSH	Wang Tao, *Songbin suohua* 淞濱瑣話 (*Trivial Words by the Song River*)
Online SKQS	*Online Siku quanshu* (Wenyuange Edition) 文淵閣四庫全書電子版

Explanatory notes on romanisation and Chinese sources

The romanisation of Chinese names and titles in this book follows the *pinyin* system. However, if quoted materials use other romanisation systems, their romanisation is kept, with names of persons or titles rendered in *pinyin* in square brackets for disambiguation purposes.

If not otherwise indicated, all translations of Chinese texts are my own, reviewed by a professional translator. The titles of Chinese primary texts first appear in this order: the romanised title in *pinyin*, the original Chinese title, and the translated English title in parentheses. For Chinese ghost stories, after their first mention in the text, the translated English title (sometimes shortened) is used. Alternatively, if a Chinese text is commonly known in the English world with a certain title (for instance the *Analects*, *The Great Learning*, or *The Peony Pavilion*), the common title is used. For secondary sources in Chinese, their titles are romanised in *pinyin* in text and the full bibliographical information can be found in the references.

The Chinese *zhiguai* collections discussed in this book were mostly published originally in multiple thread-bound *juan* (卷), each containing a dozen or more stories. Their modern editions often combine these *juan* into a single or more volumes, retaining the original *juan* number and sequence for convenience of location. To disambiguate, the *zhiguai* stories are referred to by a volume number in their modern edition (if there is more than one volume), separated by a colon from their original *juan* number, then by a full point from the page number.

1 Introduction

> In times of peace, humans and ghosts live apart, but in times of chaos like ours, humans and ghosts live together. 太平之世，人鬼相分，今日之世，人鬼相雜.
> —Feng Menglong 馮夢龍 (1574–1646)[1]

In the Ming dynasty Chinese writer Feng Menglong's eerie ghost story "Yang Siwen Meets an Old Acquaintance in Yanshan", a former Northern Song official, Yang Siwen, is stranded in the now Jurchen capital Yanshan and encounters there amongst other traces of the past the most emblematic of the fallen Southern Song dynasty: a female revenant. The revenant turns out to be Lady Zheng, the wife of Yang's sworn brother Han Sihou, who had killed herself to preserve the honour of her husband when captured by a Jurchen marshal during the turmoil of the dynastic fall. If the revenant Lady Zheng haunting the ghost-plagued Yanshan serves as an embodiment of violent historical rupture, then her following reunion with her husband Han Sihou in Yanshan stages a reunion between a traumatic past and a guilt-laden present, whose longing for each other seems to be brought to a final fruition.

Yet, Feng's story offers no such romantic resolution, for the husband, now a Southern Song diplomat, soon breaks his promise to be loyal to the deceased wife when he returns to the south with the woman's ashes. Dumping the ashes to the Yangtze River, he marries a beautiful widow whose husband had also died in the trans-dynastic turmoil. Here the melancholic tone of the story turns suddenly macabre, when Lady Zheng's mourning poem for herself is heard sung by a boatman on the Yangtze River:

> With whom can I speak of the past?
> In silence, I shed tears of blood.
> When is the saddest moment of all?
> The hour when dusk sets in.
> I gaze from the tower and pace around.
> Who knows the pain in my heart?
> Would that I fly with the wild geese home
> While south of the Yangzi spring is in bloom!

DOI: 10.4324/9781003188223-1

往事與誰論？無語暗彈淚血。何處最堪憐？腸斷黃昏時節。倚樓凝望又徘徊，誰解此情切？何計可同歸雁，趁江南春色.[2]

The poem appeared earlier in the story to affirm to Han and Yang that memories of the past are not utterly gone, and that Lady Zheng has indeed come back as a revenant. But when Han's promise with the past is broken, the ghost's poem returns as an omen for the past's revenge on the forgetful present: acting out his own oath to be loyal to the deceased, Han and his new wife are devoured by the monstrous waves of the Yangtze River.

Thus, Feng's ghost story may be read on two levels: a romantic love triangle involving a man's betrayal of and brutality toward a woman, and a subtle critique of narratives of the past. What I want to highlight is how this story is exemplary of traditional Chinese ghost stories as it perfectly mixes a gendered narrative and a narrative of the past in the figure of the ghost woman: the ghost Lady Zheng's feminine virtue and chastity throw into relief the failed masculinity of her living husband who not only accepts national humiliation but also fails the promise to be loyal to the past. Doubly inscribed with historical trauma and personal suffering, the female ghost embodies the two underlying logics of Chinese ghost stories that I will expound in this book: that stories of ghosts are concerned with problems of narrating the past, and that the ghost's returning also opens up a space for problematising and reimagining gender identities.

A ghost bearing the symptom of problems with history and gender is also the central place of horror in Rudyard Kipling's most famous imperial ghost story "The Phantom Rickshaw" (1888). Similar to "Yang Siwen Meets an Old Acquaintance in Yanshan", Kipling's story involves a surface plot in which a womaniser who refuses to admit to his past is revenged by the phantom of the woman he has abandoned, but it also contains a subtext concerning the problems with colonial historical narratives in the very figure of the woman's phantom. Indeed, competing narratives of Britain's colonial presence in India are pitted against each other at the very beginning of the story. Much as the narrator may insist on the "great knowability" of India compared to England and how men overworked to death by imperial duties is commonplace there,[3] Pansay's own narrative of being haunted by the woman's rickshaw contradicts the doctor's rationalistic explanation of his disease. To be haunted by an abandoned lover is no strange story, yet what really robs Pansay of sanity and consequently masculinity is how the dead woman's rickshaw pulled by four Indian coolies could also come back to haunt, as he exclaims, "One may see ghosts of men and women, but surely never of coolies and carriages. The whole thing is absurd".[4] What is suggested here is that injustice done on a woman may have its ghostly retributions (a familiar trope of British as well as Chinese ghost stories, as I will discuss in later chapters), but to admit that the Indian servants can also return as phantoms is to admit that the indigenous also have their own history that clashes with Britain's imperial narrative of India.[5] As with the ghost of Lady Zheng in Feng's story, the subalterns—Mrs Wessington and her Indian coolies—return as ghosts to force the present's dominant narration of history to renegotiate its relationship with the past and the ghosted.

It is now time to draw a few conclusions from these two stories. What Feng's and Kipling's ghost stories show are not only a marked similarity in plot (revenge of the ghost lover) and thematisation (relation with the past, men's injustice on women), but also some general parameters of Chinese and British ghost stories that I will examine in the following pages. First, I argue that ghosts are signs of time out of joint, and narratives of ghosts are often about a troubled, unappeasable past. It is one of my theses in this book that in both China and Britain, ghost stories can be posited as a quasi-history or para-history, indeed, the silenced other of history: their persistent gesturing towards the past reveals a desire to rethink and rebuild the historical construction of the present, yet the illicit status of the ghosts—these stories' central concern—means that they will remain forever in a struggle for legitimacy vis-à-vis the narratives of the cultural mainstream.

Second, the crystallisation of the problem with the past in the figure of the ghost woman, in both stories (and in many others as well), also suggests the genre's special function as a gendered discourse. The liaison between women and ghosts is no coincidence; as I will show later, being a narrative of the anomaly, ghost stories are traditionally associated with subaltern groups—women, invisible coolies, politically disenfranchised men, etc.—and can be appropriated by these groups in their contestation for new social roles and more cultural visibility. Ghost stories' connection with socially marginalised groups also ties with a third dimension of this weird genre that I focalise in this book—narratives of ghosts as a literature of the anomaly. In this book I explore ghost stories as embedded in and speaking to their respective literary traditions—i.e., the *zhiguai* 志怪 (records of the strange) tradition in China and the Gothic tradition in Britain—but I also conceptualise this body of writing in both countries as a literature of the anomaly,[6] and it is, I hope, one of the book's contributions to world literary knowledges to explore how this narration of the anomaly can open up a discursive space where dominant cultural narratives can be either subverted or reinforced and new cultural identities negotiated.

From "Europe and its others" to world literary knowledges

I mentioned the term "world literary knowledges" a moment ago, and it is now time to make clear what I mean by this term and how I situate this cross-cultural study of ghost stories from two vastly different literary traditions in current scholarship on comparative and world literature.

Conceived in Europe in the context of the emerging nationalism of the nineteenth century, the notion and practice of comparative literature for a long time has been Eurocentric,[7] and even the emergence of postcolonial studies since the late twentieth century and the revival of interest in world literature in the recent two decades to a large extent perpetuate instead of supplant a model of world literature imagined as composing of "Europe and the rest of the world".[8] I still remember vividly the sense of estrangement I felt as a graduate student in a seminar of a comparative literature programme at University College London. The class was sufficiently international, with more than half the students coming from outside of the UK: the Netherlands, France, Spain, Greece, Japan, Saudi Arabia, India, and China, to mention just a few. On the day we presented our research projects I was more than a little surprised to hear that the French student was working on some writer in southern Africa, the Dutch student on some writer in Malaysia, and the Spanish student on some writer in Latin America. Just as I was marvelling at my fellow students' command of languages and cultural traditions so vastly distant and different from their own, it became clear that they were working on writers from their countries' former colonies who now wrote in the colonisers' language. Suddenly the classroom looked to me like a conference of colonial powers and I, being from China which had not been a coloniser nor ever totally colonised, found no place of entry in this configuration of comparative literature mapped closely upon European powers' world expansion in the last few centuries.

Much as the sense of estrangement I felt in that classroom should be attributed to a young woman's naivety and oversensitivity in a foreign country, it does betray some of the limitations of postcolonial frameworks in comparative literary study. If the former comparative study focusing exclusively on the *rapports de fait* between a few European languages and literary traditions (the so-called "French school" of comparative literature) is now rightly deemed parochial and ethnocentric,[9] the inclusion of former colonies in the expanded landscape of world literary study by no means does justice to the "world" in "world literature". As Revathi Krishnaswamy and others have noted, the "Europe and ..." models implied in postcolonialism "perpetuate neocolonial geopolitics in the form of linguistic fields such as Anglophone, Francophone, and so on" and posits Europe forever as the centre of reference.[10] Moreover, this model also leaves blind spots, for although colonialism had forcefully shaped the geopolitical landscapes of the world since Europe's world expansion in the fifteenth century, the literary world has not always corresponded to political circumstances and there are cultures and literary phenomena that predate or go beyond the conceptual framework of colonialism.

Interestingly, the revival of interest in world literature in the past two decades, with an implied intention to democratise and rejuvenate the often elitist and Eurocentric comparative literary study, sometimes implicitly perpetuates coloniality in the literary sphere. Franco Moretti's conjectures on world literary systems based on the example of the evolution and reception of the European novel across the world reads like a story of conquest of the European coloniser over the rest of the world (though he did mention local resistances and hybridities made thereof, counter-influence from the indigenous literature does not enter his picture) reincarnated in literary terms,[11] and Pascale Casanova's model of a "world republic of letters" recognises only one capital for world literature: Paris.[12] For Casanova, the rest of the world's literatures only entered the map of world literature with the emergence of post-coloniality in the late twentieth century, for although literary traditions such as those in China and Japan have been well established long before the seventeenth century, they existed not in fierce competition with other national literatures as European literatures did, hence their "late-comer" status in the world literary space.[13] If we see world literature as an economy of exchange, interaction, and assimilation, then the maps of world literature would invariably bear resemblance to Marx and Engels's conception of the term modelled on the conquering power of capital across the world,[14] placing Europe at the prestigious centre of everything that matters (as Casanova's and Moretti's models suggest). But such a sweeping map, as Graham Huggan notes, "privileges literary history over literary analysis", obliterating national literatures preceding capitalism and homogenising specific regional literary knowledges thereof to fit a set of "pre-determined 'facts'".[15]

An alternative way to veer away from the Western hegemony in comparative and world literature studies is to turn to comparative poetics, in which non-Western poetic traditions are drawn into the map of world literature to challenge the stereotype that only the West produces literary theories whereas other parts of the world provide literary raw materials for analysis. Many scholars from Asia, South America, Africa, and elsewhere have contributed to this cause and the valuable work they do broadens our understanding of literature and literary theory. Yet as Krishnaswamy notes, even this intentionally cosmopolitan approach may have its limitations. For one thing, studies that focus on the influence of non-Western literary traditions (Arabic, Indian, Chinese, for instance) on Europe may retain the "Europe and ..." model, while parallel studies that focus on historically unrelated literary traditions often risk taking an orientalist model that homogenises a non-Western or Eastern world opposed to the West.[16] Moreover, Krishnaswamy warns that such East–West comparative poetics tend to focus exclusively on non-Western literary traditions that are more systematic (for instance Sanskrit, Chinese) and can be said to possess a "literary theory", the result of which is to create a few new non-Western "greats" in the hall of fame of literary theory. To open the field of comparative poetics to more diverse forms of literary epistemologies, Krishnaswamy proposes that we move from comparative poetics towards "world literary knowledges", in which "regional, subaltern, and popular traditions, whether latent or emergent" may be evaluated cross-culturally as "epistemologies of literature/literariness".[17]

I share with Krishnaswamy the suspicion towards sweeping East–West studies that reproduce false or misleading images of East versus West and impede on a more humanistic understanding of the commensurability of literary traditions and human experiences of different regions and societies. I also agree with her on the importance of locating the concepts of literature as "historically and culturally situated knowledges".[18] This study is an exercise practising the cross-cultural study of literary knowledges envisioned by Krishnaswamy. As a committed comparatist, I am interested in the phenomenon of literature in historically specific human societies and how it functions in the power structures of those communities, so this study will not take broad historical views such as the influence of China over British literature or vice versa but will zoom in onto a body of anomalous writing that seems to be far removed from the centre of cultural power, yet forever gestures towards that centre: the ghost story. More specifically, I read the affinities between the Chinese *zhiguai* and the English ghost story in a particular historical and social setting—the ideologically unstable late nineteenth century—and see how they respond to a set of urgent questions (gender and history) of the time. By focusing on the interaction between ghost stories, marginalised groups, and dominant contemporary cultural discourses specific to each community, I hope to tease out the commensurability of regional literary knowledges, cultural specificities of those knowledges, and a possible shared terrain of the poetics of the spectral which have been appropriated by socially marginalised people as a discursive space contesting for more visibility and power.

Literary knowledges: Gothic, ghost story, *xiaoshuo* 小說, and *zhiguai*

After delineating what this study of Chinese and British ghost stories is not, and what it aims to do, it is time to briefly survey the respective literary knowledges of each country that I intend to engage with. They are the Gothic tradition, the recent theorisation of the British ghost story, the Chinese *xiaoshuo*, and its entangled relationship with the Chinese tales of the strange, the *zhiguai*.

If there is a British counterpart of the Chinese literary tradition of *zhiguai* that features narratives of the supernatural, then it is the Gothic tradition. Originating with eighteenth-century graveyard poetry and culminating with the late eighteenth-century Gothic romances epitomised by those of Ann Radcliffe (1764–1823), Horace Walpole (1717–97), and Mathew Lewis (1775–1818), the literary Gothic has undergone tremendous thematic and formal transformations in the nineteenth and twentieth centuries and boasted canonical works as disparate as Robert Louis Stevenson's *Dr Jekyll and Mr Hyde* (1886), Oscar Wilde's *The Picture of Dorian Gray* (1895), and Bram Stoker's *Dracula* (1895), as well as those highly popular ghost stories at the Victorian *fin-de-siècle*. The sheer impossibility of theorising the Gothic as a genre is one of the famous notorieties of this amorphous phenomenon, so much so that David Punter, whose scholarship on Gothic dates to the 1980s (*The Literature of Terror* 1980, 1996) when few scholars took Gothic seriously and who also compiled two companions to the Gothic in the twenty-first century, gives up answering the question "What is Gothic" in his introduction to the 2012 companion and instead approaches the topic from what Gothic speaks of: phantoms, crypts, spectres, the uncanny, and wounds.[19]

The terms that Punter chooses to explicate Gothic—Abraham and Torok's theorisation of the phantom and crypts as veiled secrets in the human psyche, Freud's uncanny as the return of the repressed, Derrida's evocation of hauntology through the spectre—indicate the influence of psychoanalysis and deconstruction on the field of Gothic studies,[20] and it is indeed owing to these theoretical perspectives that Gothic's obsessions with cultural taboos and transgressive desires and fears, with unsettling ghosts and buried pasts, with liminality and the undecidable, begin to be recognised as important culture discourses that engage with major problems of its time. I believe it is this potentially subversive drive of the Gothic, its ability to force out an expression of the cultural unsayables, that makes it such a fascinating trope that has not only appealed to writers from the eighteenth century until now but also fuels the scholarly interest in this phenomenon from the 1990s onwards.

The expansion and innovation of Gothic studies also fertilises another previously understudied genre, the ghost story. The short story has long been regarded as a less-privileged form compared with the novel and dealing with ghosts makes the ghost story even less respectable,[21] so that for a long time it has attracted little attention even while Gothic studies have grown exponentially. Jack Sullivan's *Elegant Nightmares: The English Ghost Story from Le Fanu to Blackwood* (1978) and Julia Briggs's *Night Visitors: The Rise and Fall of the English Ghost Story* (1977) are two earlier attempts to theorise the English ghost story as a genre. Both Briggs and Sullivan treat the ghost story as primarily a nineteenth-century phenomenon, inextricably intertwined with a sense of chaos and uncertainty engendered by the clash of scientific materialism and spiritual needs of the age. Briggs posits in her book a clear differentiation between the eighteenth-century Gothic novel and the nineteenth-century short ghost story,[22] stipulating the high tide of the genre as between 1850 and 1930, yet the aforementioned expansion of Gothic studies over the past few decades has made such a separation seem unadvisable. Indeed, Briggs later gives up the separation between Gothic and ghost stories and proposes that the latter "constitute a special category of the Gothic", for one constituting element of ghost stories is "the challenge they offer to the rational order and the observed laws of nature ... reintroducing what is perceived as fearful, alien, excluded, or dangerously marginal", which is also the domain of the Gothic.[23] In this study I approach the ghost story as a subgenre of the Gothic, and I follow Briggs's model in using the most familiar term, the ghost story, to designate the body of short stories dealing with the supernatural and the strange while acknowledging that like the Gothic, not all of these ghost stories have a ghost and not even all of them engage directly with the supernatural.

Another limitation of early studies of ghost stories is the lack of attention paid to women writers and women's voices in this genre.[24] This has been partly redressed in Andrew Smith's *The Ghost Story, 1840–1920: A Cultural History* (2010) which devotes one chapter to female-authored ghost stories and their focus on love, money, and history, issues poignantly related to women's vulnerability. Yet what is more fruitful a path of enquiry is when Female Gothic criticism—a subfield of Gothic studies that focuses on Gothic's affinity with female writers, women's experiences, and feminine expressions—meets the ghost story. Indeed, shadowed by canonical male writers of ghost stories—Le Fanu, Henry James, M. R. James, Kipling, Blackwood, and even Dickens to some extent—is a vast number of female writers, some of whom enjoyed high popularity in their own time: Elizabeth Gaskell (1810–65), Catherine Crowe (1803–76), Margarete Oliphant (1828–97), Amelia B. Edward (1831–92), Rhoda Broughton (1840–1920), Charlotte Riddell (1832–1905), and Vernon Lee (1856–1953), to name just a few. As Melissa Edmundson Makala in her pioneering book on Victorian women's ghost literature notes, though the exact gender ratio of Victorian ghost story writers is impossible to determine as many women chose to write under male pseudonyms, estimations are that at least half of the Victorian ghost stories are penned by women.[25] Women's tremendous investment in ghost stories is a fact acknowledged by many, yet the great unasked critical question ("why did women write so many ghost stories?") voiced in Michael Cox and R. A. Gilbert's preface to their ghost story anthology cannot be satisfactorily answered if we do not look into the inner dynamics of this genre and the experience of women as a marginalised group.[26]

Female Gothic offers a perspective focusing on that experience. First coined by Ellen Moers in 1978 to designate the unique branch of Gothic fiction penned by women,[27] the term proves versatile yet highly contentious. Moers's restrictive definition was soon challenged and revised by later critics to relocate the "female" in Female Gothic not in the author's gender but in the work's content, speaking voice, or gendered aesthetics.[28] What I am interested in here is not defining exactly what "Female Gothic" is but what the concept can offer us in terms of thinking about the relationship between Gothic and women, and more precisely in this study, between ghost stories and women. The distinctively gendered experience of Victorian women under patriarchy, their sense of invisibility, confinement, and exclusion—in short, their analogous position with the ephemeral ghost—is something that scholars of Female Gothic and ghost stories could not overlook. Victorian women's "ghosted" position is one of the focuses of Vanessa Dickerson's *Victorian Ghosts in the Noontide: Women Writers and the Supernatural* (1996), and her study also sheds light on how writing about the supernatural, especially the ghost, could provide the "ghosted" Victorian women a public discourse voicing their concerns. Similarly, Diana Wallace posits ghost stories by women writers as a mode of Female Gothic as it is most hospitable to expressions of women's fears of male sexuality.[29] If the lowly yet potentially liberating status of supernatural writing could provide women a freer space to voice their gendered fears and desires, Makala goes one step further in proposing women's supernatural writing as a type of "social supernatural", offering women writers a channel to voice not only critiques of gender inequality but of more general social issues of economics, class, and imperialism.[30]

So why are Victorian women writers particularly drawn to writing ghost stories and what can this affinity between women and ghosts tell us about the ghost story as a participating discourse in structures of power? Part of the answer lies in the power of the spectral metaphor for marginalised and ghosted groups. To designate certain groups as ghostly foregrounds their ephemerality and vulnerability in the social sphere, yet it can also endow them with power, for the ghost itself has an ambiguous relationship with power, possessing as Esther Peeren calls it, "a compromised agency".[31] Here, an example from Chinese culture may help further illuminate the dialectical role that illegitimate entities like ghosts play in relations of power. In a study on the cult of the fox as represented in traditional Chinese literature and folklore, historian Kang Xiaofei comments on how the liminal figure of the fox can empower those marginalised social groups usually associated with this demonic being, and her insight is also applicable to the fox's neighbour in the netherworld, the ghost:

Feared yet worshipped, the fox embodied popular perceptions of marginal groups, ranging from daughters and daughters-in-law in family life to courtesans, entertainers, spirit mediums, migrants, and outlaws in society at large. ... [W]ielding the power of the fox in everyday life involved a complex process of negotiating, safeguarding, and challenging well-established social and cultural boundaries in late imperial and modern Chinese society.[32]

The British may not have a lively fox cult or customs of ancestral worship as the ancient Chinese did, which rendered liminal entities like foxes and ghosts a tangible presence in daily life, but the numerous literary ghosts populating the Gothic can be as powerful an agent, for such stories are metaphorically related to those who are perceived or perceive themselves as having a ghostly existence. A metaphor is a powerful ideological tool, argues Peeren, for it hierarchises the social position of different groups of people.[33] Yet, to be figured as ghostly is not always a disadvantage for the marginalised, as Peeren also reminds us: "All metaphors thus possess a certain potential for semantic flexibility" and "[i]n theory, ... subjects designated as ghostly ... may also work with the metaphor, reshaping it to activate other, more empowering associations of the ghost in order to go from being overlooked to demanding attention by coming to haunt".[34] The Gothic mode so hospitable to ghosts (and especially ghosts that have been wronged, misunderstood, or forgotten) is thus a fertile ground where the ambiguous and sometimes paradoxical potentials of the ghost can be teased out to mobilise new social roles and subjectivities. The Victorian women who felt themselves ghostly can thus appropriate a "spectral agency" in the literary field just as their Chinese counterparts had wielded the power of the bewitching fox.[35]

The other part of the answer to the question, I contend, lies in the ghost stories' function as a type of "unofficial history" for the marginalised. Gothic, Punter suggests, is a literary mode antagonistic to realist aesthetics and is concerned with what is inadmissible and unsayable under the dominant social mores in a certain culture.[36] Furthermore, to Punter, the Gothic's revolt against the goal of representing the "real" as stipulated in realist aesthetics also makes it a mode of history or, more precisely, what he terms as a mode of "unofficial history"; it keeps in record the inexplicable, inadmissible, and even distortions of reality as a counterpart to realist fiction, which views the world and humanity as knowable, explicable, and representable.[37] Wallace further explicates the gendered dimension of this Gothic history. The "haunting idea" that women in the past had always been "a ghostly creature too shadowy to be even that real", as Wallace notes, had been used by generations of female historians, thinkers, and writers to make sense of their condition and express their indignation.[38] Thus, Wallace proposes seeing the Gothic as a mode of history by women and for women, for Gothic's narrative of spectrality "suggests the particular power of the Gothic to express the erasure of women in history, something which may not be expressible in other kinds of language or in the traditional forms of historiographic narratives".[39] Although Wallace's focus is Gothic forms of historical fiction, her suggestion that the Gothic as a mode of writing can be seen as a "history" for women is especially illuminating for understanding the dialectical relationship between the ghost story and history, even if not all ghost stories bear a recognisable resemblance to "histories". For one way of making a ghost is by erasing someone from memory, as "Yang Siwen", "The Phantom Rickshaw", and numerous other cases in Chinese folklore can testify: the lack of a memorial, in verbal or physical form (a tombstone, a monument, or a record in official history books) will inevitably turn the deceased into a ghost.

Ghost stories as narratives about ghosts, therefore, can be conceptualised as a quasi-history or an anti-history: in the macro-scope, the ghost story, just like the Gothic, expresses in dreamlike language what is considered taboo, dangerous, or inadmissible in a certain period, constituting an alternative form of writing history. In the micro-scope, each ghost story is about that which is restless in the past and returns to haunt the present, so that to tell the story of a ghost is an endeavour against that ordering and forgetting of the past which we call history. Writing the ghost story as a disruption of the official history, and more importantly as an alternative way to form women's own histories, gives women who were traditionally excluded from the position of history-writing a sense of empowerment, for history is about power: it is an important discourse for creating order out of chaos and establishing authoritative positions.

Ghost stories can be posited by marginalised groups as an unofficial history against the official history of the cultural mainstream, and it also opens a potential space for expressions of transgressive desires, identities, and experiences. However, the seemingly fixed knot between women, Gothic, and subversion, as some of the above studies suggest, needs to be qualified, tested, and challenged in a larger cultural context to really tease out the complex dynamics between ghost narratives and power. I argue that no genre of writing is naturally subversive, and the kind of discursive moves that can be manoeuvred within ghost narratives is the result of a complex matrix of gendered narratives, history-writing, and myth-making. This is where a study combining literary knowledges in different traditions can throw light on what a nationally bounded study shadows. The following survey of the literary knowledges from China, *xiaoshuo* and *zhiguai*, further highlights the tension between supernatural writing and cultural orthodoxy extant in narratives of ghosts, while at the same time complicating the simple equation that the supernatural disrupts the normative.

The Chinese *zhiguai*, a short story genre dedicated to "recording the strange" since its birth in the chaotic Six Dynasties period (third to sixth century CE),[40] had enjoyed continuous popularity among Chinese male literati class over a millennium. More importantly, *zhiguai* is not only an important mode of traditional Chinese fiction but also the very early specimen of it.[41] The underlying tension between Chinese fiction and the orthodox discourse ever since the former's inception provides an important backdrop for understanding the similar entanglement between *zhiguai* and its other in the orthodox discourse: the official history. Therefore, before an examination of the genre *zhiguai*, I would first explicate the concept *xiaoshuo*.

While the "fictive" nature of fiction is self-evident in the English word, it is a different matter for the Chinese *xiaoshuo*, the term now used as an equivalent for the English word fiction, for *xiaoshuo* in its origin had little to do with fictionality yet much to do with didacticism. Literally, *xiaoshuo* means "minor or small talks".⁴² The term first appeared in the philosophical text *Zhuangzi* 莊子 (c. third century BCE): "Those who dress up their small tales to obtain favour with the magistrates are far from being men of great understanding" 飾小說以幹縣令，其于大達亦遠矣.⁴³ Here, *xiaoshuo* appears in a polarised position against men of great understanding. Later, in a summative review of arts, the Han-dynasty historian Ban Gu 班固 (32–92 CE) explains the origin of *xiaoshuo* as the works of *baiguan* 稗官 (petty officials) who went along the streets and collected the talks of the common people, so that this trivial talk may occasionally serve as critiques or comments for the ruler and ministers.⁴⁴ The trivial and petty nature of *xiaoshuo* as a discourse was still extant, yet different from Zhuangzi's condemnation, *xiaoshuo* had already gained some validity, as the same text also cites the *Analects* to speak for *xiaoshuo*: "Even in inferior studies and employments there is something worth being looked at; but if it be attempted to carry them out to what is remote, there is a danger of their proving inapplicable. Therefore, the superior man does not practice them", 雖小道，必有可觀者焉；致遠恐泥，是以君子不為也.⁴⁵ Being thus fashioned as a petty official (*baiguan*), the *xiaoshuo* writer in the beginning was positioned against the superior man in the orthodox power centre. Assigned the job of collecting the trivial talks of the mass to serve the ruler, he was at once aware of the inherent didacticism in his task and its lowliness compared with the mission of the superior man.⁴⁶ Although the scene of petty officials collecting trivial street talks may be largely imaginary and what was collected was far from our modern understanding of *xiaoshuo* as fictional narratives, the close connection between *xiaoshuo* and *baiguan* was firmly established, and the two terms were sometimes used interchangeably.

When *baiguan* was used as a substitute for *xiaoshuo*, it was often compounded with another word: *yeshi* 野史, literally meaning "unofficial or wild histories" as opposed to the *zhengshi*, official or proper histories. The compound word *baiguan yeshi*, used to denote those texts that we would regard as fiction (or *xiaoshuo*) today, helps to elucidate the proximity of fiction and historiography in traditional thinking and the two basic tenets in the concept of traditional Chinese fiction: that it is meant to be didactic (in its status as minor persuasion by petty officials) and that it is supposed to be a kind of history, although an unofficial and unverifiable one. Conceptualised as such, *xiaoshuo* intrinsically exemplifies both a centripetal and a centrifugal force vis-à-vis the orthodox discourse in the power centre. On the one hand, it endeavours to be recognised by the orthodox as a useful minor discourse, while on the other hand, it is wild and riotous, an unofficial history likely to contradict and disrupt the coherence of the official history.

This understanding of *xiaoshuo*'s etymological proximity with petty officials and wild histories foregrounds two features of the Chinese *zhiguai*, its didacticism and historiographic feature, as the latter was not only the earliest specimen of *xiaoshuo* but also for a long time its representative. The time of *zhiguai*'s birth was a period of social instability and the subject matters of *zhiguai* are equally riotous—encounters with ghosts, metamorphosis of humans and beasts, carnivalesque sexual gratifications—all being matters famously shunned by Confucius.[47] The first *zhiguai* writers themselves are very often historians, and their borrowing from the techniques of historiography in this new genre and their investment in *zhiguai*'s ability to admonish and teach as history are conspicuous in many of their prefaces.[48] Scholars may differ regarding how *zhiguai* had evolved from existing genres,[49] but the genre's close relation with historiography is undisputed, and this affinity was only later severed when the Six Dynasties *zhiguai* works were removed from the *shi* (history) category in the traditional bibliographical system to the *xiaoshuo* category after the Tang dynasty.[50] However, given the conceptualisation of the nature of Chinese *xiaoshuo*, it is little surprise that some later *zhiguai* works still maintain a trace of historiography and a lingering desire to relocate themselves within the Confucian discourse, however unseemly and unorthodox their subject matter may be.

Another dimension in understating *zhiguai* as a dissenting as well as conforming discourse vis-à-vis the cultural orthodoxy is to look at the identity of its makers. Written in the classical (instead of vernacular) Chinese modelled on the style of historiography, *zhiguai* since its inception is a genre of the male literati class and highly relevant to literati identity-building. The Six Dynasties *zhiguai* writers came from the displaced literati class who lived in an age of great political instability when their cultural centrality was challenged. In a sense, the jostling of competing worldviews (the Confucian moral system, Buddhist karmic retribution, Taoist marvels) in *zhiguai* at this period was the perturbed literati's way of wrestling in a world where order had collapsed. The Tang dynasty (618–907 CE) *chuanqi* by the newly emerging educated bureaucratic class developed the pithy records of strange into elaborately plotted tales of supernatural romance, and were often used to manifest their authors' literary talents before their superiors or as products of literati group creation.[51] The socialising and identity-affirmation functions of conversing about the supernatural were still extant in the Qing dynasty (another high point for this genre),[52] as manifested in *zhiguai* collections of Ji Yun 紀昀 (1724–1805) and Wang Shizhen 王世禎 (1634–1711). At the same time, another important function—to reinvent for oneself in the literary world the identity of the historian only accorded to those who have entered the centre of power—was introduced by the Qing dynasty writer Pu Songling 蒲松齡 (1640–1715) in his *Liaozhai zhiyi* 聊齋誌異 (Strange Tales from A Chinese Studio, prefaced 1715)[53] and later imitated by many. Unlike Ji Yun and Wang Shizhen who had been government officials and imperial degree-holders, Pu was at the very margin of the elite literati class, as he never entered officialdom and was only an "elite" for his education's sake. For such a marginalised literatus, to write in the *zhiguai* genre symbolically manifests the author's literati identity: re-appropriating the petty official of minor talks into the "historian of ghosts", Pu could do in the world of anomalies what only the Confucian ideal, the *shi* (士) class could do—regulating the world out of chaos. In Pu's work, the two dimensions of *zhiguai* as a regulating as well as an identity-building discourse are intertwined: it offers a space for recording and controlling the anomalies so that order can be established upon them, and it is precisely through this process that the endangered literati identity and masculinity can be adjusted, reaffirmed, and reconstructed.

Throughout its history, *zhiguai* was a genre for and by the male literati class and crucial to their cultural identity to various degrees. The subject matter of *zhiguai*, anomalies that have been regulated outside of the orthodox Confucian order of things, creates a dynamic zone where the narration and reinterpretation of the supernatural provide new models of knowing and being. Sing-chen Lydia Chiang remarks that "the *zhiguai* is the discourse of the others".[54] Yet, at the same time it is also a discourse of the (male literati) self, helping to establish the self through imagining and controlling the other. Chiang also points out the double function of the anomaly for *zhiguai* writers: "the act of recording an anomaly accords it reality, significance, and power. Furthermore, to write about anomalies is not only to empower them but also to harness their potency".[55] This understanding of narrating the anomaly bears directly on the insight we gain from Female Gothic criticism, previously reviewed: if to write about the supernatural provides for Victorian women—themselves "ghosts in the noontide", to use Dickerson's phrase—a discursive field to express their vulnerability and social critique that may otherwise be viewed as transgressive, then *zhiguai*'s dialectical relation with the cultural orthodoxy reminds us that the potency of the anomaly is not reserved for women only but also applicable to males who feel themselves marginalised. Moreover, the female ghost is also a favourite figure of the Chinese literati writers. Yet, if the female ghost in British women's Gothic writing figures women's cultural invisibility and a precarious agency of power, it has a more complex relationship with the cultural orthodoxy and *zhiguai* writers. For the ghost is the quintessential anomaly under Confucian discourse, coming back only when something goes wrong. Being the abjected other of the Confucian norm, the ghost's appearance both critiques the validity of the orthodox and is a production of it, negatively defining what the norm is or could be. Thus, the narration of female ghosts by male authors complicates the possible equation between ghost narratives and liberation for women.

If we look at the ghost in Chinese *zhiguai* over the centuries, its increasing domestication, eroticisation, and romanticisation chart the whole range of the Chinese literati's imagination of the opposite sex and of the self. The ghosts in the Six Dynasties *zhiguai* often appear as a sign of warning or some heinous devil that needs a Taoist priest or Buddhist monk to exorcise so that some religious teaching can be elicited from the tales.[56] The malignancy of literary ghosts is considerably subdued in the Tang *chuanqi*, which often adds a romantic dimension to the encounters between human males and alien females. The Ming-dynasty dramatist Tang Xianzu's 湯顯祖 (1550–1616) masterpiece *The Peony Pavilion* 牡丹亭 (variously titled "The Return of the Soul" 還魂記, 1598) crystallises the quintessential "amorous ghost"—a young woman who pines away for love and is resurrected through a man's love.[57] Woman, otherworldly beauty, death, and sex constitute the formula. For advocates of the so-called "cult of *qing*" in the late Ming and the early Qing dynasties, *qing*, or more narrowly love, is the fundamental regulating moral principle in the universe and a death-defying force, of which the loving female revenant is the perfect embodiment.[58] The body of the female revenant, veiled with the extra allure of death, offers male connoisseurs of literature not only erotic pleasure but also a model for ideal authentic subjectivity.[59] The female ghost, the quintessential anomaly placed at the opposite of the human male, thus encompasses the whole range of the male desires and fears: she can be the abjected other regulated out of the Confucian norm, the desired other as an object of love or worship, or a transcendental other figuring an ideal self. Likewise, narrations of ghosts and other transgressive entities not only offer the marginalised male literati a discursive space to reconstruct their cultural identity and renegotiate their position with the official history, but itself is a gendered discourse where the regulating boundaries between men and women, self and the other, norm and the anomaly may be either challenged, redrawn, or reinforced.

The above examination of Gothic and *zhiguai* show prominent commensurability between these two traditions of the supernatural; more importantly, the intersection of gender, anomaly, and cultural marginality in this body of writing also shows that similar discourses may have different positionality with one another in different social contexts. It is from this difference that I hope to extract, in the book's study of ghost stories by Chinese and British writers written in the *fin-de-siècle*, a tentative sketch of a common poetics of spectrality that has certain ideological functions for the marginalised group (be they male or female). That this can be done is based on two premises of this book: first, both Gothic ghost stories and *zhiguai* deal with the anomaly—represented by the ghost—and a narration of the anomaly opens discursive space for formulating the norm; second, the book's particular focus, the chaotic late nineteenth century in Britain and China, offers an appropriate window for examining the various ideological forces at play in the alchemic ghost narratives. As Feng Menglong's ghost woman succinctly reveals, times of chaos call for ghosts, for it is in unstable times that established social narratives such as gender and history can be challenged and remoulded.

The late Victorian and the late Qing: chaotic times, furious ghosts

The late nineteenth century is a critical transitional period for Britain and China as both countries witnessed something of a "crisis of faith" of opposing natures: in Britain, the decline of religious faith beginning with the Enlightenment was further exacerbated by Darwinism, which in turn spurred a revival of supernaturalism; while in China, as a consequence of repeated defeats by Western powers in wars since the mid-nineteenth century, there arose among scholarly elites increasing doubts about the superiority of Chinese culture and a questioning of the orthodox state ideology. The *fin-de-siècle* in both countries was permeated with a sense of crisis, as established concepts ranging from the cosmic order, unity of history to notions of gender and the self all underwent re-examination. In this ideological uncertainty, the ghost, an oxymoron and something intrinsically hostile to categorisation, serves as the figure that best captures the anxieties of the time. The ghost becomes, as Dickerson notes, "one of the 'signs of the times', a marker of social, historical, and philosophical positionality, an emblem of 'the perplexed scene where we stand'".[60] Consequently, narratives about ghosts in this transitional period also served as a way to negotiate with the perplexed self in the forging, as Andrew Smith remarks that "[d]uring the nineteenth century the ghost story became *the* form in which conventional cultural assumptions about identity politics were challenged".[61] An important dimension of the perplexity that perturbed the self was the contestation of masculinity and femininity which, as I will show, was a direct consequence of the ideological turbulence in each society.

If one of the consequences of the nineteenth-century crisis of faith was the revived interest in assorted occultism that made the Victorian age a notable haunted age, the other was the continuous debate regarding women's roles in the home and society and more crucially, notions of femininity. Moreover, these two ideological shifts are often intertwined. The spiritual uncertainty of the age contributed to the popularisation of supernaturalism, evidenced first by phrenology, then mesmerism, and finally during the late nineteenth century by the advent of spiritualism in which female mediums figured prominently and earned precariously through the ghost a position of authority.[62] Thomas Carlyle's (1795–1881) repudiation of William Holman Hunt's (1827–1910) painting *The Light of the World* (1851–53) probably best encapsulates how a questioning of God was intertwined with the questionable status of male supremacy, and consequently the indignation against women's oppression. What infuriated Carlyle was Hunt's Christ figure, to him apparently "false" for it was modelled on two women: Christina Rossetti (1830–94) and Elizabeth Siddal (1829–62).[63] Ironically, just as Carlyle feared, the Victorians were increasingly feeling that the "Man-God" may be false, and that women may have been wronged. If the icon of the ideal woman in the Victorian age was Coventry Patmore's "angel in the house", the century had also witnessed increasing resistance to that image, manifesting in a series of debates on women's nature coordinated under the "Woman Question" and agitations for women's rights: the Lunacy Law Act Reform Association was founded in 1873 aiming at revising the legal mechanism that allowed husbands to put deviant wives away in asylums,[64] the Married Women's Property Act in 1882 recognised women's legal independence within marriage,[65] and the Contagious Disease Acts which endorsed apparent double standards for men and women, were repealed in 1886.[66] All these social reforms culminated in the suffrage movement in the 1890s and the unsettling *fin-de-siècle* anomaly: the New Woman.

Accompanying all these agitations for women's rights in various social fields was the urgent issue of redefining femininity, and in this instance the burgeoning ghost story had much to offer. The experience of one spiritualist, Louisa Lowe, who was also the founder of the Lunacy Law Reform Association, showcases how the expression of women's repressed indignation and patriarchal regulations of deviancy are closely connected with the liberating yet dangerous act of speaking through the ghost. As a spiritualist medium, Mrs Lowe recorded in her "passive writing" her conversation with the Holy Spirit about her husband's strange behaviours at night:[67]

16   *Introduction*

> Father, Father of mercies, I am weary of life, weary of the spirits' lies. ... Let me die. My poor weary child, the spirits have not all lied, thy husband was on the roof in and out of the chimney half the night ... Father, Thou saidst Satan helped him to slip in and out like an eel. Who my friend and comforter, doubled him up like an opera hat; but how can a great big six-feet man get in and out a chimney like this? My child, no one doubled him up; he unbuilt the upper part of the chimney, and built it up again.[68]

For a modern reader, the latent sexual undertone clearly reveals her dormant anger at her husband's suspected adultery, yet for her contemporaries and especially her clerical husband, the provocative language was only a sure sign of her insanity, which soon legitimated her husband to put her in an asylum.[69] If the spiritualist medium's role is to converse with the ghost and utter through the ghost what is inexpressible, the situation of female writers of ghost stories is not so different, for they too conversed with literary ghosts and brought to light through the ghost what was otherwise inexpressible. As Owen remarks, "utterance was central to the business of mediumship", and "giving voice to the unutterable" was thus the valuable gift that the ghost bestows on both types of mediums.[70]

Analogous to the Victorian crisis of religion and ideological instabilities, late nineteenth-century China also witnessed a crisis of faith of another nature: the declining of a Sino-centric worldview and the ensuing masculinity anxiety.[71] A very important aspect of the Chinese worldview had been based on the faith in the centrality of Chinese culture in the world,[72] anchored deeply in the millennia-long centre–periphery dichotomy underpinning Chinese perceptions of the self and the other. Historically, the superiority of Chinese culture had been challenged during dynastic transitions when the Han Chinese empire was conquered by what were perceived as alien peoples, yet to the Han people in the new regime, the subsequent acculturation of the alien rulers could at least conversely testify to the superiority of Chinese culture. However, the Qing government's total defeat in the two Opium Wars (1839–42, 1856–60) at the hands of Britain and the subsequent forced opening-up of treaty ports for the first time put that cultural confidence into question. Apart from Western military intrusions, the decade-long war of the Taiping Rebellion (1850–64) dealt another blow to the already declining Qing dynasty.[73] The war devastated the country's wealthiest Jiangnan area, leaving a generation of Chinese people in trauma and, more importantly, arousing alarming doubts regarding the legitimacy of the current Qing rule among the intellectuals.[74]

Such alarming cultural and national crises generated a great anxiety over Chinese masculinity among the literati class. In many cultures nationhood and manhood have been correlated, as the analogy between a nation and a male-dominated household mutually legitimises and defines the function of the ruler in each case.[75] For the Chinese male literati, however, the orthodox Confucian ideology provided a role model closely measured on man's relationship with his nation, composed of hierarchised life goals starting from "cultivating one's person" (修身), "regulating one's family" (齊家), to "ordering well one's state" (治國), and finally "keeping the whole kingdom tranquil" (平天下).[76] Such syncretisation of nationhood and manhood leaves male literati desperately impotent to rescue both in times of war and dynastic fall.[77]

What aggravated these intertwined national and masculinity crises was the Chinese literati's fear of feminisation in front of Westerners, something unprecedented in Chinese history. In a gendered imagination of nationhood, the confrontation of nations in war is envisioned as a clash of genders, resulting in the feminisation of the defeated side. Wang Tao 王韜 (1828–97), one of the late Qing *zhiguai* writers I study in this book, records an anecdote of such an encounter in his travelogue. While he was working with James Legge translating Chinese classics in Scotland, one day a group of local children in the street pointed at him and called him a "Chinese lady", probably misled by his scholar's long robe, a not-so-masculine attire in Western eyes.[78] Wang records the incident in a light manner, yet immediately his tone turns self-pitying:

> The identities [of the female rabbit and the male rabbit] are all in irresolution.[79] Sailing alone across wide oceans and sojourning in this foreign land, I could not fly like a true male and have to couch like a female. Now listening to the children's talk, [I wonder] isn't it a prophecy of my destiny?
> 撲朔迷離，隻身滄波，托足異國，不為雄飛，甘為雌伏，聽此童言，詎非終身之讖語哉?[80]

Wang indeed had much to lament for himself: setting out as an ambitious Confucian scholar to "rectify the world", he was not only excluded from officialdom but moreover turned into a political exile stranded in an alien land far away from home.[81] Yet what is significant here is that all these frustrations boil down to an eminent masculinity anxiety, and, worse still for Wang, a fear of emasculation when being looked at as the "other" and having his body misinterpreted by Westerners.

Wang's experience in Scotland was unique in that he was among the first few late-Qing Chinese who had been abroad and looked back at Chinese culture from an outsider's perspective.[82] However, his experience did play out the repressed fear of feminisation in many Chinese male literati. This was the time when the Chinese male literati were forced to reconsider their identity, reorient their relationship to their country and adjust themselves to the changing demands of masculinity. In reaction, many turned to *zhiguai* writing, which traditionally had served as a means of alternative identity-building and for the time being, provided the space needed to reconstruct their besieged masculinity and imagine a gendered encounter between China and the West revalorised through mythical motifs.

Organisation of the book: strategies and trajectories

The ideological uncertainties in both Britain and China in the late nineteenth century had engendered tremendous anxieties and perturbation over notions of gender, and those who felt an urgent need to redefine or revalorise their gender identity—the marginalised literati class in China and women writers in Britain—had turned to the versatile ghost story. The following chapters focus on four representative ghost story writers of this period: Chinese writers Xuan Ding 宣鼎 (1832–80?) and Wang Tao and British writers Vernon Lee (1856–1935) and E. Nesbit (1858–1924). These writers are representative in that they all engaged closely with the radical social changes of their time and participated in the negotiation between the past and the present, the self and the other, and between tradition and modernity through their literary creation of a "ghost's history".[83] Wang and Xuan were typical of the first generation of Chinese intellectuals caught between tradition and new challenges: the Taiping Rebellion had a decisive impact on their life path, and both writers acutely felt the shock of encountering the West in their sojourn in and around Shanghai. Although they champion their inheritance of the tradition of "history of ghosts" started by Pu Songling, as I will show in the following chapters, this homage marks simultaneously an interest in and a scepticism toward Chinese history and tradition. The British writers, on the other hand, were women who actively lived outside of contemporary restrictive notions of women's roles. Apart from her career in fiction writing, Vernon Lee was the author of more than forty books and numerous essays traversing art history, philosophy, aesthetics, and travel writing—a female public intellectual perhaps would better fit her own understanding of her identity. E. Nesbit, apart from being a successful writer of children's literature, was one of the founding members of the socialist Fabian Society and an advocate for social reforms. Whatever their positioning in the various political debates on the issue of the New Woman that characterised late nineteenth-century Britain, their lives and especially their ghost story writing already formed a part of the history that made for a new understanding of femininity and sexual differences.

Although each of the chapters takes one writer as its primary focus, I treat them not as closed case studies but each as expressing one voice in an ongoing conversation about the malleable relationship between ghosts and pressing gender discourses. I locate two overarching strategies for negotiating with gender identities that run through the writers' works: a re-evaluation of the construction of (personal or collective) history and an appropriation of popular myths. By tracing the variations of these strategies across the chapters, I draw out the invisible trajectories of history-writing and myth-making traversed by the ghost stories of different writers, opening up each writer's treatment of the ghost for response, challenge, and refutation from other writers.

As mentioned before, both types of ghost stories in China and Britain can be posited as a type of unofficial history for the marginalised groups: in China, ghost stories were used by the marginalised literati as a "history of ghosts" to reaffirm or challenge the history of the state, while in Britain the women writers appropriated the fantastic space of ghost stories to reinstate women's distinctive voice and experience into a private history of their own. To narrate an alternative history, to challenge the official history, to re-inscribe the self into history and finally to reimagine new gender roles through that narration—these are the common drives that underline all four writers' ghost stories. Yet, at the same time some prominent patterns emerge. As I demonstrated above, gender identity perhaps is more conspicuously associated with national history in the Chinese case; thus, the late-Qing literati turned to *zhiguai* to reimagine a dynastic history in which their endangered masculinity can find new meaning or get reaffirmation. The late-Qing reformist thinker Wang Tao was one such writer. Chapter 3 examines Wang's *zhiguai* writing in which Wang persistently invokes groups of people antithetical to orthodox state history. The encounter with these spectres of history makes possible a critique and subsequently a departure from official state history in which China is always perceived as the centre of the world and the dynastic transformation is always justified. These reconsiderations of Chinese history bring forth a model of masculinity that is more open to the outside world and is therefore for Wang a more suitable type for facing the imminent challenges from the West.

However, in this negotiation of masculinity and national identity through ghost stories, the male writer is constantly imagining a feminine other, against which his own masculinity is reaffirmed and through which his own words can be spoken. Just as women are excluded from the position of historians, the female ghost, too, is excluded from the position of making her own voice heard in this, supposedly "her true history as a ghost". Positioned diagonally against male literati's appropriating of the female ghost's story as "hi(s)story", Chapter 4 looks at Vernon Lee's dismantling of this type of history-making through her ghost stories about men writing the ghosts' history. Lee's own experience in contesting for a voice of the female historian informs her ghost story writing, in which men's construction and manipulation of the image of women is taken to task. The male historian in Lee's stories is presented as a counterpart of the perturbed male literati in China: with a desire to revitalise his endangered masculinity, he wills out the female ghost to help substantiate his own version of history. The validity and supposed objectivity of man-made history is thus exposed as a gendered fiction. Freed from the yoke of historiographic authority, the female ghost can finally make her presence felt through haunting a space just between history and fancy.

Until now I have conceptualised ghost stories as a kind of quasi-history. Here I propose that in its active appropriation of existing mythic patterns and soliciting power from them, the ghost story can be conceptualised as a kind of mythopoeia—an artistic remaking of narrative patterns whose cultural veracity is already pertaining to myth. And by myth, I mean not only stories concerning a sacred past or cosmic origin, but more broadly the underlying patterns of some basic narrative plots which over time have solidified into a self-fulfilling fiction, exerting a considerable ideological force in the cultural field they are active. As a highly conventionalised genre, ghost stories abound with such camouflaged mythical narratives, as it is a melting pot of recurring plots, symbols, and archetypal figures, themselves the legacy of a long literary tradition and bearing the imprints of the dominant ideologies of the time.

The ghost story writers in the following chapters write with a consciousness of their literary legacy, and they constantly recycle and remould a set of plots already pertaining to mythic status: the cultural hero who sacrifices himself for his community and is resurrected as a god (especially in Xuan's stories), the perilous amorous encounter between a human male and a spectral female (a plot common to all four writers), the ghost lover returning from the dead (in Lee and Nesbit), and the popular Victorian myth of the fallen woman (Nesbit). More specifically, Chapter 2 (on Xuan) and Chapter 5 (on Nesbit) can be read as variations of a similar mythic drive, creating different national and gender identities for their author. Faced with the imminent danger of a dynastic collapse, Xuan Ding, like Wang Tao, returns to Chinese history in his *zhiguai* stories. But instead of questioning the validity of historical narratives, Xuan turns to those who should have been glorified by national history; moreover, he immortalises his historical figures into mythic gods. This mythology about the integrity, nobility, and patriotism of various cultural heroes becomes a literary pantheon in which the contemporary perturbed literatus can not only reunite with his heroes and spiritual fathers, but in their presence he also regains his standing vis-à-vis a threatening other: the intruding Westerners.

In contrast to Xuan's myth of the cultural hero which charts the man's ascent from death to immortality, Nesbit focuses on the popular Victorian myth of the fallen and dead woman: the transgressive woman falls to death, expurgated of her sins by death, and is resurrected by her male lover as a passive goddess. Twisting and reverting the familiar cautionary tale about model womanhood into a macabre Gothic nightmare, Nesbit not only exposes the hypocrisy embedded in the original patriarchal myth but also envisions new possibilities for women. Through manipulating old myths in her fragmentary histories of women, Nesbit's tales serve as a mythography, yet in creating new myths for women, they are also a lively mythopoeia.

While history and myth are the two major strategies I examine in the writers' reconstruction of gender identities, they certainly are not an exhaustive inventory of what the ghost story can do, nor does my discussion of the strategies used by specific authors cover the whole dimension of each author's work. History and myth are important analytical perspectives through which to consider the ghost literature's potential as a destabilising as well as constructive discourse, since to write stories of ghosts as (national or private) history or myth indicates the author's attitudes toward the relationship between the past and the present, and between the self and the alterity that is the ghost. While this introduction begins with the warning that "times of chaos call for ghosts", ultimately, through the following journey over various narratives of ghosts, I wish to arrive at the point where it is clear why our time needs ghosts, too.

Notes

1 Feng, "Yang Siwen yanshan feng guren" 楊思溫燕山逢故人, in *Yushi mingyan* 喻世明言 (Wise Words to Enlighten the World, [c.1621] 1994), 252. The translation is my own. Unless otherwise indicated, all translations of Chinese texts in this book are mine.
2 Feng, "Yang Siwen", 250. The translation is from Feng, *Stories Old and New: A Ming Dynasty Collection* (2000), trans. Shuhui Yang and Yunqin Yang, 447–8.
3 Kipling, "The Phantom 'Rickshaw", *The Phantom Rickshaw and Other Tales* (1888), 7. https://archive.org/details/phantomrickshawo00kiplrich.

4 Kipling, "The Phantom", 17.
5 While Simon Hay in *A History of the Modern British Ghost Story* (2011) argues that this type of imperial ghost story insists that "[T]he history that matters", "even in colonized lands, is white history" (131), I contend that the appearance of the phantoms of the abandoned woman together with her indigenous servants indicate that indigenous history could haunt and meddle with white men's affairs, which is much more unnerving than simply a woman ghost returning to revenge a personal grievance. To rephrase Hay's own explication of the power matrix in imperial ghost stories as "gendered otherness standing in for racial otherness" (145), I suggest that in Kipling's as well as the late-Qing Chinese ghost stories to be examined in this book, gendered otherness and racial otherness mutually reinforce each other through the figure of the female ghost.
6 A concern with the anomaly is a defining feature of the Chinese *zhiguai*, which has been denominated by scholars as accounts of anomaly; see Robert Ford Campany, *Strange Writing: Anomaly Accounts in Early Medieval China* (1996) and Sing-chen Lydia Chiang, *Collecting the Self: Body and Identity in Strange Tale Collections of Late Imperial China* (2005).
7 The well-known history of comparative literature's nineteenth-century inception and practice in Europe is too long to rehearse here. On comparative literature's early history, see David Damrosch, Natalie Melas, and Mbongiseni Buthelezi ed., *The Princeton Sourcebook in Comparative Literature* (2009), Part 1; see also Haun Saussy, "Exquisite Cadavers Stitched from Fresh Nightmares: of Memes, Hives and Selfish Genes" (2006), in Saussy ed., *Comparative Literature in an Age of Globalization*, 3–42 for a synthesis.
8 On recent debate on world literature, see David Damrosch ed., *World Literature in Theory* (2014). On a critique of the notions of world literature as proposed by Damrosch, Moretti, and Casanova, see Graham Huggan, "The Trouble with World Literature", in Ali Behdad and Dominic Thomas eds., *A Companion to Comparative Literature* (2011), 490–506.
9 See Susan Basnett, *Comparative Literature: A Critical Inquiry*, Chapters 1–2 for an account of the "French school" and "American school" of comparative literary studies.
10 Revathi Krishnaswamy, "Towards World Literary Knowledges", *Comparative Literature*, 62.2 (2010): 402. See also Rey Chow's critique of the "Europe and Its Others" model in comparative literary studies, "The Old/New Question of Comparison in Literary Studies: A Post-European Perspective", *ELH* 71.2 (2004): 289–311.
11 Moretti, "'Conjectures on World Literature' (2000) and 'More Conjectures' (2003)", in David Damrosch ed., *World Literature in Theory* (2014), 159–79.
12 Casanova, *The World Republic of Letters* (2004).
13 Casanova, "Literature as a World", *New Left Review* 31 Jan Feb (2005): 71–90. Casanova's closely Europe-based model for the conceptualisation of world literature has been criticised. See for instance Aamir F. Mufti, "Orientalism and the Institution of World Literatures" that challenges Casanova's "Europe and the rest" model; Alexander Beecroft, "World Literature without a Hyphen: Towards a Typology of Literary Systems" that proposes six models of world literature systems opposed to Casanova's single model based on European literatures since the seventeenth century, and Karen Thornber, "Rethinking the World in World Literature: East Asian and Literary Contact Nebulae" in *World Literature in Theory* (2014), 460–79, David Damrosch ed.
14 Marx and Engels, *The Communist Manifesto* (2019), 41.
15 Huggan, "Trouble with World Literature", 496.
16 Krishnaswamy, "World Literary Knowledges", 407.
17 Krishnaswamy, "World Literary Knowledges", 408.
18 Krishnaswamy, "World Literary Knowledges", 408.
19 Punter, "The Ghost of a History", in Punter ed., *A New Companion to the Gothic* (2012), 2–3; see also Punter ed., *A Companion to the Gothic* (2000).

22 Introduction

20 Peter Buse and Andrew Scott's edited anthology *Ghosts: Deconstruction, Psychoanalysis, History* (1999) offers a synthesis of the intersection of the three.
21 The very marginality of the short story in British literature has been re-appraised by many scholars as an important feature of the genre that lends to its freedom to transgression. See for instance, Emma Young and James Bailey, Introduction, *British Women Short Story Writers: The New Woman to Now* (2015) for a review of the three "waves" of short story criticism.
22 Briggs, *Night Visitors*, 13.
23 Briggs, "The Ghost Story", in Punter ed., *A New Companion to the Gothic*, 177, 176.
24 Sullivan's study highlights only three ghost story masters: Sheridan Le Fanu, M. R. James, and Algernon Blackwood, while Briggs's monograph, though much broader in scope, focuses predominantly on traditional male masters of the genre and discusses only one female writer, Vernon Lee.
25 Makala, *Women's Ghost Literature in Nineteenth Century Britain* (2013), 14.
26 Cox and Gilbert, Introduction, *The Oxford Book of Victorian Ghost Stories* (1991), xiv.
27 Moers, "Female Gothic", in Fred Botting and Dale Townshend eds., *Gothic*.
28 See respectively, Alison Milbank, *Daughters of the House: Modes of Gothic in Victorian Fiction* (1992), Susanne Becker, *Gothic Forms of Feminine Fiction* (1999), Ann Williams, *Art of Darkness: A Poetics of Gothic* (1995). For a review on Female Gothic criticism, see Diana Wallace and Andrew Smith, "Introduction: Defining the Female Gothic" in Wallace and Smith eds., *The Female Gothic: New Directions* (2009).
29 Wallace, "Uncanny Stories: Ghost Story as Female Gothic", *Gothic Studies* 6.1 (2004): 57–68.
30 Makala, *Women's Ghost Literature*, 7.
31 Peeren, *The Spectral Metaphor: Living Ghosts and the Agency of Invisibility* (2014), 3.
32 Kang, *The Cult of the Fox: Power, Gender, and Popular Religion in Late Imperial and Modern China* (2006), 7. Fox and ghost are almost synonyms in Chinese folklore and *zhiguai* writing, as the variant title of *Liaozhai zhiyi—Stories of Ghosts and Foxes*—indicates.
33 Peeren, *The Spectral Metaphor*, 5.
34 Peeren, *The Spectral Metaphor*, 7–8.
35 I borrow the word "spectral agency" from Peeren. See Peeren, *The Spectral Metaphor*, 16–24.
36 On the Gothic mode as anti-realism, see Punter, *Literature of Terror* (1996), vol. 2, 183–5; Simon Hay also contends that the ghost story can be conceptualised as the shadow of the realist novel; see Hay, *A History*, especially Chapter 2.
37 Punter, *Literature of Terror* (1996), vol. 2, 185–8.
38 Wallace, *Female Gothic Histories: Gender, History and the Gothic* (2013), 2. See also Wallace, "Uncanny Stories".
39 Wallace, *Female Gothic Histories*, 2.
40 *Zhiguai* literally means records of the strange. A similar type of story is called *chuanqi*傳奇, "tales of the marvellous", which has more elaborate plots. On the evolution from *zhiguai* to *chuanqi*, see Lu Xun, *Zhongguo xiaoshuo shilüe* (1973), especially Chapter 8. Some scholars maintain that *chuanqi* and *zhiguai* have different origins. See Jianguo Li, "Tang bai sikao lu" (1998), Xiaoyong Zhan, *Qingdai zhiguai chuanqi xiaoshuoji yanjiu* (2003), 10–19, for a differentiation of the two. The hair-splitting differentiation between *zhiguai* and *chuanqi* is not particularly germane to this study, which takes a semantic angle instead of a formal one. I discuss both types of stories and for the sake of convenience would refer to them solely as *zhiguai*, as the term captures an important dimension of the genre: the fascination with the strange. Whatever contention there may be about their separate origins, it is indisputable that both types share similar narrative subjects: things of the supernatural. The Qing-dynasty writers often included both types of stories in a single collection, an indication that writers of such stories did not bother to make the differentiation.

41 Kenneth J. Dewoskin sees the Six Dynasties *zhiguai* as marking the birth of Chinese fiction. See Dewoskin, "The Six Dynasties Chih-Kuai [*zhiguai*] and the Birth of Fiction", in Andrew Plaks ed., *Chinese Narrative: Critical and Theoretical Essays* (1977), 21–2.
42 Tak-hung Leo Chan in *Discourse on Foxes and Ghosts* (1998) renders *xiaoshuo* into "inconsequential conversations" or "minor persuasions" (7) to illustrate the didactic nature of this Chinese concept.
43 Zhuangzi, "Waiwu, or What comes from Without", in Legge trans., *Sacred Books of China: The Texts of Taoism* (1962), vol. 2, 134.
44 Ban Gu's original text is 小說家者流，蓋出於稗官。街談巷語，道聽途說者之所造也，quoted from Lu Xun, *Zhongguo xiaoshuo*, 8.
45 *Confucian Analects*, Book XIX ("Zizhang"), Chapter IV, in Legge translation, *Confucius: Confucian Analects, The Great Learning & The Doctrine of the Mean* ([1893] 1971), 340–1.
46 It is mainly in this line that Tak-hung Leo Chan argues that *xiaoshuo*, or "minor persuasion" in his rendering, is didactic in nature (*Discourse*, 7). Although later *xiaoshuo* had evolved fully from historiography to fiction, its didacticism was still persistent and invariably influenced the motives of the *zhiguai* writer.
47 Confucius's famous reticence on ghosts is recorded in the *Analects*: "子不語怪力亂神"— "The subjects on which the Master did not talk, were: extraordinary things, feats of strength, disorder, and spiritual beings" (Legge trans. *Confucian Analects*, 201).
48 See Tak-hung Leo Chan, *Discourse*, 7–8.
49 On the origin of *zhiguai*, see Dewoskin, "Six Dynasties Chih-Kuai"; Robert Ford Campany, *Strange Writing*, 162–4; Chiang, *Collecting the Self*, 13–15. Dewoskin and Campany mainly differ as to whether the earliest writers created this genre with a self-awareness of its fictionality (Dewoskin) or regarded it as factual (Campany).
50 See Lu Xun, *Zhongguo xiaoshuo*, 4.
51 On the socialising function of the Tang dynasty *chuanqi*, see Zongwei Li, *Tangren chuanqi* (1985), 134–7, 50.
52 Tak-hung Leo Chan, *Discourse*, 28–9.
53 Hereafter referred to as *Liaozhai*.
54 Chiang, *Collecting the Self*, 16.
55 Chiang, *Collecting the Self*, 12.
56 See Muzhou Pu, "The Culture of the Ghost in the Six Dynasties Period" and Yuan-ju Liu "Allegorical Narrative in Six Dynasties Anomaly Tales: Ghost Sightings and Afterlife Vengeance", in Muzhou Pu ed., *Rethinking Ghosts in World Religions* (2009).
57 The term "amorous ghost" is borrowed from Anthony Yu, "'Rest, Rest, Perturbed Spirit': Ghosts in the Traditional Chinese Prose Fiction", *Harvard Journal of Asiatic Studies* 47.2 (1987): 423. In his article Yu offers a discussion of the amorous ghost figure in Chinese fiction throughout history. Plots may vary, yet the ghost is almost always female.
58 On the "cult of *qing*", or "cult of love", see Paolo Santangelo, "The Cult of Love in Some Texts of Ming and Qing Literature", *West and East* 50.1/4 Dec (2000): 439–99; Martin W. Huang, "Sentiments of Desire: Thoughts on the Cult of Qing in Ming-Qing Literature" *Chinese Literature: Essays, Articles, Reviews* 20 Dec (1998): 153–84. In the context of this so-called cult, *qing* is a multifarious concept that at times can mean emotion, love, desire, or even lust. More on the cult of *qing* in Chapter 2.
59 On authenticity as an expression of the ideal self gendered as female, see Maram Epstein, *Competing Discourses: Orthodoxy, Authenticity, and Engendered Meanings in Late Imperial Chinese Fiction* (2001), 303–6.
60 Dickerson, *Victorian Ghosts*, 13.
61 Smith, *The Ghost Story*, 4.
62 See Dickerson, *Victorian Ghosts*, 17–21 and Janet Oppenheim, *The Other World: Spiritualism and Psychical Research in England, 1850–1914* (1985), 207–17. On Spiritualism and women's role in it, see Alex Owen, *The Darkened Room Women, Power and Spiritualism in Late Victorian England* (1989).

24 *Introduction*

63 See A. N. Wilson, *The Victorians* (2003), 159.
64 Owen, *The Darkened Room*, 196.
65 Owen, *The Darkened Room*, 3.
66 On the Act and the struggle for its repeal, see Wilson, *The Victorians*, 308–11.
67 "Passive writing" is a technique through which spiritualist mediums sought communication with ghosts. In these practices, the medium tried to achieve a state of mental void which was regarded as a prerequisite for the reception of spiritual instruction, before she wrote down whatever involuntarily came into her mind (Owen, 205).
68 Quoted in Owen, *The Darkened Room*, 186.
69 Mrs Lowe was committed to an asylum in 1870 by her husband, released in 1872 after much appeal to medical and legal authorities and afterwards she became an activist in the Lunacy Reform movement. On the implications of Louisa Lowe's story, see Owen, *The Darkened Room*, Chapter 7, 168–201.
70 Owen, *The Darkened Room*, 213.
71 On the late-Qing crisis, see Fairbank and Liu eds., *The Cambridge History of China: Late Qing 1800–1910* (1985), translated by Guangjing Liu, vol. 10.
72 On the Sino-centred world order *tixanxia* (All under heaven), see John King Fairbank, "A Preliminary Framework", in *The Chinese World Order: Traditional China's Foreign Relations* (1968), 1–19, Fairbank ed., and a reconceptualisation of *tianxia* in Ban Wang, "Introduction", *Chinese Visions of World Order, Tianxia, Culture and World Politics* (2017), 1–22, Ban Wang ed.
73 The Taiping Rebellion started in 1850 and swept many southern provinces, finally taking Nanjing as its headquarters from 1853 to 1864. The war ranks as one of the bloodiest wars in human history, with an estimated figure of war deaths ranging from twenty to thirty million. See Xiaobing Li, "Taiping Rebellion (1850–64)" in *China at War: An Encyclopaedia* (2012).
74 See Hao Chang, *Chinese Intellectuals in Crisis: Search for Order and Meaning (1890–1911)* (1988), translated by Like Gao and Yue Wang, 6–10.
75 On nationhood and masculinity, see Todd W. Reeser, *Masculinities in Theory: An Introduction* (2010), 171–99.
76 See Legge, *Confucius*, 57.
77 On the equation of nationhood and manhood in China, see Martin W. Huang, *Negotiating Masculinities in Late Imperial China* (2006), especially Chapter 4; Xueping Zhong, *Masculinity Besieged: Issues of Modernity and Male Subjectivity in Chinese Literature of the Late Twentieth Century* (2000).
78 Wang, *Manyou suilu* 漫遊隨錄 (Casual Records of My Travels [1890] 1982), 144.
79 Here the phrase Wang uses is derived from two lines of verse about the difficulty of telling a male from a female: "[when holding them by the ear] the male rabbit kicks his hind legs while the female rabbit squints her eyes; yet when the male and the female are walking together on the ground, how can one tell who's the male and who's the female?" (雄兔腳撲朔, 雌兔眼迷離; 雙兔傍地走, 安能辨我是雄雌?)
80 Wang, *Manyou suilu*, 144.
81 Before his journey to Europe upon Legge's invitation, Wang was forced to escape to Hong Kong with the help of his British missionary friends in Shanghai for his alleged involvement in the Taiping Rebellion. More on this incident in Chapter 3.
82 A famous late-Qing reform advocate, Wang was among the first generation of traditionally educated Chinese intellectuals who encountered and absorbed Western learning in treaty ports like Shanghai. They were what Paul Cohen calls the "treaty-port intellectuals" in *Between Tradition and Modernity: Wang T'ao and Reform in Late Ch'ing China* (1974).
83 "Modernity" for me is a plural concept because it is fundamentally determined by a culture's perception of its own tradition, and the Chinese concept of modernity in the late Qing was vastly different from the British one. As I will show in the following chapters, it is closely related with recognising the West as a referential "other".

2 "Among dark woods and black fortresses"
Xuan Ding's mythologisation of national history

The seventeenth-century *zhiguai* writer Pu Songling makes a touching yet ghostly call for comradeship at the end of his highly personal preface to *Liaozhai*: "Aren't those who know me among dark woods and black fortresses!" 知我者, 其在青林黑塞間乎![1] The phrase "among dark woods and black fortresses" is derived from a line of a Tang-dynasty poem expressing the foreboding of a dear friend's death.[2] The dear friend's disembodied soul, travelling across dark woods and black fortresses to meet the poet in his dream, seems to be an omen of the friend's death. Therefore, as Judith Zeitlin notes, while Pu makes the call for friendship among his potential readers at the end of the preface, he is also bitterly aware that the truly knowing friend might only be found among ghosts.[3] The popularity of *Liaozhai* during the Qing dynasty led many admirers, sincerely or not, to respond positively to Pu's call for comradeship in the prefaces of their own *zhiguai* collections. Both Xuan Ding and Wang Tao, the two late-Qing *zhiguai* writers who were singled out by Lu Xun in his pioneering *Zhongguo xiaoshuo shilüe* (A Brief History of Chinese Fiction) as "pure imitators of *Liaozhai*",[4] made overt or implicit references to *Liaozhai* in their *zhiguai* prefaces. Were they truly identifying themselves as Pu's followers, himself now a dead soul "among dark woods and black fortresses", or were there other ghosts that they were responding to? The two late-Qing writers were faced with a totally changed world where phenomena stranger than the *Liaozhai* were becoming an everyday reality, and a mere endorsement of Pu's heritage—a voluntarism[5] embodied by the transcendental ghost—proved insufficient to help the contemporary men cope with their current crises. Therefore, while ghost stories continued to offer the late-Qing literati a space for alternative identity-building, new strategies were invented in this old genre to make sense and take control of the strangeness of the day.

An optimistic belief in the centrality of human will underlies the voluntaristic cosmos created in Pu's *Liaozhai*, yet such a reassuring cosmic order was visibly under attack by Xuan's time when unprecedented disasters like the Taiping Rebellion made human will seem ignorable and cosmic order arbitrary. But *Liaozhai* did provide the besieged late-Qing literatus an important spiritual resource—the writing of *zhiguai* as a process of self-mythification and identity-affirmation, which was the strategy that Xuan borrows from *Liaozhai* to develop new literary myths in his *zhiguai* stories. Departing from the ideal ghosts in Pu's voluntaristic cosmos,

DOI: 10.4324/9781003188223-2

Xuan's ghost stories, as I will show below, excavate a legion of neglected heroes from Chinese national history and elevate them from the pathetic status of ghosts to a literary pantheon of patriotic fatherly gods. This literary god-making not only renders national history into a mythical history, in which the contemporary man can unite with and gain power from his spiritual ancestors and cultural heroes, but also endows him with a mythical identity. Moreover, the mythologisation of national history is not simply a nostalgia for the splendid past, as it serves a practical purpose for the besieged late-Qing writer in his contemporary confrontation with threatening Westerners: it reinstates him at the advantageous central position vis-à-vis the Western other and offers him a familiar rhetoric to domesticate the strange with the conventional male–female encounter plot, at the end of which the Chinese man could reaffirm his masculinity and triumph over the aliens.

The great tradition: *Liaozhai zhiyi* and the cult of *qing*

As a homage to Pu's *Liaozhai* and a close engagement with the *zhiguai* tradition underlie both Xuan Ding's and Wang Tao's ghost stories and inform their appropriation of history, it is important to understand first what the heritage of *Liaozhai* is for its late-Qing followers. As an early-Qing *zhiguai* collection, *Liaozhai* distinguishes itself conspicuously from many other Qing-dynasty *zhiguai* in its celebration of the strong and subjective *qing*, or emotions, forming part of a continuum from the late-Ming "cult of *qing*" and its highly idealised and romanticised portrayal of the ghost figure.[6] Further, the emphasis on individual freedom and subjectivity in the cult of *qing* also informs how Pu fashions his *zhiguai* writing and establishes his own identity through it. In *Liaozhai*, Pu exalts the *zhiguai* genre as a serious art form for creating the author's ideal self and an alternative, better world, which differs greatly from other contemporary *zhiguai* writers who often take a dismissive attitude to the genre in their own prefaces.[7] This emphasis on literature's creative power, as mentioned above, is also the spiritual resource of *Liaozhai* that Xuan's and Wang's works to various degrees inherit.

Since the cult of *qing* stands at the thematic centre of *Liaozhai*, it merits a brief explanation to forward my following discussion of the voluntaristic cosmos crystallising in the ghost figure—the most important heritage of *Liaozhai*. While the philosophical discussions surrounding *xing* (inborn nature) and *qing* (emotion) can date back to the earliest Confucian texts,[8] two prominent late-Ming writers, the fiction writer Feng Menglong and the dramatist Tang Xianzu (1550–1616) are the direct influences of Pu and they each preach one facet of *qing* that Pu imbues in his ghost stories.

The "cult of *qing*" partly got its name from Feng. In his preface to the voluminous anthology *Qingshi* 情史 (History of Love),[9] Feng elevates *qing* into a cosmic force that bears the very secret of the universe:

> If heaven and earth do not have *qing*, nothing can be generated. Everything lacking in *qing*, is unable to initiate anything. Life forever renews life, for

qing is a force never dying. ... I will establish the "cult of *qing*", to educate everyone in the world.

天地若無情， 不生一切物,一切物無情， 不能環相生， 生生而不滅，由情不滅故, ... 我欲立情教,教誨諸眾生.[10]

Feng puns on the word "*jiao*", which can mean both a "cult" and a "cult-ivation". As the centre of this mysterious cult, *qing* is the fundamental cosmic power that regenerates everything in the world.[11] Yet Feng also envisages *qing* as pertaining to the cultivation of all kinds of model human relationships, encompassing not only the bond between lovers but also between father and son and emperor and his subjects. In other words, *qing* is foundational to the very structure of a hierarchical society.

While Feng still contemplates *qing* as totally compatible with the existing social establishments, Tang goes further to make *qing* the antithesis of *li* (reason). In the preface to his play *The Peony Pavilion* (1598), Tang preaches on *qing*:

We know not whence *qing* begins, but it goes deep once it begins. *Qing* can kill what is alive and relive what is dead. If it cannot make one willing to die, or to resurrect what is dead, then it is not supreme *qing*. Why would *qing* in a dream be considered not true *qing*?

情不知所起，一往而深. 生者可以死，死可以生. 生而不可與死，死而不可複生者，皆非情之至也. 夢中之情，何必非真.[12]

and he concludes with a serious claim: "What must not exist in reason, must exist in *qing*!" 第雲理之所必無，安知情之所必有邪![13] *Qing* for Tang becomes a force that defies reason, thus opening up to the world of the fantastic. *The Peony Pavilion* is representative of the literary trend in the wake of the cult of *qing* in many ways and in a sense its loving heroine capable of transcending death foreshadows the remarkable female ghost in *Liaozhai* who often towers over her less resolute male partners.

Liaozhai not only partakes of the valorisation of *qing* as a transcendental force guiding human relationships, life and death, and even cosmic regeneration; moreover, in extending *qing* into the fantastic world of ghosts and foxes, it makes new contributions to the cult of *qing* through its various supernatural characters. The fantastic world for Pu is the privileged world that opens to people with abundant *qing*, and the eroticised and idealised female ghost becomes the apotheosis of desire and the perfect crystallisation of *qing*.[14] Furthering Tang's antithesis of *qing* and reason, Pu exalts the remarkable female ghost sometimes to a heroic figure brave and resourceful enough to go against normality—variously showcased in Pu's stories as the rule of life and death, social rituals, or conventional moral proprieties.[15] Many of Pu's stories deal with strong *qing* that can motivate lovers to brave death, as in "Liancheng" 連城 (1:3.363) and "Liansuo" 連瑣 (1:3.331); while in stories like "Lianxiang" 蓮香 (1:2.220) and "Zhang A-duan" 章阿端 (2:5.627), the female fox's or ghost's love for her human lover is so profound that she either willingly induces her own death or evades the cycle of reincarnation to continue the romance. All these are manifestations of Tang's claim that "If it cannot make one willing to die, or to resurrect what is dead, then it is not supreme *qing*".

But at the same time *Liaozhai* is also an heir of Feng's strand of *qing*, in which *qing* is imagined as a moral force governing both human relations and the cosmos and the vital connection between the two, thus the ultimate regulating force in the universe.[16] Apart from the amorous female ghost representing *qing* going against reason, *Liaozhai* also presents a group of ghosts who have suffered injustice, continue fighting corruption even in the underworld, and are finally able to restore justice. In this sense, ghosts become the agent of justice, the witness of a higher providence even when the corruption in the human world and the underworld may contemporarily obscure it. If in the Confucian patrilineal patriarchal ideology, the ghost exists as a symptom of something having gone wrong,[17] this subaltern status also gives the ghost a subversive power to make trouble in the human world and the world beyond. In this sense, the appearance of ghosts is a sign of hidden injustice but can also work as a catalyst for the restoration of justice. "Kao Chenghuang" 考城隍 (The Examination of City God, 1:1.1), the very first story of the nearly 500 stories in *Liaozhai*, relates how a frustrated yet upright scholar passes the underworld examination to become a City God, which brings home Pu's conviction in a ghostly justice.[18] The scholar writes in the examination his understanding of morality as "doing good deeds with external purposes, even good deeds will not be rewarded; doing evil deeds without deliberate intention, even evil deeds will not be punished" (有心為善，雖善不賞；無心為惡，雖惡不罰1:1.1), which pleases the examining gods and wins the scholar the position of City God. The story reveals how much Pu invests in human intention: it is at the centre of his moral system and plays a decisive role in retribution. This and other stories about ghostly justice actually share a similar spirit with Pu's stories of the amorous ghost: in the latter, the ghost is the crystallisation of supreme *qing* which can go against reason, while in the former, the ghost is the crystallisation of justice which may go against social establishments. In both cases, the ghost is the condensation of intense human will that can have an impact on cosmic order.

The various manifestations of *qing* in *Liaozhai* imply a correlative cosmology in which a correspondence is believed to exist between human wills and actions and the cosmic order.[19] It is a voluntaristic worldview where human beings reside at the centre and human will is perceived as the essential force behind every action in the cosmos. Moreover, Pu's distinct innovation of the cult of *qing* is to elevate ghosts to the centre of this voluntaristic cosmos: the resolute and loving ghost woman embodies the radical *qing*, therefore is not only a site of eroticised femininity but also the icon of an ideal male self;[20] the unrelenting revenging ghost, on the other hand, embodies the agent of justice and expresses the possibility of a morally comprehensible cosmos where human intention profoundly determines man's relation with the world.

The late Qing period under investigation in this study in many ways resembled the late Ming which cultivated the cult of *qing*; both were times of upheaval when the social and political orders were seriously threatened by alien military intrusions. Could Pu's cult of *qing* and his alternative fantastic land peopled by foxes and ghosts still help to reaffirm an otherwise besieged sense of self for the late-Qing literati? The next section will show how the old cosmos is severely under attack in Xuan's stories, where a bleaker view of the world replaces the confident voluntarism and the traditional "centre–periphery" framework underlining perceptions of China's position in the world risks collapsing. Following Pu's steps, both Xuan and Wang turned to ghosts—their true friends "among dark woods and black fortresses"—to cope with the imminent challenges to their masculinity and national identity, yet while Xuan turns his focus from the erotic female ghosts to those neglected father ghosts, Wang's historical ghosts, as I will discuss in the next chapter, are caught in a world of multi-layered realities, some of which are evidently informed by a materialistic view borrowed from the West while some are still anchored in the fantastic world of *zhiguai*.

A collapsing heaven

A glance of Xuan's preface to his *Yeyu qiudeng lu* (Records of Rainy Nights under Autumn Lights, 1877),[21] which is a touching quasi-autobiography,[22] shows that Xuan was at least similar to Pu in two important aspects. Both had lived a typical "frustrated scholar's" life, though Xuan's circumstances were aggravated by the unique phenomena of his age, the Taiping Rebellion and Western intrusion in China, and both rely heavily on the strategy of self-mythification in their fashioning of themselves as *zhiguai* writers.

Born in 1832 into a wealthy family in the Jiangnan town Tianchang (now in Anhui Province), Xuan received a traditional scholar's education before his life took a downturn at the age of twenty, when his foster father's death left the family in financial crisis. In the 1850s, the Taiping Rebellion swept the whole Jiangnan area, smashing the local economy and causing great civilian casualties, shattering any hope for Xuan to continue the traditional scholar's path into officialdom. For around ten years he lived in destitution, sometimes fighting the Taiping troops in the Qing army and sometimes making a meagre living by selling his paintings in Shanghai. From his thirties, he served as secretary to several local magistrates in Shandong and Jiangsu provinces for another wandering ten years. Xuan's own preface to *YYQD* gives a dramatic account of how he turned into a writer: when he was standing upon the ruins of a pavilion dedicated to the poet Du Fu 杜甫 and looking at Confucius's hometown Qufu in the distance, he suddenly realised that it was his fortieth birthday and immediately fell ill (*YY* 1:13). The evocation of Du Fu and Confucius—both names reminding one of the traditional scholar's duty to serve one's country—in contrast to Xuan's own frustrating life must have been an agonising blow to him and proved to be the epiphanic moment in the creation of a writer. Fifteen days after falling ill, Xuan suddenly rose from his bed to write *zhiguai* stories and gradually healed himself through writing (*YY* 1:4). Before long, he quit his secretary job and worked as an independent writer and painter. His first *zhiguai* collection, *Yeyu qiudeng lu*, was published by the

Shanghai publishing house *Shenbaoguan* in 1877; a second collection entitled *A Sequel to Yeyu qiudeng lu* 夜雨秋燈續錄 was published posthumously by *Shenbaoguan* in 1880.[23]

This dramatic account of an author's life depicted in Xuan's preface reads almost like fiction, yet it is deliberately rendered in this way to achieve what Pu did in his preface to *Liaozhai*: to establish the image of a frustrated talent, who was excluded from the traditional career of a Confucian scholar, yet belonged to a lineage of upright social outcasts like Qu Yuan 屈原 (340–278? BCE), Han Fei 韓非 (c. 281–33 BCE) and Sima Qian 司馬遷 (145 BCE–?).[24] By emulating Pu, Xuan also gains himself a place in this veritable literary galaxy of non-conforming writers; but more importantly, by appropriating Pu's strategy of self-mythification,[25] Xuan presents his act of writing *zhiguai* as not only therapeutic but also something mythical yet predestined. After narrating his mother's dream vision of a Taoist priest preceding his birth,[26] he further confirms his mythical identity by accounting how his studio had been one day visited by a butterfly fairy, who told him: "you were a Taoist priest of the Chongxu Temple on the Luofu Mountain in your previous life, and you got punished for playing with the pen; now you are playing with the pen again!" 子生前為羅浮沖虛觀道士，以弄筆頭獲過，今又弄筆耶! (*YYQD* 1:14) The butterfly episode seems crucial in Xuan's self-chosen literary persona as he later named his studio "The Studio Visited by the Butterfly Fairy" (仙蝶來館). The literati's studio, as John Minford notes, is more than just a physical space but also "a gestalt", and the literati often "encoded their own personal sense of identity into a 'studio name'".[27] Thus by incorporating a fairy into his studio name, both the master of the "Butterfly" studio and the stories produced therein gain a mythical status affirmed by a "fairy". This heavy reliance on artistic myth-making in the construction of personal and even, as I will show later, national history, will be an important strategy for re-establishing the self in Xuan's ghost stories.

However, despite these continuities between Xuan and Pu manifested in their prefaces, the optimism in Pu's work—a human-centred voluntarism and the celebration of *qing*—is obviously running thin in *YYQD*.[28] If ghosts as either the embodiment of supreme *qing* or agents of justice help to establish a harmonious relationship between heaven and man in Pu's literary world, this reassuring world order is collapsing in Xuan's stories. Stories of amorous female ghosts are rare in *YYQD*,[29] and the few revenging-ghost stories often downplay or even deny the effectiveness of human intention in the ghosts' quest for justice.[30] These unsuccessful revenge stories expose Xuan's lack of confidence in the ghost as an agent of justice and his suspicions towards a unitary cosmic order which, as Paolo Santangelo notes, "envisages continuous interaction and reciprocity between heaven and man, with a strong moral connotation".[31] In Xuan's stories, not only personal vendettas can be easily thwarted, but the whole notion of a responsive and morally comprehensible universe was under question. "Zhong Xiaomei zhuan" 鐘小妹傳 (The Story of Zhong Xiaomei, 2:8.379)[32] is such a story, showing serious forebodings that the old heaven is collapsing while a new order is yet to arise.

"Zhong Xiaomei" depicts a cosmic battle between a Chinese goddess, Zhong Xiaomei, and a league of ghosts, yet by anachronistically marrying timeless mythical narratives with a bleak contemporary political situation, it also links an incomprehensible cosmic evil with Western threats. The goddess is the younger sister of the legendary "Ghost-Extinguisher" Zhong Kui,[33] who had neglected his duties for a long time, leaving humans prey to ghosts. Dissatisfied with her brother's negligence, the goddess descends from heaven to deliver the human world from evil. Yet just as she is about to pursue the escaped ghost lord at the end of a seemingly won battle, a letter from Zhong Kui arrives to bid her return, explaining that "the time [to vanquish the ghost lord] has yet to come, and that's why I had left him crawling" 特時未至，姑不與較耳 (YYQD 2:8.382). The enigmatic message produces an immediate change in the fierce goddess, who quickly returns to heaven, leaving the human world prey to the surviving ghost lord. It is here that the humorous story takes on an ominous tone and allusions to the foreign origin of the ghost army enter the picture. The narrator Xuan Ding, who by now is only alluded to as a friend of the protagonist Zong Haifan, comes to the front and becomes a spokesman for the author to sing a poem celebrating the goddess's heroic feat:

> Mountain devils and wood spirits are crawling,
> And myriad ghosts are howling in their caves,
> Snatching and gnawing people in broad daylight.
> [They] took our Rouge Mountain,
> So our women lost their rosy complexion.
> [carrying] Silken banners and embroidered umbrellas [they] are coming from the sea,
> Hidden among their tinkling bracelets are daggers and spears.
> 山魈木魅方縱橫，眾鬼啾啾啼鬼窟，白晝人裹攫人食.
> 奪我胭脂山，婦女無顏色. 錦旗秀傘海上來，環佩珊珊雜戈戟.
> (YYQD 2:8.382)

The phrases used in connection with the ghost army—"Rouge Mountain" and "our women lost their rosy complexion"—have a heavy connotation of foreign invasions in Chinese history. They appear in a Tang-dynasty scholar's annotation to Shiji's (The Book of History, c. 91 BCE) description of how the Han-dynasty emperor Wudi had finally won over the intruding nomadic people Xiongnu (匈奴) and took over their Qilian Mountain and Yanzhi Mountain, where a ballad sung by the defeated Xiongnu was recorded: "Losing our Qilian Mountain, our herds can no longer breed; Losing our Rouge Mountain, our women lost their rosy complexion" 失我祁連山，使我六畜不蕃息. 失我焉支山，使我婦女無顏色.[34] As the ballad was widely anthologised in poetry collections in later dynasties, the phrases "Rouge Mountain" and "our women lost their rosy complexion" have over time crystallised into a default reference to war, defeat, and loss of sovereignty. Xuan's recycling of these set phrases here immediately transforms the goddess's battle against the ghosts into a contemporary context: the confrontation between nations where the loss is on *our* side.

As critics have noticed, Xuan's allusion to the "Rouge Mountain" in the story indicates that the battle against the ghosts must be conceptualised in the late-Qing political scene, in which China was perceived as falling prey to a dangerous enemy "coming from the sea".[35] Yet apart from expressing an alarm to foreign invasion, the story also conveys forebodings for calamities on a cosmic scale. It is important to note the reversal in Xuan's appropriation of Xiongnu's song: the song recorded by Zhang Shoujie is the winning side's testament to its own victory by vicariously imagining and adopting the voice of the defeated, while in Xuan's poem, it is *we Chinese* losing *our* Rouge Mountain to another group of invaders. The change of subjects over the claim of the imagined Rouge Mountain subtly reveals that depending on time and situation, the Xiongnu, the Chinese, and the Westerners can all be invaders and the invaded. This perceptible situational fluidity may thus explain the goddess's sudden halt: everything in the universe ought to follow its destiny, and even someone as evil as the ghost lord still needs to wait for his time to be finally vanquished. Much as the narrator laments the goddess's missed victory, he has to recognise the unsatisfactory situation as part of a cosmos where unimaginable evils are unavoidable and even as necessary as the good.

In Xuan's ghost world, not only the fate of individuals, but also that of nations is subject to inexplicable catastrophes, and all these are still part of the cosmic order. Here we see how far this outlook has departed from Pu's voluntarism: human intention no longer sits at the centre of the universe and the destiny of individuals and countries are largely beyond the subject's comprehension or control. It also shows what a different world Xuan was facing to that of Pu: the earlier writer could appeal to the host of ghosts to mitigate the frustrations in a personal life, whereas in Xuan's time the familiar world order was collapsing: the traumas in the Taiping Rebellion, the unprecedented Western invasion, and the waning myth of China's centrality in the world all make the belief in the transcending force of fantastic figures less sustainable. An ecstatic romance with the phantom heroine was not enough to salvage the scholar's endangered sense of masculinity (thus the lack of amorous female ghosts in Xuan's stories) when men themselves were threatened to become ghosts in upheavals like the Taiping Rebellion and Opium Wars. To mend the Chinese man's collapsing heaven, new strategies need to be devised. Like Pu, Xuan seeks to regain his standing in the current world with the help of ghostly friends "among dark woods and black fortresses", but unlike Pu, Xuan's salvation project is anchored in mythologising the past as well as the present: by excavating a group of neglected heroic ghosts, he turns the personal and the national history into a myth; and by taming the Western threat with the mythical plot of a human–demon encounter, he revitalises the Chinese self against a feminised and demonised other.

Ghosts, gods, ancestors

A ghost is what could not be assimilated into the Confucian system, and therefore women as the outsiders of the patrilineal clan are naturally more prone to become ghosts compared with men, who possess the centre of the clan as either authoritative ancestors or rightful heirs. But occasionally men may also become ghosts in the circumstances of bad deaths, although at the same time, they have the opportunity of being sanctified as gods.[36] Both anthropological studies of Chinese folk religion and the elite Confucian discourse show that the seemingly rigid boundaries between entities of the otherworld—ghosts, gods, (dead) ancestors—are indeed fluid, and something as lowly as a ghost may also transform into its structural opposite and vice versa.[37] This categorical fluidity of the hierarchy not only implies an inherent deconstructive potential in the orthodox structure, but also indicates the possibility for ghosts to be re-assimilated into positions of authority as ancestors and gods. The latter informs Xuan's project of constructing a mythical national history through its neglected ghosts.

In anthropologist Stephen Feuchtwang's study of Chinese folk religion, the three types of spiritual entities, gods, ghosts, and ancestors, are shown to be "arranged in pairs of cross-cutting oppositions",[38] each displaying the opposite traits of the other two categories. Yet despite the hierarchy, they can be transformed into their opposites, as Wolf summarises: both ghosts and ancestors may appropriate the status of gods—ghosts of luminaries may somehow occasionally become gods and enjoy offerings, and ancestors to their own descendants are like domestic gods, offering protection and receiving due sacrifices; ghosts and ancestors, one despised and propitiated while the other carefully worshipped, are only relative categories based on the worshiper's perception of them as insiders or outsiders, so that "one man's ancestor is another man's ghost".[39]

While folk religion belongs to the lower ranks of society, the ideology of the elite Confucian scholars does not differ too much from the villagers' syncretic understanding of ghosts, gods, and ancestors. Despite Confucius's famous reticence on ghosts and spirits, Confucianism establishes the worshipping of ancestors and sanctified gods (such as the god of Mount Taishan) as an indispensable part of its social hierarchy. The Southern Song scholar Chen Chun 陳淳 (1159–1223) attempts to reconcile the disparate meanings associated with the term "ghosts and gods" in his neo-Confucian textbook *Beixi ziyi* 北溪字義 (Explanation of Words by Beixi). In the entry "ghosts and gods" 鬼神, he categorises four different meanings of the term: 1) as an alternative terminology for yin and yang in Confucian sages' yin–yang metaphysics; 2) as referring to religious sacrifices for one's ancestors or other sanctified deities; 3) as used in wanton sacrifices for someone else's ancestors or improper deities; 4) as referring to evil spirits and monsters.[40] It is easy to detect a similarity between Chen's categorisation and the situational fluidity between gods, ghosts, and ancestors observed by anthropologists. What differentiates Chen's category two from categories three and four is whether the sacrifice is sanctified and proper, and what distinguishes an ancestor from a ghost for the villagers is whether the spirit is taken as an insider or a stranger.[41] The implication is that ghosts, gods, and ancestors are just relative categories, separated from each other only by such referential qualities as inside/outside or orthodox/unorthodox. Under certain circumstances, what is sanctified and proper may turn spectral, and what is ghostly may also acquire the status of gods.

That the seemingly rigid hierarchy between ghosts, gods, and ancestors contains its own undoing has further implications. If the authoritative history can be represented by and imagined at the family level as the peaceful transmission from ancestors to descendants, the differing posthumous fates of the ancestor as either turning into a god or a ghost imply that history itself is liable to transform in two directions: either being consecrated into a mythology of gods or despised and ousted as non-history—the unofficial history of ghosts. In times of chaos many people could die a bad death and turn into ghosts and even the deceased heroes of a community are not safe: their memory could be forgotten or suppressed in the contingencies of dynastic transformation. The late Qing was precisely such a time of chaos, a time when "people and ghosts mingle freely" and the glorious Chinese history was under the risk of turning spectral when the notion of China's centrality was challenged in its encounter with the West. This threat to national history prompts Xuan to turn particularly to historical figures in his *zhiguai* stories, and through a series of artistic myth-making, he endeavours not only to salvage history, but also to turn national history into a glorious myth.

Building a pantheon of fatherly ghosts

In times of crisis, history, the community's public memory of its past, offers people in crisis not only past examples of triumph and solution but also a conceptual model to make sense of and even reshape their contemporary problem. As historian Paul Cohen observes, to appropriate stories of the past to solve the problems of the present is a widely used strategy in different communities worldwide.[42] Cohen attributes this phenomenon to the power of story instead of the power of history, for while this story of the past must claim some historicity (not entirely made up) to have its resonance in the present, it is also a story substantially modified from its "true" version with the historians to match the present's requirements, so that it is more a "mythologisation" or "fictionalisation" of the past rather than an evocation of history.[43] Cohen's insight is illuminating in understanding both Xuan's and Wang's obsession with dynastic falls in their ghost stories, for the catastrophic ending of previous dynasties speaks to the late-Qing writers' perception of their own current crisis. Yet if the strategy Cohen observes may be called giving myth the power of history, Xuan's strategy is slightly different: he gives history the power of myth. Instead of making a myth of the past that passes as history, Xuan elevates the national history itself into a myth. In this process, the distinction between history and mythology is not evaded but deliberately made to collapse: the national history, its heroes, and their protected contemporary descendants are all consecrated to form a glorious national myth, but at the same time it also inadvertently reveals the inherent mythical nature of official history in its original construction.

Two stories in Xuan's *YYQD*, "Shendeng" 神燈 (Spirit Lanterns, 1:4.215) and "Ji Song mo wei wen xinguogong mingmu" 稽聳歿為文信國公冥幕 (Ji Song after His Death Became the Secretary of Minister Wen Tianxiang, 1:5.259), are direct derivatives of various official versions of local history in the tumultuous late Ming and late Song, but they reveal different levels of mythologisation and contingency inhering in the orthodox historicisation process

The main plot in "Spirit Lanterns"—how a Ming-dynasty military leader, Wo Tian, died fighting Japanese invaders east of Xuan's hometown, Tianchang—is firmly grounded in the historical background of the Japanese invasions in the Jiajing period (during Emperor Shizong's reign). Japanese maritime invaders, more commonly known as the *wokou*, were a constant nuisance to Chinese coastal regions throughout the Ming dynasty and posed a particularly serious threat in the Jiajing period, when the Ming empire had been in obvious decline.[44] In the spring of the 36th year of Jiajing (1557), large troops of Japanese landed on several spots along the coastal line of Jiangsu province and within a month they had marched eastwards to the wealthy Jiangnan town Yangzhou. The Ming armies proved impotent in their defence against the Japanese. When the Japanese were just about to move further westward to the neighbouring town Tianchang, Yangzhou Captain Wo Tian led an army to strike the Japanese on the east of Tianchang and died in the battle. The Japanese consequently occupied Tianchang, but they soon moved northwards.[45] A major battle was won by the Ming army in July that year when an Anhui general drove the fleeing Japanese back to the sea.

The Yangzhou Captain Wo Tian possesses a peripheral position in this history of national defence. As a relatively low-ranking military officer, Wo's death was insignificant to the overall Ming history and his reputation was ignorable compared with other highly famed military leaders like Qi Jiguang. But as a part of the Ming official apparatus who died in a battle against foreign invasion, as a rule his death still deserved a mention in official Ming historiography. Wo's name appears in several Ming historical records of this 1557 *wokou* invasion, but the description is scanty, usually one sentence long, recording the name of Wo and other deceased amid a series of defeats met by the Ming army.[46]

It is in the local histories that Wo gets a more reverent representation and an individuation that lifts him above the legion of nameless deaths in war. In *Jiangnan tongzhi* 江南通志 (General Records of the Jiangnan Area), the reader is informed that a temple dedicated to Wo was built in Tianchang by the municipal government and a Ming-dynasty magistrate named Sun Yiren wrote an article to commemorate the occasion.[47] Sun's article itself is an act of official history-building, and what is interesting is how this official historicisation of the dead hero blends together biographical details, melodrama, and myth-making. After giving a biography of Wo, Sun's article portrays Wo's death in a tragic yet mythic colour: just as Captain Wo had thwarted the advancement of the Japanese and was about to achieve a vital victory, the weather suddenly turned and the Ming army was trapped in a thick fog. Subsequently Captain Wo was killed in the ambush. Nevertheless, Tianchang people still considered Wo their saviour, for his strike had seriously frightened the Japanese who then left Tianchang quickly, saving the town from a massacre. The article ends by arguing for the legitimacy of building a temple for Wo:

> According to the sacrificial rites of past emperors, a person is eligible to receive public worship [in the following circumstances]: if he brought rites and law to the people, if he died in defending the emperor, if he made major

contributions to the country, and if he saved the people from great disasters or dangers. Wo Tian died in saving us from great catastrophe; as his loyal spirit stands intact for thousands of years, so he deserves non-stop sacrifice in a temple for thousands of years.

夫先王之制祀, 禮法施於民則祀之, 以死勤事則祀之, 以勞定國則祀之, 以能禦大災捍大患則祀之. 公之死豈惟禦災捍患而已哉, 耿耿忠義垂之千古而不磨, 廟貌血食當歷千古而弗諼也.[48]

Through official sanctifications such as Sun's article, the building of the temple, and the further verbal archiving of all the above in *Jiangnan tongzhi*, Wo Tian is no longer a faceless name in Ming histories of Japanese invasion but part of the local official memory pertaining to godhood. Sun's verbal commemoration charting the hero's life, death, and posthumous official sanctification in particular shows how official history-building of the state is inseparable from myth-making: Wo could qualify as a local god because the practice is historically sanctified by "past emperors", and he certainly would not be the last hero thus being made a god.[49] Represented by such heroic figures as Wo, official state history is no less than an official state myth.

Once a myth is made, it obtains a life of its own and can in turn fertilise history and folklore. Xuan's "Spirit Lanterns" evidences a new phase of the Wo Tian myth and itself continues the long line of history-making blended with myth-making. The first part of the story, which recounts Wo's heroic deeds, corresponds to Sun's article mentioned earlier as well as the records in a Qing-dynasty compilation of Tianchang county history which Xuan probably had read,[50] yet the ending departs from historical records into a new myth embedded in contemporary history. The narrator Xuan Ding tells us that Wo's story has by his time become part of the local lore: the spirit of Wo would appear annually in the wild as numerous spirit lanterns, and they were seen by local peasants as a harbinger of the coming harvest. Moreover, the narrator himself bears witness to the protective power of Wo as a god: when he returned home after the Taiping troops had left, he found every household in town had been damaged except Wo's tomb, a miracle only accountable by the god's protection. Here we see the mutual fertilisation between myth, folklore, and history: the mythical traces of Wo Tian as "spirit lanterns" in Xuan's story (real or imaginary) become a new archive for the deceased hero and prevent him from being forgotten, and the mythologised dead himself turns into an icon of patriotism and loyalty, an auspicious protector of the version of history he stands for when social stability was shaken by riots like the Taiping Rebellion. In this collaboration of official and individual myth-making, whether the narrative is fictional or historical becomes unimportant, since all these narratives lend legitimacy to the kind of ideology promoted by Wo's story: the hero dies defending his country from foreigners, and such a heroic death not only elevates the deceased to godhood, but also protects the community he dies for.

However, not all dead heroes can fit in both official and private memories of the past, and it is here we witness the orthodox ideology's suppression of its other through "history"—the official act of regulating and forgetting the past.

While Captain Wo's status as a national hero is unquestionable as he died fighting foreigners, the other story about dead heroes, "Ji Song after His Death Became the Secretary of Minister Wen Tianxiang", foregrounds three virtuous deceased whose orthodoxy as national heroes could be contentious. The story allows three historical figures—two being patriotic heroes during the fall of the Southern Song and the third a Ming-dynasty local magistrate who survived the Ming–Qing transition—to meet anachronistically in Tianchang.

The pivotal hero of the story is Wen Tianxiang 文天祥 (1236–83), a high-ranking minister in the last years of the Southern Song and an important figure in the Song's defence against the Mongols. Such a renowned cultural icon certainly needs no more glorification. What Xuan does in this story is to excavate the lesser-known local heroes Ji Song and Luo Wanxiang by connecting them with Wen, taking a similar history-to-myth trajectory as "Spirit Lanterns". The story begins with the narrator recounting in quick pace what he has read about the last years of the Southern Song and then digresses to introduce a little-known figure: Ji Song. Ji was the head of the Ji village outside of the Tianchang township. When a troop of Southern Song delegates was carrying the emperor's instrument of surrender to the Mongol capital—an act viewed as blatant treason by loyalists such as Wen Tianxiang—Ji Song attacked the delegates when they passed his village, out of the indignation of a loyal subject. He then tells the reader where the Ji village is situated in the contemporary time (north of Tianchang) as additional evidence to validate the authenticity of this record. Further evidence is provided at the end of the story, in the narrator's commentary section, where Xuan quotes a poem by Wen Tianxiang narrating a dangerous episode in the latter's perilous southward journey fleeing from Mongol pursuit:

> I temporarily anchored my boat by the Ji village under an arched moon,
> When a villager, shocked, asked who I was.
> [Suspicions cleared, he told me] the Mongol horses had just been seen this morning,
> By the main road along the green hills.
>
> 小泊稽庄月正弦，庄官惊问是何船.
> 今朝哨马湾头出，正在青山大路边.
>
> (*YYQD*, 1:5.261)

This poem was also collected in Wen's poetry collection *Zhinan lu* 指南錄 (Heading South, prefaced 1276), where Wen's explanatory notes reveal that the "villager" in the poem was Ji Song and that after knowing his identity the latter had made great efforts to escort him safely to the sea.[51] What is interesting here is the shuffle of places between Ji and Wen in Xuan's record: while initially the only historical record of Ji's heroic deeds were found in Wen's note, through Xuan's re-narration and added contemporary observation, Ji is removed from the peritext to the centre of the text, whereas Wen's poem becomes the validating commentary to testify to Ji's heroism. Thus, a commoner like Ji holding no official position and no place in official history obtains the central position in Xuan's retelling.

If thus far Xuan still relies on existing historical records to narrate his story, the rest of the story crosses with the life of the Ming local magistrate Luo Wanxiang, and the narrative then takes off from history into the realm of myth. We learn through the narrator's introduction that Luo had been a Tianchang magistrate well-respected by his citizens during the last years of the Ming dynasty. After the Ming–Qing dynastical change, Luo retreated anonymously to Ji village outside of Tianchang in the style of a *yimin* 遺民 (loyalist recluse).[52] One day in a dream, he was invited to a grand temple, where a god of regal countenance asked him to compose a few couplets. The same dream repeated, until one day Luo accidentally found out in the City God Temple that the City God looked exactly the same as the god in his dream. After a while, he dreamed of the City God again, but this time the City God was irritated by his repeated refusal and was only appeased by his secretary, who at this point revealed himself to be Ji Song, and the City God no other than Wen Tianxiang (*YYQD* 1:5.259–60).

The three historical figures evoked here are of varying standing: while Wen is a pivotal figure in history and an icon of patriotism, Ji is just a civilian anonymous in official histories, and Luo a little-known local magistrate whose position as a loyalist Ming *yimin* is at best viewed with suspicion by the succeeding Qing regime; yet in this mythic dream, all three are synthesised into the same rhetoric of loyalty and patriotism. Despite his incredulity at the City God episode, the narrator further consolidates the three heroes' equally divine standing towards the end of the story, where after a description of the current negligence of Magistrate Luo's tomb, he laments:

> I have always intended to restore Magistrate Luo's tomb, plant trees, and erect a tablet on it and record his deeds in writing, and build a statue of him just opposite that of Ji Song and by the side of Wen Tianxiang, so that all three of them can enjoy sacrifices in the temple till eternity!
> 余時擬出資，為公加封植，立崇碑，敘其事，且肖其像于信國右，宛于稽公對峙，血食千秋。
>
> (*YYQD* 1:5.261)

The last appeal to eternal sacrifice is reminiscent of magistrate Sun Yiren's commemoration of Wo Tian quoted above, yet it was exactly the lack of official commemoration that led to the heroes' current pitiable status.

The repeated confirmation of the three heroes' equal standing as gods in this story also evidences the difficulty of doing so outside the realm of literature. The sad fact is, even those sanctified deceased could easily pass into oblivion and turn into uncared-for ghosts, let alone those who had a troubled relation with official history and never received official sanctification. Outside of Xuan's literary myth, Ji's name appeared only sparsely in a few local histories (*Jiangnan tongzhi* for instance), and a Ming literatus had already lamented how utterly he was forgotten even in his own hometown.[53] Luo's career as a Tianchang magistrate appeared in a short paragraph in a local history, yet his loyalty as a *yimin* was not officially recognised, and his tomb stood in a swamp by Xuan's time.[54] Xuan's story, by imagining the three heroes' compatibility in a synchronised mythical temporality, rescues Ji out of oblivion and recognises Lu as another figure of loyalty just as the Song dynasty heroes were.

The differing posthumous fates of the two Ming-dynasty heroes Wo and Luo (one sanctified by government officials while the other being forgotten by his countrymen) show how precarious the notion of loyalty and patriotism can be. While it is easy to recognise a hero who died in a battle against foreigners, it is more difficult to recognise someone who died as a loyalist to a previous dynasty that the current one has overthrown. The lament for the contingency involved in heroic figures' historical visibility has been famously voiced by the Grand Historian (太史公) Sima Qian in his "Boyi liezhuan" 伯夷列傳 (Biography of Boyi). To Sima, what is lamentable is that only those lucky enough (Boyi, Shuqi, and Yanyuan are his examples) to be praised by Confucius could be canonised as cultural heroes whereas other "inglorious Miltons" only die anonymously "in their caves".[55] Using the story of Boyi as a declaration of his own principle of historiography, Sima implicitly affirms the historian's role in maintaining and distributing historical justice; in other words, the historian is to substitute the sage as the one to confer canonicity and should shoulder the responsibility of saving those virtuous heroes from oblivion.[56]

In inheriting from "Historian of the Strange" Pu Songling, Xuan's "Spirit Lanterns" and "Ji Song" expand the Grand Historian's mission of distributing historical justice to the world of neglected ghosts.[57] If official historians like Sima could rescue from historical records those virtuous figures they believe should have been transmitted, the shifting official ideology means that much could be suppressed or omitted in such records. Without what Stephan Feuchtwang calls an "archive"— any verbal or physical trace that "can be called upon for a narrative, a commemoration, or a new myth or legend",[58] those who could have been elevated into ancestors and gods are in danger of becoming ghosts; hence there is the need of "historians of ghosts" like Xuan, whose ghost stories attempt to amend the fissures of official history by mythologising the ghosts of the cultural heroes into protective and authoritative fatherly gods. The mythologised heroes are at the same time elevated into the mythical ancestors of the nation, their death embodying and reinforcing the orthodox values promoted by official history: loyalty to one's people, nation, and emperor. In this sense, Xuan's mythologisation of national history not only supplements official history with what it may have missed, but also consecrates its values.

If, as Mircea Eliade maintains, the religious man through reciting myths relives the sacred time and reunites with his heroes and gods,[59] then Xuan's myth of these neglected fatherly ghosts, apart from being a resistance to history's forgetting, is also a re-actualisation of the national heroes' courage and nobility. Through making and retelling these myths, the contemporary perturbed man can unite with these spiritual ancestors and appropriate their strength. In this sense, even if the voluntarism inhering in Pu's ghost world is no longer abiding in the late Qing, Xuan still manages to mend the collapsing heaven with narratives of ghosts. By excavating and consecrating the neglected heroic ghosts into gods,

Xuan mythologises the national history and reinforces the ideologies represented by these fatherly ghosts: the nobility of sacrificing for one's country, and the perseverance and immortality of the virtuous souls which protect China from invasion and defeat. This impulse to reaffirm and consecrate one's history reveals a contemporary need, for an age obsessed with rarifying its past is an age uncertain of its present. The reconstructed past gives the Chinese descendant a confidence in his cultural centrality, and this is precisely what he feared most in losing in the late Qing, as a vital blow to the Chinese worldview of the time was the collapse of the centre–periphery mental structure which affirms China's centrality and superiority vis-à-vis what were perceived as China's barbarian others. As I will show in the next section, applying a similar mythic strategy as used in his project of salvaging history, Xuan tames the inevitable encounter between the Chinese self and the threatening foreign others into the familiar narrative pattern of masculine/norm versus feminine/demon.

Taming the strange at home: foxes and snakes

As a genre about knowing the anomalies, *zhiguai* is greatly influenced by a centre–periphery conceptual framework that has a remote origin in the *Shanhai jing* 山海經 (The Classic of Mountains and Seas).[60] In this so-called *Shanhaijing*-pattern,[61] the knowing and collecting self is firmly established in a central position vis-à-vis the strange creatures and peoples on the peripheries who are made known. More importantly, the act of knowing and narrating the strange becomes what Robert F. Campany calls a "cosmic collecting", an act of regulation and subjugation that lends legitimacy to the centre and hierarchises the relation between the self and the others.[62] Such a "centre/norm versus periphery/strange" conceptualisation has had profound influence on Chinese literature and travel writing involving an imagination of foreigners and foreign lands. The superiority of the Chinese centre is repeatedly confirmed and consolidated in the Chinese subject's outgoing journeys, and the lands and peoples he encounters on the peripheries are all reminiscent of the specimens recorded in *The Classic*, once again offering the Chinese subject the mental satisfaction of prior knowledge.[63] A prominent example is the Qing-dynasty novel *Jinghua yuan* 鏡花緣 (Flowers in a Mirror, 1819), in which the wondrous foreign lands that the Chinese travellers encounter are all prefigured by *The Classic*. *Liaozhai* also contains a few stories of Chinese men's overseas adventures, in which the alien peoples are described as heinous savages, rendered strange and monstrous from the point of view of the "civilised" Chinese centre.[64]

Accompanying this "centre–periphery" pattern in Chinese literary imagination of foreigners is a gendered discourse that tends to feminise the encountered other in contrast to a masculine Chinese self. Eric J. Leed considers travel a "gendering activity", and he aptly terms the travels of European colonisers a "spermatic journey", "stimulated by a male reproductive motive, ... through the agency of women".[65] Similar gender tropes can also be found in much traditional Chinese travel writing and fantastic fiction.[66] Just as the ancient Greeks projected their fear of women on the imagined Amazons, the Chinese had an equivalent legend about the "Kingdom of Women" which features disproportionately highly in literature about the overseas.[67] Even when the "Kingdom of Women" does not appear in recognisable forms, the overseas is still imagined as a land of sexual promiscuity where the Chinese man can have easy access to native women's bodies.

The centre–periphery dichotomy inherited from *The Classic* and the gendered pattern of travel writing have become prominent tropes in the literary imagination of the overseas by the Qing dynasty. The two tropes often go hand in hand and re-enforce each other: the foreign lands are imagined as strange lands on the peripheries of the Central Kingdom, where strange creatures and hypersexualised foreign women await the Chinese traveller and reward him with treasure and sexual gratification. Informed by these conceptual frameworks, Qing-dynasty *zhiguai* stories involving the overseas often display a cyclical pattern: the Chinese protagonist goes overseas, finds fortune and/or sexual rewards in a fantastic foreign land, and returns to China as a knowledgeable rich man. In this cyclical pattern, China is the starting and ending point of the journey, the eternal mental centre however far away the traveller goes from home, and the alien lands and peoples he encounters are only curios he collects on the way to prove the central and superior state of the self. Such gendered and hierarchised representations of aliens do find examples in Xuan's collection. In "Mohe gaoyinü zhen fo pusa" 摩訶縞衣女真佛菩薩 (The Great Buddha in White, 2:6.267), a Chinese scholar lands on an island of intelligent parrots where the only creature with a human body is a lady who has visited Tang-dynasty China. In the story "Situ ruyi langjun" 司徒如意郎君 (Mr Situ, 2:4.193), the destitute son of a Chinese magistrate easily charms the daughter of a high minister of the Kingdom of Women and wins fortune and sex solely for being a Chinese male. Sinocentric conceit cannot be more blatant. The images of aliens in these stories are conventional in their superficiality—they are a flattering mirror to reflect the aggrandised image of the Chinese self.

However, despite these familiar tropes, Xuan's stories also show glaring departures from this comfortable image of the overseas. In "Beiji pilin dao" 北極毗鄰島 (The Island of the Northern Extreme, 1:4.211), the image of the overseas subtly shifts from a knowable land of treasure to a source of fear and threat. The story unfolds in the familiar cyclical pattern summarised above, yet at the end of the Chinese man's journey he brings home no beauty or fortune but the warning that a league of demons is to incarnate in the form of Taiping leaders and shatter the Chinese order. In the aforementioned "Zhong Xiaomei", the fear of aliens is dramatised into a new level that the "centre–periphery" model is no longer able to contain: without going overseas to encounter aliens, the Chinese have been plagued by foreign ghosts for years and even the goddess Zhong Xiaomei could not vanquish them.

When the aliens have already transgressed the border between the centre and periphery and appeared at home, the centre–periphery model inherited from *The Classic* is no longer able to subjugate the strange. To tame the new strange, Xuan fits the encounter with the West at home into another familiar mythic structure in *zhiguai*: the gendered encounter between a human male and a supernatural female (often a ghost or a fox spirit). Moreover, Xuan elevates one discourse in this model—the gender category—above categories of normality and the anomaly to become the final regulating force that can defeat and subjugate the threatening other. This gendered structure not only leads the Chinese self to victory but also doubly affirms what he fears most in losing when confronted with a rival other—his masculinity.

The story "Bai Laochang" 白老長 (The Old White Snake, 1:4.175) epitomises how an encounter with Westerners is imagined as a gendered encounter with a demonic other. The story begins with a formulaic setting in *zhiguai*: a lone scholar in his studio is approached by a beautiful woman at night. The woman is dressed in Western attire and tries to seduce the scholar Fan Xiyan, and the latter, although knowing her to be a fox intuitively, cannot resist her charm and soon becomes emaciated through having sex with her. Fan's whole family is alarmed, yet can do nothing to drive away the fox.

Such a human-male versus fox-female plot, as many critics remarked, has become "formulaic and predictable".[68] In Patrick Hanan's apt summary, this type of "demon story" is composed of three actors (man, demon, exorcist) and four actions: meeting, lovemaking, intimation of danger, and intercession by the exorcist.[69] The fox woman and the ghost woman readily occupy the "demon" position in this formula and share many similarities: both are decidedly in the realm of yin in contrast with the realm of yang as inhabited by the human male, and both are often imagined as female sexual vampires adept in the art of *caibu* (采補), i.e., to copulate with human males to rob them of their yang essence (semen).[70] This convergence of foxiness and femininity in the image of the fox woman certainly is the worst projection of men's fear of female sexuality—female sexual appetite is demonised as the bestial fox, bewitching on the surface yet corrupting in essence; yet at the same time, to merge the demonic with the feminine also helps men to contain the threat of what is alien and unknown, because it now has the familiar name and form of a woman, the lower end of the gender hierarchy.

Xuan's fox woman is built on this familiar formulation of the female demon, but his fox also has a new attribute: she is a Western woman. Foreignness translates well into foxiness in this tale: the exotic Western dress of the woman strengthens her charm as a vixen, and her promise to make Fan rich by conversion to Christianity is reminiscent of the old belief that a fox demon may bring wealth to a family.[71] Although aliens are shown in this story as so alarmingly close that they are intruding into Chinese studios at night, they still wear the familiar garb of the vixens. By imposing on Western threat the contour of the mythical fox story, Xuan has considerably subdued and contained the danger of the aliens, for myth provides paradigms. The Westerners are demonised and feminised in familiar terms, and with familiarity comes the solution.

The solution to the fox problem resides in the internal dynamic of the demon-encounter story. After the intimation of danger, an exorcist will usually appear to help save the man and destroy the demon. An exorcist promptly appears to the Fans in Xuan's story, but instead of a usual Taoist priest or Buddhist monk, the exorcist is an old white snake demon disguised as an old man named Bai Laochang. Bai easily drives away the fox, but the fox does not admit defeat and comes back with a group of demon helpers. Each time they are defeated by Bai's tongue-sword, yet each time they return with a larger army, until in the end the fox even coaxes a county magistrate to be on her side. At this stage, the battle is significantly upgraded: it is no longer between the fox and the Fan family but between the county magistrate, a pillar of governmental authority, on one side, and Bai the snake demon on the other.

This unusual alignment of warring sides blurs the usual distinction between normality and the anomaly, for the county magistrate, the representative of orthodoxy and order, sides with the demonic fox, while Bai the snake-demon becomes the protector of justice.[72] What is more significant is the hyper-phallic weapon through which Bai repeatedly defeats his enemies: a tongue-sword. Bai's tongue is turned into a deadly weapon, a giant sword in his battles with the fox's army; later, the physical tongue-sword becomes a symbolic one that renders the magistrate speechless with an eloquent reprimand; in the final battle, the tongue turns into a sword of flames and consumes all the fox's demon followers (*YYQD* 1:4.177). After Bai's spectacular display of triumphant masculinity, the story ends with conventional conjugal bliss: scholar Fan marries Bai's daughter, and the repentant fox is mercifully accepted as Fan's concubine. However, romance is not the focus of the story, as the narrator's comment at the end emphatically endows the snake's triumph with a historical significance by connecting the snake's flames with the fires of E-pang Palace and the Red Cliff, two significant events in China's dynastic history that signalled the defeat of one political regime by another (*YYQD* 1:4.178). Moreover, the narrator's implied analogy between Bai Laochang and the dragon—"hasn't he turned into the sacred dragon and disappeared into the clouds?" (*YYQD* 1:4.178)—also indicates that the snake demon's victory is viewed symbolically as a victory of the Chinese nation, and the snake man is exalted into an icon of national backbone.

Equally important with the imagined national confrontation in "Bai Laochang" is the gendered pattern that Xuan gives to this confrontation and his modification of conventional gender stereotypes, which reveals another important dimension in the contemporary Chinese literati's confrontation with Western challenges: their masculinity anxiety. While the Western threat is sexualised as a female seducer, the protector of the Chinese family is valorised as a powerful and hyper-masculine male demon. It is worth noting that Bai himself is a snake demon and shares a similar status with the vixen in the hierarchy of demon (or ghost), man, and god. Like the fox, the familiar image of the snake demon in folklore and literature is a seductress, the most famous of which is the legendary White Snake Lady.[73] The early specimens of the White Snake legend fit well into the demon story formula summarised above.[74] Xuan's white snake Bai Laochang may well have been influenced by the legend of the White Snake Lady, and Bai's daughter occupies precisely the position of the snake seductress in the original tale. But turning on the tradition, Xuan foregrounds in the story the masculine and warrior-like father instead of the beautiful daughter, and it is the snake warrior's hyper-masculinity that transforms the anomaly into the orthodox. Masculinity is not only the trait that the story celebrates, but itself has become a transcending signifier that redefines the norm and the anomaly. Represented as male instead of female, the once anomalous snake now stands in a position of orthodoxy as opposed to the feminised and demonised Westerners. So far, the anxiety caused by the intruding aliens is successfully domesticated into a battle between familiar tropes: masculinity/orthodoxy versus femininity/anomaly, and the story can be read as a besieged Chinese man's salvation of his masculinity and cultural identity in which gender tropes and anomaly tropes fertilise each other to re-establish the advantageous position of the Chinese male self.

Xuan's white snake story also shows the snake as a liminal and multifaceted figure. The snake motif has many variations across cultures. While the Chinese culture has the legend of the seducing White Snake, Western literary imagination has the lamia myth which too portrays the snake as a stealthy *femme fatale*. However, the snake is a figure encompassing both the feminine and the phallic, embodying a sexual fluidity which may well melt into its other. While Xuan's "Bai Laochang" capitalises on the phallic aggressiveness of the snake and turns it into a symbol of masculinity, in Chapter 4 I will examine Vernon Lee's fantastic story "Prince Alberic and the Snake Lady" which also builds on the motif of the seducing snake but turns the snake lady into an icon of idealised maternal abundance featuring a sexual fluidity. Both stories show the subversive potential of the anomaly: being liminal entities abjected from the normal, they are good materials for shaping alternative gender models.

Is Xuan a genuine friend of Pu Songling "among the dark woods and black fortresses"? The answer is a partial yes. Xuan is a sincere admirer of Pu, and his works do show numerous traces of continuity from Pu's *Liaozhai* tradition—the tradition that fashions *zhiguai* writing as the frustrated literatus' self-chosen identity as well as his solitary yet heroic battle against a collapsing world. Yet, if Pu stages his battle through the amorous ghost as the quintessential embodiment of *qing*, Xuan's project of reconstructing the self is based on revisiting national history. History becomes vital to one's understanding of the present especially when the current version of seeing the world proves insufficient and familiar conceptions of the self are challenged. Xuan's approach to revalorise his besieged masculinity and Chinese cultural identity in a chaotic age is a myth-making of national history through excavating and consecrating a group of fatherly ghosts. Through mythologising these ghosts, the Chinese man reunites with his gods and heroes, and through mythical narratives of the encounter with a demonic female, he tames the threatening other and revalorises the Chinese self. Such an approach, while successful in Xuan's case, will prove less sustainable for Wang, who had stepped outside of the comfortable position of the Chinese centre and embraced open-mindedly the aliens on the "peripheries". Wang's reformation of *zhiguai* stories shows a greater departure from tradition and a less confident defence of his cultural identity, as the moral legitimacy of *zhiguai* itself is questioned in his *zhiguai* collections, as is the coherence of the official version of Chinese history.

Notes

1 Pu, *Liaozhai zhiyi huijiao huizhu huiping ben* (2nd ed. 2011), Youhe Zhang ed., 3. Citations of *Liaozhai* in this book all refer to this edition.
2 The phrase is borrowed from Du Fu's 杜甫 (712–70) "Meng Li Bai" 夢李白 (Dreaming of Li Bai): "the ghost came from the dark maple woods; the ghost returned to the black fortresses" 魂來楓林青，魂返關塞黑.
3 Zeitlin, *Historian of the Strange: Pu Songling and the Chinese Classical Tale* (1997), 51.
4 Lu, 188. Scholars have found that the version Lu read as Xuan's *Yeyu qiudeng lu* 夜雨秋燈錄 (Records of Rainy Nights under the Autumn Lamp 1877, 1880) were counterfeits, in which at least half of the stories were collated from other books; therefore, Lu's comment on Xuan was not wholly justified. See Xin Song's preface to *Zhengxu yeyu qiudeng lu* (1987), 15–16.
5 The term voluntarism is used here slightly differently from its connotation in the Western context where the emphasis is on human will over rationality. See Richard Taylor, "Voluntarism", in Donald M. Borchert ed., *Encyclopaedia of Philosophy* (2006), vol. 9, 714–17.
6 *Liaozhai* is distinctive from Ji Yun's *Yuewei caotang biji* 閱微草堂筆記 (Jottings from the Studio of Close Scrutiny,1789–98) and Yuan Mei's 袁枚 (1716–98) *Zibuyu* 子不語 (What Confucius Would Not Discuss, c. 1788) in its much more romantic portrayal of the ghost. For a comparison of the three High Qing *zhiguai* writers, see Santangelo, "An Introduction to *Zibuyu*'s Concepts and Imagery", in *Zibuyu, or "What the Master Would Not Discuss", According to Yuan Mei (1716–98): A Collection of Supernatural Stories* (2003), 1–160 and Tak-hung Leo Chan, *The Discourse on Foxes and Ghosts*, 160–7.
7 More on Pu's apology for the *zhiguai* genre in Chapter 3.
8 On a re-evaluation of the concept of *qing* before Neo-Confucianism, see Zongyi Zheng, "Xingqing yu qingxing", in Bingzhen Xiong and Shou'an Zhang eds., *Qingyu mingqing: daqing pian* (2004), 23–32. On ramifications of *qing* in Chinese philosophy through Neo-Confucianism to the cult of *qing*, see Martin Huang, "Sentiments of Desire", 154–74 and Epstein, *Competing Discourses*, 62–119.
9 The anthology contains stories about love from the pre-Qin period to Feng's contemporary Ming dynasty, some gleaned from other sources and some written by Feng.
10 Feng, *History of Love*, vol. 1, 1–2.
11 Chengzhou Fu, "Qingjiao xinjie", *Researches on Ming and Qing Dynasties Novel* 1 (2003): 40–3.
12 Tang, "Mudan ting tici" 牡丹亭題詞 (Preface to *Peony Pavilion*), in *Tang Xianzu shiwenji* 汤显祖诗文集 (Poetry and Prose of Tang Xianzu, 1982), vol. 2, 1093.
13 Tang, "Mudan ting", 1093.
14 On the hyper-feminine and eroticised ghosts in *Liaozhai*, see Zeitlin, *The Phantom Heroine: Ghosts and Gender in Seventeenth-Century Chinese Literature* (2007), 24.
15 Because of the rebelliousness exhibited by these supernatural heroines, for a period in the mainland of China Pu was hailed as a "progressive" proto-feminist writer. Later scholarship has revealed how much of this assumption may be a misunderstanding (see Luo Hui, "The Ghost of *Liaozhai*"). Continuing the long literary tradition in which the male literati adopt a female subjective position, the idealised otherworldly women in *Liaozhai* are as much a projection of the male literati's ideal self as their idealised imagination of the other sex. On the remarkable woman representing an ideal subjectivity, see Keith McMahon, *Polygamy and Sublime Passion: Sexuality in China on the Verge of Modernity* (2010), 16–17.
16 On *Liaozhai* reconciliation between the fulfilment of desire and returning to order, see Wai-yee Li, *Enchantment and Disenchantment: Love and Illusion in Chinese Literature* (1993), 89–151.

17 In folk religion, people who die a good death would not become ghosts; only those who die a violent death or as unmarried virgins would become ghosts—this is part of the reason for the greater number of female ghosts in *zhiguai*. Unmarried women had not been properly integrated into either the father's or the husband's clan, thus becoming an outcast of the Confucian patrilineal family. See A. P. Wolf, "Ghosts, Gods and Ancestors", in Wolf ed., *Religion and Ritual in Chinese Society* (1974), 131–82.
18 The City God in Chinese folklore is imagined as a local judge in the underworld appointed from among the virtuous dead and serving as a counterpart to the secular city magistrate. On City God worship, see Tuyou Zheng and Xianmiao Wang, *Zhongguo chenghuang xinyang* (1994). Both commentators of *Liaozhai*, Dan Minglun and He Shouqi point out the significance of this story in determining the moral tenor of the book at the very beginning (1:3). On a comparison of *Liaozhai*'s and *Zibuyu*'s treatment of destiny and divine justice, see Santangelo, "*Zibuyu*'s Concepts and Imagery", 145–6.
19 See John Henderson, *The Development and Decline of Chinese Cosmology* (1984).
20 Contrary to Western notions of masculinity which rely on a clear distinction from femininity, scholars have observed the correlative yin–yang cosmology in China and in its implication, the fluid boundary between femininity and masculinity. This may explain the not infrequent phenomena in Chinese literature where the male literatus chooses to speak through and identify with a female figure. See for instance Alison H. Black, "Gender and Cosmology in Chinese Correlative Thinking", in *Gender and Religion: On the Complexity of Symbols*, 166–95, Caroline W. Bynum, Stevan Harrell, and Paula Richman eds.; Huang, *Negotiating Masculinities*, 1–4, and Kam Louie, *Theorising Chinese Masculinity: Society and Gender in China* (2002), 9–10.
21 Hereafter referred to as *YYQD*.
22 Apart from a few details, this preface contains basically all we know about the author's life. For biographical information for Xuan, see Shihao Yu, "Xuan Ding yu Yeyu qiudeng lu yanjiu", MA thesis, 2005 and "Xuan Ding jiashi ji shengping shiji xinzheng", *The Research on Ming and Qing Dynasties Novels* 1(2012): 138–50.
23 Zhenguo Zhang hypothesises that Xuan died shortly before the publication of the *Sequel*, probably at the end of 1879; see Zhang, "Xuan Ding shengzu nian ji wenxian yicun lüekao", *Journal of Chuzhou University* 11.2 (2009): 5–6. The two collections were later published as a whole under the title *Yeyu qiudeng lu*. For this study, I mainly consulted the 1995 Huangshan shushe edition, in two volumes, each containing eight *juan* (卷), in accordance with the original two *Shenbaoguan* collections. All quotations refer to this edition. *YYQD* in this study refers to the original two collections regarded as a whole.
24 These are the writers evoked in Pu's preface to *Liaozhai*. On Pu's re-appropriation of the "solitary indignation" (孤憤) tradition in his preface, see Zeitlin, *Historian of the Strange*, 50–1.
25 On Pu's strategy of self-mythification in his preface, see Zeitlin, *Historian of the Strange*, 54.
26 A similar "dream-vision" story is used in Pu's preface to allude to the author's mythical Buddhist identity (*Liaozhai*, 1:1).
27 Minford, Introduction, in *Strange Tales from a Chinese Studio* (2006), xix. Pu's studio name "Liaozhai", his *zhiguai* collection named *Liaozhai zhiyi* (literally "Strange Stories of Liaozhai"), and his autobiographical preface "Self-record of *Liaozhai*" 聊齋自志 are a perfect example of how the studio, the ghost stories produced therein, and the author who created them fuse into one indissoluble literary persona.
28 Some scholars however see a continuity of the cult of *qing* in Xuan Ding. See Zhenguo Zhang, "Lun Xuan Ding *Yeyu qiudeng lu* dui *Qingshi* de chengxu he chuangxin", *Study on Pu Songling Quaterly* 1 (2009): 149–58.
29 Only a few among more than one hundred stories of *YYQD* involve a possible romance between men and ghosts, for instance, "Donglin mu" 東鄰墓 (1:1.19), "Yao Shisan

lang" 晁十三郎 (2:1.1), "Shi Qiaoqiao" 石翹翹 (2:1.26), "Ye bushou" 夜不收 (2:8.400), and "Youfang niangzi" 幽芳娘子 (2:2.102).
30 See for instance these stories: "Jiang Xiaoyu" 姜小玉 (2:6.271), "Mizhu" 宓珠 (1:4.217), "Yuhong ce" 玉紅冊 (1:1.44), and "Lieshang Jinxiao" 烈殤盡孝 (1:3.110).
31 Santangelo, "*Zibuyu*'s Concepts and Imagery", 70.
32 "The Story of Zhong Xiaomei" was originally published separately in *Shenbao*'s literary magazine *Huanyu suoji* 環宇瑣記 in around 1874–6 (see Yu, "Xuan Ding"). One story in *YYQD*, "Jiulianzhou gaohui" 九蓮洲高會 (The Grand Banquet of Nine Immortals, 2:8.378) is a sequel to this story, so the Huangshan shushe edition includes the earlier story as an appendix to "Jiulianzhou". "Jiulianzhou" recounts a goddess's visit after reading the author's "Zhong Xiaomei" story. It claims that the "Zhong Xiaomei" story was written by Xuan's friend Zong Haifan while the attached poems were his own. However, judging from the way the protagonist (this friend) is addressed in the story, its author is unlikely to be the friend. I agree with other scholars and treat "Zhong Xiaomei" as Xuan's writing.
33 In folklore, Zhong Kui was "the Great Ghost-Extinguisher" appointed by the Jade Emperor to extinguish all evils and vices marauding as ghosts in the human world. Two popular novels about Zhong Kui attributed to a "Yanxia sanren" remain. See Yanxia sanren, *Zhongkui zhuan* 鍾馗傳 (1980).
34 In Zhang Shoujie 張守節, *Shiji zhengyi* 史記正義, vol. 110, 22, *Online SKQS*. The Yanzhi Mountain (homophone to "rouge mountain") is famous for a kind of flower used to make rouge, therefore "our women lost their rosy complexion".
35 See Hongji Xue, "Cuotuo bushang lingyunzhi, qieyu baiguan jie huanyuan", *Social Science Front* 3 (1988): 252–60.
36 One common instance of such is the City God, who very often was promoted from the virtuous dead or luminary figures in the locale. See C. Stevan Harrell, "When a Ghost Becomes a God", in Wolf ed., *Religion and Ritual in Chinese Society* (1974), 193–206. On rare occasions victimised women after death may also obtain godhood, referred to as "*yinshen*" 陰神, a lower ranking local god; see Yuan-ju Liu, "Liuchao *zhiguai* zhong de nüxing yinshen chongbai zhi zhengchanghua celüe chutan", *Thought and Words: Journal of the Humanities and Social Science* 35. 2 (1997): 93–132.
37 On the interstices of gods, ghosts, and ancestors, see Wolf, "Gods, Ghosts, and Ancestors", Stephan Feuchtwang, "Domestic and Communal Worship in a Taiwan Town", and Harrell "When a Ghost" in Wolf ed. *Religion and Ritual in Chinese Society* (1974).
38 Feuchtwang, "Domestic and Communal", 106.
39 Wolf, "God", 146. On deceased human beings acquiring the status of City God, see also Zheng and Wang, *Zhongguo chenghuang*, 51–65.
40 Chen, *Explanation of Words by Beixi* (1983), entry "Ghosts and Gods", 55–66. I consulted Wing-tsit Chan's English translation for my wording. See Wing-tsit Chan, *The Neo-Confucian Terms Explained: The Pei-Hsi Tzu-I [Beixi ziyi]* (1986), 156–63.
41 Confucian classics emphasise too the distinction between the inside and the outside in dealings with ghosts and gods. Confucius said in *Analects* that "For a man to sacrifice to a spirit which does not belong to him is flattery" 非其鬼而祭之,諂也. See *Confucius*, in Legge translation, 154.
42 Cohen, *History and Popular Memory: The Power of Story in Moments of Crisis* (2014).
43 Cohen, *History*, 194.
44 Records of *wokou* can be found in numerous Ming-dynasty historiographies. See for instance Huang Fengxiang 黃鳳翔, *Jiajing dazheng leibian* 嘉靖大政類編 (Major Political Events in the Jiajing Years [1597] 1995 rpt.), "Nanwo" 南倭 (*Wokou* in the South). For a contemporary history, see Zhongyi Fan and Xigang Tong, *Mingdai wokou shilüe* (2004).
45 Huang Fengxiang, *Jiajing dazheng*, 757, and Fan and Tong, *Mingdai wokou*, 125.

46 Apart from *Jiajing dazheng leibian*, records of Wo's death can be found in Tu Shan comp., *Mingzheng tong zong* 明政統宗 (Ming Dynasty Political History [1615] 2000 rpt.), vol. 27, 33–4.
47 Huang zhijuan 黃之雋 and Zhao Hong'en 趙弘恩, comp., *Jiangnan tongzhi* [1987 rpt.], vol. 42, 370. The book is a Qing-dynasty compilation of local histories.
48 Huang and Zhao comp., *Jiangnan tongzhi*, vol. 42, 371.
49 Shelly Chang notes that the deification of historical heroes was a distinctive feature of the Chinese mindset and an effective way of political and social control by authoritarian Confucianism. See Chang, *History and Legend: Ideas and Images in the Ming Historical Novels* (1990), 191–5.
50 The Qing compilation *Jiaqing beixiu Tianchang xianzhi gao* 嘉慶備修天長縣志稿 (Draft for A Full History of the Tianchang County in Jiaqing Years) was first complied by Zhang Zongtai 張宗泰 in 1819.
51 Wen, *Wenshan ji* 文山集 (Work of Wenshan), vol. 13, "Jizhuang jishi" 稽莊即事 (Ji Village), 61, *Online SKQS*.
52 Records of Luo can also be found in Huang and Zhao, *Jiangnan tongzhi*, vol. 118, 55–6, and Zhang Zongtai, *Jiaqing beixiu Tianchang xianzhi gao*, vol. 6, 111; Xuan's narrative so far corresponds with these historical records. *Yimin* refers to the loyalists to a fallen dynasty who lived on in the new dynasty in recluse. More on *yimin* in Chapter 3.
53 Cheng Minzheng 程敏政, "Diao Jizhuang ci" 弔稽莊詞 (A Eulogy to the Ji Village), in *Huangdun wenji* 篁敦文集 (Work of Huangdun), vol. 60, 16, *Online SKQS*.
54 According to *Jiaqing beixiu Tianchang xianzhi gao*, vol. 6, 111, a temple dedicated to Luo and another local personage had been built, yet Luo's tomb was uncared for, and the temple could not compare with Wo Tian's in grandeur.
55 Sima, *Shiji* [2003 rpt.], vol. 61, "Boyi liezhuan", 401: 伯夷、叔齊雖賢, 得夫子而名益彰; 顏淵雖篤學, 附驥尾而行益顯. 巖穴之士, 趨捨有時, 若此類名湮滅而不稱, 悲夫. (Although Boyi and Shuqi were virtuous, their names got transmitted far and wide only after Confucius's praise; although Yan Yuan was a dedicated scholar, his virtuous deeds were only made known when he followed Confucius. For those recluses, their conducts and behaviours were so governed by moral principles, yet their names all passed into oblivion: it is indeed lamentable.)
56 On an analysis of "Biography of Boyi" and history as a unique tenet in Chinese philosophy to ensure justice and immortality, see Shaojie Shan, "Boyi liezhuan zhong de gongzheng linian yu yongheng linian", *Journal of Renmin University of China* 6 (2005): 129–37.
57 For instance, in "Zhonghun rumeng" 忠魂入夢 (Visited by a Loyal Spirit in a Dream, 1:1.41), Xuan narrates a nocturnal encounter with the ghost of a Ming loyalist whose memory was utterly suppressed in local history and only survived fragmentarily in folklore as a ghost; in "Guilin gaoshu sanyi" 桂林皋署三異 (Three Strange Cases in the Guilin County Office, 1:1.39), Xuan records his informant's sighting of a headless ghost. Although the ghost is rumoured to be a nameless Ming loyalist, for the lack of actual evidence, even the narrator is suspicious of this claim and lumps the spirit in the group of demons.
58 Feuchtwang, *The Anthropology of Religion, Charisma and Ghosts: Chinese Lessons for Adequate Theory* (2010), 129.
59 Eliade, *The Sacred and the Profane* (1959), 81–2, 91–5.
60 *The Classic* is an ancient Chinese text of geography, fantastic creatures, mythology, and magic. The Han-dynasty scholar Liu Xin 劉歆 recorded the legendary origin of *The Classic* as such: Great Yu, the founder of China's first dynasty Xia, commanded his minister Boyi 伯益 to record all the mountains and seas and creatures in the far corners of his land so that his people may know about them and would not feel afraid (See Ji Yun, et al., "*Shanhai jing* tiyao" 山海經提要). However, modern scholars generally hold that the book was written by different writers over time, probably from the Warring States period to the early Han dynasty. See Tao Fang, Preface, *Shanhai jing*

(2009). The various legendary creatures recorded in *The Classic* are a well of resources for later Chinese supernatural literature.
61 On the "Shanhaijing-pattern" in *zhiguai*, see Yongqiang Liu, "Mingqing xiaoshuo zhong de shewai miaoxie yu yiguo xiangxiang", *Literary Heritage* 4 (2006): 133–43.
62 Campany, *Strange Writing*, 103–8.
63 On a critique of the Sinocentric conceit in Chinese literary imagination of foreign lands, see Yongqiang Liu, "Mingqing xiaoshuo", 136–8.
64 One example is "Yecha guo" 夜叉國 (The Yaksha Kingdom, 1:3.348).
65 Leed, *The Mind of the Traveller: From Gilgamesh to Global Tourism* (1991), 217, 114.
66 See Emma Jinghua Teng, *Taiwan's Imagined Geography: Chinese Colonial Travel Writing and Practices 1638–1895* (2004), 173–5 and "The West as a 'Kingdom of Women': Woman and Occidentalism in Wang Tao's Tales of Travel", in Joshua A. Fogel ed., *Traditions of East Asian Travel* (2006), 70–96.
67 "The Kingdom of Women" features in *The Journey to the West*, the Ming-dynasty novel *Sanbao taijian xiyang ji* 三寶太監西洋記 (Zheng He's Expedition in the Western Seas, 1598), *The Flowers in the Mirror*, as well as the two stories of Xuan to be discussed below.
68 Kang, *Cult of Fox*, 74.
69 Hanan, *The Chinese Vernacular Story* (1981), 44. Hanan's book deals with the vernacular story in particular but his formula applies readily to many *zhiguai* stories.
70 On the close link between fox and sex, see Kang, *Cult of Fox*, and Huntington, *Alien Kind: Foxes and Late Imperial Chinese Narrative* (2003), 177–89. The imagination of women's vampirism in sexual intercourse may originate with the Taoist concept that sexual intercourse is a transmission of yin and yang life energies between woman and man. See Robert Van Gulik, *Erotic Colour Prints of the Ming Period, with an Essay on Chinese Sex Life from the Han to the Ch'ing [Qing] Dynasty, B.C.206–A.D.1644* (1951).
71 Kang, *Cult of Fox*, 83–7.
72 Hongji Xue interprets the battle as an allegory for the confrontation between Chinese commoners and Western colonisers, with the county magistrate representing the Qing government manipulated by Westerners. See Xue, "Cuotuo", 253.
73 On the evolution of the White Snake motif, see Jinlan Fan, "Baishezhuan gushi xingbian yanjiu" (1991).
74 See, for instance, in Li Fang 李昉 comp., *Taiping guangji* 太平廣記 (978 CE), vol. 458 ("Snake III"), "Li Huang", 10–13, *Online SKQS*.

3 "These are what Westerners refuse to believe"

Wang Tao's uncanny history[1]

Friedrich Nietzsche (1844–1900) proposes three types of history that may serve the living in "On the Use and Disadvantages of History for Life" (1874): the monumental, the antiquarian, and the critical.[2] If the mythical national history reconstructed in Xuan Ding's ghost stories can be said to belong to Nietzsche's monumental history—looking back for monumental moments in the past to offer paradigms for the historical present, then Wang Tao's history of ghosts to be investigated in this chapter fits more with Nietzsche's critical history: the present man feels oppressed by the immortality of past traditions and customs, and through a criticism of history he seeks to break away from the past and embark on a new journey.[3] Being an important late-Qing reformist political thinker and one of the first Chinese intellectuals who had stepped outside of China and advocated learning from the West, Wang was aptly termed by his biographer Paul Cohen as a man "caught between tradition and modernity"; yet, conceptualising what tradition and modernity meant in the late-Qing context, it is also apt to say that Wang was a man caught between Chinese and Western cultures. Working with British missionaries in Shanghai, Hong Kong, and Scotland, Wang had helped in the translation of the Bible into Chinese and Confucian classics into English. This unique immersion in both Chinese and Western cultures gave Wang a valuable opportunity to step out of a Sinocentric mentality and to re-evaluate his own culture from an outsider's perspective; yet, at the same time, it could also be a source of perturbation and disorientation.[4] Wang's understanding of and fascination with Western culture made it more difficult for him to valorise his own cultural identity through simply demonising the Western other as Xuan does, and it also prompted him to adopt a more critical attitude towards Chinese history and tradition. Instead of glorifying a mythical national history, Wang casts doubts on official history and the orthodox values endorsed by that history through his *zhiguai* writing.

More particularly, Wang's critique of national history in *zhiguai* is realised through portraying the ghosts of two groups of people who have had a troubled relationship with dynastic history: the *yimin* (loyalists) who went on a mental or physical exile during dynastic changes and the chaste women who became victims of dynastic wars. The former group expresses a persistent yearning for escaping from historical succession into a temporal stasis, while the silent sufferings of the latter expose the futility and cruelty of the *yimin* discourse, whose essence is clinging to the past at whatever cost. By exposing the uncanny side of official history and of the loyalty discourse upheld in this history, the contemporary Chinese man may break away from tradition and begin an outgoing journey to confront his Western rivals.

Critical history and monumental history, Nietzsche admits, are practical ways to appropriate history for the present, yet both approaches have their limitations: monumental history is no less than a myth-making of the past whose reconstruction of the past is prone to beautification and distortion, while the severance with one's roots and tradition in critical history can be dangerous to one's current sense of being. Particularly for Wang, breaking away from tradition has its cost, as it strips the subject of the once reassuring central position sanctified in tradition when he confronts a powerfully rivalling other. Caught between Chinese and Western epistemologies, Wang's ghost stories crystalise the perilous mental journey that late-Qing Chinese intellectuals undertook to re-evaluate and reform the self. This is a deeply troubled journey, departing from the old *zhiguai* tradition yet never landing in the imagined Western land; instead, it witnesses a constant oscillation between different interpretative frameworks, the result of which is an unsettling, fantastic literature per Tzvetan Todorov's definition,[5] embedded in layers and layers of *zhiguai* intertextuality and offering no definite claim of reality for its author or reader.

Wang's highly unconventional attitude towards the *zhiguai* tradition was closely correlated with the author's irregular life path deviating from a traditional Confucian scholar's. Born into a scholarly family in Fuli county near Suzhou in 1828, Wang was trained, as was Xuan Ding and most Confucian scholars of the time, for a career path in officialdom. In 1848, Wang went to visit his father then working in Shanghai, and the newly opened treaty port offered him the first window into a larger world. The 20-year-old Wang was immediately fascinated with the vitality of this rapidly urbanising city, and the advanced printing facilities of the London Missionary Press where Wang's father worked left an indelible impression on him.[6] One year later, his father's death prompted him to find a job in Shanghai, and he soon became an employee of the London Missionary Press, helping Dr W. H. Medhurst 麥都思 (1796–1857) translate the Bible into Chinese. From 1849 to 1862, Wang witnessed Shanghai being transformed into the new commercial and cultural centre of southern China with its fashionable urban and Westernised style of life, as he himself turned gradually into one of the first generation of "treaty-port intellectuals".[7] To work for foreigners—then a self-degrading act for a Chinese scholar—was Wang's first deviation from the Confucian scholar's path, and a greater crisis was yet to come. In 1862, when Shanghai was under threat of the Taiping army based in Nanjing, the Qing government confiscated in a raid a letter written in the name of Huang Wan (黃畹) to one of the Taiping leaders in Suzhou offering strategies for defeating the Qing army. The Qing authority believed Wang to be the author of this letter, although the latter denied it all his life. This was the incident that exiled Wang from the Chinese mainland for more than 20 years. With the help of the British Consul in Shanghai, Sir Walter Henry Medhurst 麥華陀 (son of the missionary Medhurst),

Wang was able to narrowly escape from government persecution to Hong Kong.[8] For the next 20 years, he mainly stayed in Hong Kong but he had the opportunity to travel to Europe in 1867 at James Legge's invitation and stayed in Scotland for two years helping Legge translate Chinese classics into English.[9] Upon returning to Hong Kong, Wang established *Xunhuan ribao* 循環日報 (1874–1947), the first Chinese-language newspaper run by the Chinese, and in the following ten years he published numerous articles introducing Western science, history, and political systems as well as advocating for China's reform.[10] By the time he returned to Shanghai in 1884, Wang had been widely recognised as an expert on "Western Learning".[11]

Such an unconventional life path was indeed unique for a late-Qing intellectual, and Wang's importance in China's ideological transformation is unquestionable. However, never holding any official position and exiled from China proper by political authorities most of his life, Wang's lifelong self-identified persona was still that of *"wenren"*— man of letters, and he did write many literary pieces, mainly *zhiguai* stories and travel writing. Wang published three *zhiguai* collections in his life—*Dunku lanyan* 遁窟讕言 (Unverified Words from the Cave of Retreat, 1875), *Songyin manlu* 淞隱漫錄 (Random Records by the Song River, 1887), and *Songbin suohua* 淞濱瑣話 (Trivial Words by the Song River, 1893) and two travel writing collections *Manyou suilu* 漫遊隨錄 (Casual Records of My Travels, 1890) and *Fusang youji* 扶桑遊記 (Records of My Travels in Japan, 1880).[12] Compared with his highly famed political treatises and European histories, Wang's literary output, especially his *zhiguai* writing, received much less academic attention until the last two decades.[13]

The dearth of scholarship on Wang's *zhiguai* writing was possibly a result of a contemptuous misconception about late-Qing *zhiguai* that had dominated Chinese academia for a long time: it either perceived late-Qing *zhiguai* as mere imitations of their earlier-Qing models, or denounced these as tales of superstition, the worst dregs of a "feudal" China soon to be replaced by the enlightenment of science and democracy in the Republican era.[14] More problematic in Wang's case is that this old genre dedicated to ghosts and foxes seems to be especially backward and incompatible with its supposedly progressive author, who spent most of his life advocating practical learnings to the world. However, an important goal of this study is to explore the multi-layered functions of *zhiguai*, and I argue that it is precisely the anomalousness of *zhiguai* that can better encapsulate the complexities and strangeness of the encounter between China and the West as experienced and made sense of by Wang's generation of transitional intellectuals. In Wang's hands, the traditional genre to "record the strange" is reshaped to negotiate between China's past and present, to envisage China's inevitable conflict with the West, and finally to serve as the last shelter for the besieged Chinese man's masculinity and cultural identity. This embracing of diverse discourses in Wang's *zhiguai* writing, as I will show in the following sections, creates textual conflicts in which one way of understanding the world is constantly in danger of being supplanted by another. The result is a disconcerting mode of fantasy in Tzvetan Todorov's sense, which oscillates between a natural and a supernatural interpretation of the fictional world and constantly forces its reader to question his or her own epistemological premises.[15]

Battling worldviews: the supernatural besieged

At the end of his preface to *SBSH*, the last of his three *zhiguai* collections, Wang depicts an imaginary meeting with the great *zhiguai* master Pu Songling, who takes him into the woods and praises him: "You have exceeded me; perhaps now I've finally found a successor to *Liaozhai?*" 子突過我矣，《聊齋》之後有替人哉 (*SBSH* 2). However, this seemingly proud identification with *Liaozhai* is immediately dismissed in the following sentence where the author begs his reader to regard his writing merely as the "playful words of a dying man" 將死遊戲之言 (*SBSH* 2). This contradictory view regarding the *zhiguai* heritage and one's own relation with it underlies the prefaces of Wang's three *zhiguai* collections, and such a paradoxical framework ushers the reader into a very different *zhiguai* world which, instead of providing a reassuring alternative fantastic cosmos such as Pu's (and to a lesser extent Xuan's) *zhiguai* did, foregrounds the irresolution between competing worldviews.

As a mediator between a book's potential reader and the text proper, the authorial preface of a book, according to Gérard Genette, is an important paratext that performs two functions for the author: to instruct the reader why to read the text and how to read it properly.[16] While both functions are more or less present in most *zhiguai* prefaces, *zhiguai* preface often expresses another authorial intention: to explain from the author's perspective why "I" have written the book. In other words, before putting expectations on the reader, a *zhiguai* work is expected firstly to justify its own existence. It is not difficult to understand this apologetic move considering the embarrassing position of the genre. As Tak-hung Leo Chan notes, the lowly status of *zhiguai*, unbefitting a serious scholar, means that a *zhiguai* writer often needs to use various legitimisation strategies in the preface to justify his writing this very book.[17] Zeitlin offers a cogent analysis of Pu's apologetic moves in his "Self-Record of *Liaozhai*" (聊斎自志), in which a recourse to the established ghost-collecting tradition is blended with a touching autobiography to lend legitimacy to the author's natural affinity to ghosts. Zeitlin argues that Pu's preface to *Liaozhai* is no less than the "Historian of the Strange's self-introduction" and fashions the writer himself "into a lens through which the book would be refracted for his readers".[18] Building on this insight and Genette's, I would further argue that Pu's preface emphatically starts the tradition of identity-building through *zhiguai* writing, where the autobiographical preface serves not only as an apology for the genre but also a self-mythification which glosses both the *zhiguai* writer and his *zhiguai* stories with an aura of the mythic.[19] As discussed before, this model has been diligently observed in Xuan's preface to *YYQD*, and as I will show below, is still a central tenet in Wang's prefaces to *DKLY*.

A slightly different legitimisation act is to argue from the didacticism of ghost stories.[20] This is a position more akin to the Confucian tradition of "moralising by poetry" (詩教) and the one held by Ji Yun in his *Yuewei*.[21] A less confrontational justification is to trivialise the act of *zhiguai* writing or to overtly term it simply as amusement. Both Ji Yun and Yuan Mei adopted this approach. While Yuan admits in his preface to *Zibuyu* his personal obsession of "collecting stories pleasing to the heart and shocking to the ear" 乃廣采遊心駭耳之事,[22] Ji seems to consider it unbefitting to even write a preface for *Yuewei*, leaving only a few lines of notes before each of its volumes.[23]

A close adherence to such traditional legitimisation acts can be traced in Wang's two prefaces to *DKLY*, his first *zhiguai* collection and in a sense a juvenile work compared with *SYML* and *SBSH*.[24] Preface I, a piece in verse composed mainly of couplets with dense allusions, is clearly modelled on Pu's "Self-record of *Liaozhai*" and advances the traditional legitimation moves: a reference to the tradition of supernatural literature and a description of the author's bleak studio "Dunku" (The Cave of Retreat) in Hong Kong. The scholar's studio, as mentioned earlier, is a defining element of the scholar's self-chosen identity, and it is particularly prominent in the strand of *zhiguai* writing influenced by Pu.[25] In Preface II, Wang connects his somehow passive "retreating from the world" (gesturing to the "cave of retreat" in the book title) to the traditional Confucian scholar's active mission of "rectifying the world" (*DKLY* 3), and his claim lies in his faith in the moralising force of supernatural stories:

> because they aim at persuasion and admonishment and connect with customs and rituals; they praise the good and punish the evil, exalt the chaste and degrade the licentious, enlighten the foolish and the stubborn and excite women and children, so that the ghost chronicler's work is not so different from the wooden bells of the moralists—what I record in this book is just like this.
> 亦緣旨寓勸懲，意關風化，以善惡為褒貶，以貞淫為黜陟，俾愚頑易于觀感，婦稚得以奮興，則南董之槧鉛，何異於逌人之木鐸？斯編所寄，亦猶是耳.
>
> (*DKLY* 3–4)

If the author of *DKLY* is still a loyal disciple of Pu and to some extent of Ji Yun, both of whom believe in the use of talking about ghosts, Wang's preface to *SYML* is a defiant assault on such traditions. As discussed in the previous chapter, *The Classic of Mountains and Seas* has set up the prototype for "collecting the strange" in the *zhiguai* tradition, yet at the beginning of the preface to *SYML*, Wang sets out to dismantle the aura of *The Classic*, and he did so by using Westerners and their knowledge as a reference:[26]

> Today the Westerners have set foot on the extremes of the world, but they have not found fantastic creatures with round heads and square feet, stretching to the heaven and to the earth as described by *Shanhaijing*. Therefore, what the book says is not believable. *Qilin*, phoenix, turtle, and dragon, these are the four holy creatures honoured by the Chinese, but the Westerners say there

is no *qilin* among furred animals, no phoenix among feathered animals, and no dragon among scaled animals.

然今西人足跡，遍及窮荒，凡屬圓顱方足、戴天而履地者，無所謂奇形怪狀如彼所云也. 斯其說不足信也.　麟鳳龜龍，中國謂之四靈. 而自西人言之，毛族中無所謂麟，羽族中無所謂鳳，鱗族中無所謂龍.

(*SYML* 1)

Wang then continues the polemic and extends it to a comparison of Western and Chinese beliefs and behaviours. According to Wang, the Westerners are good at practical knowledge, scientific investigation, accurate observation, and machine-making, all of which can benefit the people and strengthen the country, while the Chinese "do not do this, but seek such ends in fractured, illusory, and unverifiable lands—this is not merely the folly of curiosity, but pertaining to absurdity!" 不此之務，而反索之於支離虛誕、杳渺不可究詰之境，豈獨好奇之過哉，其志亦荒矣 (*SYML* 2).

Wang's exaltation of Western practicality over Chinese supernaturalism is unequivocal. By now, Wang has positioned himself on the opposite side of the traditional apology for talking about ghosts endorsed by both Xuan and the great master Pu Songling. The last redeeming virtue of supernatural stories that he had clung to in *DKLY—zhiguai*'s didacticism, is also dismissed as expedient and impractical:

> The sage used the supernatural as a moral lesson, but this is only a lesson for the foolish ones—in the human world there is the law of the emperor, while in the netherworld there is the law of ghosts and spirits, so the foolish ones are intimidated to follow proper conducts by the just punishments and awards of the supernatural. … The self-deluded create all kinds of strange stories, so that the cave of the fox is made to look like an alternative world. All these are what the Westerners resolutely refuse to believe, for they hold that illusory words are not as good as practical deeds.
>
> 聖人以神道設教，不過為下愚人說法：明則有王法，幽則有鬼神，蓋惕之以善惡賞罰之權，以寄其懲勸而已⋯自妄者造作怪異，狐狸窟中，幾若別有一世界. 斯皆西人所悍然不信者，誠以虛言不如實踐也.
>
> (*SYML* 1)

By now, Wang has nullified every merit of talking about the supernatural: they are not real, they do not serve as good moral lessons, and they do not do the country good. It seems that he is not writing a preface to a *zhiguai* collection but a polemic on it. One may ask, what kind of a framework is the author building for the understanding of his *zhiguai* stories? The answer, as I will show below, is precisely a paradoxical one which constantly requests the reader to replace one way of contemplating the world with another, yet where no single way of knowing is to have the final claim to superiority, and by extension, to reality.

Wang's next move is somewhat surprising, for without resolving the fissure between Western practicality and Chinese supernaturalism in his re-staging of *zhiguai*, he begins a sketch of his life foregrounding the injustices he has suffered. This is a relatively conventional move following what Pu does in his preface: appealing to the tradition of solitary indignation, the *zhiguai* writer fashions himself as an upright genius who with no solace in the human world has to seek friendship among ghosts and foxes.[27] Wang portrays a similar image of himself: once an ambitious man eager to serve his country with practical knowledge, his candour and unconventionality only brought him enemies and slanders (*SYML* 2).[28] What can one do with such a frustrating life? Wang's solution is familiar but not so compatible with the worldview he has set up in the previous part—he resorts to literary creation:

> When [one is] direly trapped, one must find a way out; when [one is] desperately depressed, one has to command his energy [to some channel]. When one ends up unrecognised by the world, one has to go to the deepest of the mountains and the heart of the forests, and his sorrows, agonies, melancholia, and delicate sentiments have to be commanded to a book. If not finding this in China, I seek it in the extremes of the world and the strange lands; if not finding it in my contemporaries, I go to the origins of history and towards the far ends of future; if I cannot find it among creatures like me, I seek it among ghosts and foxes, immortals and Buddha, grasses, trees, birds, and beasts.
>
> 困極則思通，鬱極則思奮，終於不遇，則惟有入山必深，入林必密而已，誠壹哀痛憔悴婉篤芬芳悱惻之懷，一寓之於書而已. 求之於中國不得，則求之於遐陬絕嶠，異域荒裔；求之於並世之人而不得，則上溯之亙古以前，下極之千載以後；求之於同類同體之人而不得，則求之於鬼狐仙佛、草木鳥獸.
>
> (*SYML* 2)

After deciding that the fantastic world of ghosts and foxes is illusory in the first part, Wang now appeals to the traditional apology of *zhiguai* writing and stages the fantastic world as the last resort for a frustrated man. For this frustrated being, the ordinary world as it is offers him no solace, and his true friend, once again as the author admits, must be found among "dark woods and black fortresses".

Certainly, beliefs in the supernatural and fictional narrations of the supernatural are different things;[29] while Wang certainly is not a supporter of the former, his act in even writing fictitious supernatural stories still seems suspicious. Wang's exaltation of what he believes to be Western practicality in the first part of his preface has debunked every conventionally evoked merit of recording the strange, ironically accomplishing the very opposite of the traditional authorial task in *zhiguai* prefaces—explaining why "I" should NOT write this book. The final resort to *zhiguai* writing as the last shelter for a frustrated scholar, however, is a return to tradition—the long tradition of conceptualising writing as the result of the author's "solitary indignation" emphatically promoted in Pu's *Liaozhai*,—yet it is also part of the tradition that Wang has just broken with. This partial retreat to tradition exposes the inherent perils of Wang's outbound mental journey troubled by the incompatibilities of a Western outlook and a traditional Chinese one.

There are yet larger implications embedded in Wang's paradoxical treatment of *zhiguai*. If Xuan has resorted to a pantheon of ghosts to mend a cosmos beleaguered by Western intrusion, we see two incompatible cosmoses wrestling with each other in Wang's *zhiguai* world: on one side, there is the rational world navigated by Westerners where no supernatural creatures exist and only practical knowledge does anyone good—this is the world that Wang, as a man admiring Western efficiency, lived and believed in; on the other side, there is the cosmos backed up with an entire genealogy of supernatural writing and a tradition of fashioning alternative identities and enclaves through writing the supernatural—this is the world that a disillusioned and displaced Chinese literatus can resort to, and Wang retreats to it in the end.

Symbolically, Wang's polemic on *zhiguai* traces a circular movement that returns to its starting point—writing *zhiguai* as a way of alternative identity-building, and in a sense Wang's own life journey is refracted in this pattern: starting as an ambitious man to rectify the world, yet ending as a frustrated man retreating to the "mountains" and "forests".[30] Wang's polemic on *zhiguai* illustrates vividly Longxi Zhang's insight that spiritual pilgrim is often conceptualised as a homecoming, but the return to home is also a reversal and a renewal, for the ending point is already subtly changed from the starting point.[31] Likewise, Wang's retreat to the *zhiguai* world is not a return to pure tradition, for the places where he envisions he can seek his peace of mind include not only China but also a larger outside. Indeed, the wonderlands in Wang's writing stretch far beyond the traditional peripheries of Chinese culture to include Western countries like Italy, France, Britain, and Switzerland. The West may not offer the Chinese intellectual his urgently needed sense of security, but it does offer him a reference to reorient his own identity.

Wang's preface to *SYML* sets up for the reader a heterogeneous world where competing discourses coexist. More importantly, prefaces as a threshold leading to the text proper affect also how meaning is made and understood in the stories they lead to. The following *zhiguai* stories by Wang that I examine expectedly also bear that mark of hesitation between disparate discourses, opening up a fantastic space where epistemological certainties are undermined, and new possibilities can be imagined. In the next section, I focus on Wang's stories dealing with the uncanny spectres of Chinese history, where the persistent evocation of *zhiguai* rhetoric and historical precedents and a deferral and deviation from the expected path expose the fissures in a reassuring glorious Chinese history, so that a break with history and tradition may be imagined.

Encountering the spectres of history: the remains and the revenants

Ghost narratives, as discussed earlier, are essentially narratives about the past and about making peace or trouble with the past. Writing ghost stories, ghost chroniclers make history serve the living by either looking up history for past greatness which the present can emulate, or critiquing history so that the present can escape from the burden of it. But if Xuan is interested in excavating neglected ghosts and re-entering them into a mythical history, Wang's ghost stories turn to two groups of people who have had a troubled relation with the official version of history: the male loyalists and the female revenants. By observing these people's alienation from official history, Wang calls into question the process of official history-making as well as the orthodox values upheld by that history; at the same time, the frequent evocation of past dynastic falls also helps to give expression to the unsayable masculinity anxiety acutely felt by the late-Qing male literati.

Male remains

In Wang's *zhiguai* stories, an explicit or covert reference to China's dynastic history is realised through alluding to the *yimin* 遺民 identity of some characters (often immortals).[32] By placing these *yimin* on some utopian island encountered in a contemporary protagonist's overseas travels, these stories reveal a yearning to escape to a temporal stasis outside of historical succession. As *yimin* make themselves the embodiment of a fossilised past, the evocation of *yimin* in Wang's stories bears some resemblance to Xuan's strategy of myth-making of a monumental past. However, for Wang's protagonists, the sojourn on the immortal's island is temporary and invariably they have to return to a mundane everyday world, exposing the inherent impossibility implied in the *yimin* discourse: history is inescapable and a clinging to the past in an imagined vacuum space out of history is no longer valid in the contemporary changing world.

To understand the embedded critique of official versions of national history in these stories, it is necessary to first put *yimin* into its cultural and political context. *Yi* means to leave behind, to be lost, and remaining, so *yimin* literally means "the remaining people". A polysemic word, it most often refers to the group of people "left behind by history" in China's dramatic dynastic changes. Sometimes, the "leaving behind" is a self-willed, strongly-posed political gesture: living as a recluse and refusing participation in the new political regime testify to the subject's loyalty to the previous dynasty and rejection of the new one.[33] *Yimin* carved out for themselves a symbolic vacuum space in history by sheer will: they absented themselves from contemporary life and observed the customs of a previous dynasty, so that while they actually lived simultaneously with the changed world, they had made themselves the living remains of what was already dead. David Der-Wai Wang aptly summarises *yimin*'s antithetical status to history: "*yimin* points to a political subjectivity dislocated from time".[34]

In theory, each dynastic change would produce its own *yimin*, but in reality, the most conspicuous *yimin* groups emerged during the Song-Yuan (Mongols) and Ming-Qing (Manchus) dynastic changes: both were occasions when what were perceived as an alien people replaced the Han Chinese as the new rulers. For the Han Chinese *yimin* of the Song and Ming living under alien rule, they regarded their loss as not only that of their nation but of the whole Chinese civilisation.

Yimin is a term with strong moral and political connotations and this identity actually affords little accessibility to common people—the refusal to participate in the new regime implies that the subject at least has had the right to participate in the first place: namely one has to be a male, scholarly elite or a man of prestige. But in this study I use the term in a broader sense to denote the group of people who deliberately or unconsciously leave themselves behind history; while they preserve the practices and cultures of a past time and keep a moment of Chinese history alive, they themselves become the living dead—the remains of history. If we adopt this concept of *yimin*, we will find that such figures appear frequently in Wang's three *zhiguai* collections. The immediacy of the particular political struggle of *yimin* softened, the *yimin* characters in Wang's stories blend with their fantastic setting and even merge with another literary motif: the Peach Blossom utopia.

Indeed, if we examine the "Taohuayuan ji" 桃花源記 (Record of the Peach Blossom Spring, 421) written by Tao Qian 陶潛 (365–427), we will find it to be yet another *yimin* story. Set in the Taiyuan era of the Eastern Jin when *coups d'état* were frequent and violent, the story depicts a utopian village hidden inside a cave blissfully oblivious of the violent dynastic successions of the world outside, and this possibility of living in a temporality forgotten by history and unperturbed by political struggles must be especially appealing to Tao's contemporaries. In this sense, the Peach Blossom utopia is a *yimin* story without the *yimin* discourse: it expresses the desire to escape from contemporary political turmoil rather than the desire to cling to a historical past, as Tao Qian's villagers preserve no loyalty to any political regime.

The encountering with *yimin* in an immortal's island in Wang Tao can be read as a capsule Peach Blossom story, yet this flirtation with a limbo outside of history is only temporary and Wang's protagonist always returns to the mundane reality however much he may marvel at the wonders of the immortals' island, for he has another, more urgent identity: the overseas traveller. The cyclical *Shanhaijing*-pattern of the traveller's tale discussed in Chapter 2 is the other substructure of Wang's overseas stories; but while Xuan reforms the *Shanhaijing*-pattern to portray the overseas as unspeakably evil and hostile to China, Wang's overseas islands signify a land of promise and wonder. The typical protagonist in Wang's stories would be a contemporary young man as ambitious and practical-minded as the author himself. He decides to see the wonders of the world, takes a modern steamship, and sets out; he suffers a shipwreck, lands on an apparently uninhabited island, and then meets some benevolent immortals, who prove to have been Chinese *yimin* of the Ming or Song dynasty or even earlier times. The utopian island is such a perfect limbo outside of history that both the immortals and the protagonist find their previous engagements with worldly affairs so shallow and repulsive; but unlike the immortals, the protagonist has to return to the human world in the end, just as the Wuling fisherman does in the original Peach Blossom Spring story.

Such a formula can be traced in Wang's "Xianren dao" 仙人島 (The Immortals' Island, *SYML* 1.13), "Min Yushu" 閔玉叔 (Scholar Min, *SYML*

3.113), and "Xiaoxia wan" 銷夏灣 (A Summer Resort, *SYML* 12.566). "A Summer Resort" is an exhibition of fossilised Chinese history: the protagonist, Ji Zhongxian, first meets two old men on the island in attire so antique it is as if transported from the mythic origins of Chinese history (implied to be the legendary "flood period"); both their speech and writing are incomprehensible to Ji (*SYML* 12.568). Unable to communicate with him, they invite over another islander, a hermit also in antique attire but speaking a language that Ji can at least understand. He tells Ji that he had been a follower of the Southern Song loyalist Wen Tianxiang and how he had drifted to this island after the critical Yashan maritime battle with the Mongols. The chaotic history of the collapse of the Southern Song is lightly evoked in the hermit's recollection, and the narrative then swiftly turns to an indulgent description of the island's wonders as the hermit shows Ji around. In this fantastic island forgotten by emperors and historians, the remains of different dynasties live peacefully together, each preserving the relics of their own epoch. The long Chinese history seems to be thus reincarnated in these human bodies and kept intact, while reminiscences of floods and wars are overshadowed by the fantastic wonders that the island can offer.

Wang's *yimin* stories reflect some undercurrents of the late-Qing intellectuals' perception of the self and other. To meet Chinese *yimin* in an overseas island is to meet with a past self; if in Xuan's overseas stories the other is portrayed as a demon lurking on China's periphery, here in Wang's immortals' island inhabited by Chinese *yimin*, the wondrous other is submerged within the familiar self. Moreover, to see a Chinese face and costume in a place far away from China offers, for a late-Qing traveller, an urgently needed reassurance of China's continuous cultural and political influence in the world, while the actual political climate then in Asia clearly indicated the opposite.[35] Yet Wang's evocation of Chinese history does not stop at self-aggrandisement. The remaining people of the past, while reminding one of the superiority of Chinese culture, also haunt as an uncanny spectre to the contemporary traveller. Embodying what is already dead, the *yimin* are truly the spectres of China's dynastic history, and as spectres their very presence reminds one of a constantly present absence, namely the cruel and violent historical fissure that makes the spectre in the first place. As anachronic entities, spectres defy the lineal succession between past and present and make the very notion of history—an ordering of the past to make sense of the present and future—problematic. Here, Wang's fantastic *yimin* stories, by reference to both the Peach Blossom Spring motif and the traveller's tale, draw out the tension with history already inherent in the Peach Blossom Spring myth: *yimin* seek to deny the succession of history, yet their very existence firmly implicated in history presupposes the inescapability of history and its violence. The *yimin* as spectral remains, therefore, embody the impossible desire of escaping from history and at the same time being predicated on it.

This paradoxical drive towards history inherent in *yimin* stories also reflects Wang's contradictory sentiments towards the past: a simultaneous desire for re-enacting past splendours and a fear of witnessing a return of past dynastic falls.

In this sense, the spectres of history embody for Wang the late-Qing literati's sense of uncertainty when the self was thrust into a chaotic world of competing discourses. The ambiguous ending of "The Immortals' Island" exemplifies this conflict between a mythologised version of Chinese history and the recognition of an alterity to it. After 20 years of happy abode on the immortals' island with an immortal wife, the protagonist Xu Mengtu is urged by the wife and his parents-in-law to return to the human world as predestined.[36] Reluctantly, Xu obeys. Thirty years later, a message from the wife asking him to return to the island rekindles his desire to travel overseas, but this time he is ridiculed by a sailor: "Nowadays the sea ships are all steered by, Westerners and sea voyages are all scheduled; all the overseas islands they reach are already inhabited. Wide as the oceans are, how can there be any deserted islands for the immortals to live on? Stop your daydreaming!" 今時海舶，皆用西人駕駛，往還皆有定期，所止海島皆有居人，海外雖汪洋無涯，安有一片棄土為仙人所駐足哉？子休矣! (*SYLM* 1.16). But Xu is adamant. He books a voyage to America, yet before he departs, Taiping troops raid his village, and Xu is killed by Taiping soldiers when he leaps from his hiding place to protect his travel fund.

Different narrative conventions jar disconcertingly in this strange brew of old and new wine. Traditional plot conventions like predestination are flagged up repeatedly in the tale: Xu's marriage with the immortal wife, his unwilling departure from the island, and the promised return to the immortals' island are all preordained by destiny, according to Xu's immortal parents-in-law (*SYML* 1.15). However, although such formulas are partly enacted, a full realisation of the genre expectation is always delayed and finally denied, as if Wang deliberately lures his reader into a familiar world only to expose the unstable foundations of it. If to portray *yimin* as immortals exhibits a desire to turn history into myth and a hope for divine intervention in human lives—strategies tried by Xuan and Pu respectively—the thwarting of this hope exposes the impotence of such a history-turned-myth. Moreover, the futility of Xu's effort is further ridiculed by the incongruity between the fantastic logic that governs the immortals' island and the contemporary industrialised, navigated, and Western-dominated human world he is stranded in. This new world is no longer regulated by the correlation between heaven and man (as implied in the cult of *qing*) but by physical forces powered by steam engines. However much the protagonist may long for the immortals' island, the Westerners' mastery of the sea is a sad truth that he must acknowledge and put up with.

The brutal ending of Xu's fantastic adventure fully exposes the incongruity of competing worldviews in the chaotic late Qing. The world of immortals pales against bloody contemporary atrocities, as Xu's efforts to fulfil his destiny are first hindered by Western navigation of the sea and then cut short by the Taiping raid. Xu's ending of being killed in the act of protecting gold is doubly ironic: since he is a hermit supposedly contemptuous of money, to guard money at the cost of his life is a considerable shame; and the fact that his possessiveness of gold is caused by his eagerness to re-join his beloved wife only heightens the irony—the immortal wife's message for reunion does not miraculously bring about reunion as expected but indirectly kills the husband. Is the man who longs today for an immortals' island really a fool to be mocked? Were Xu given the opportunity to begin his journey, would he be able to find the way back to the immortals' island? Or rather, is Xu really killed by the bandits? Can it be a disguise staged by the immortal wife to help achieve the reunion, so that while we are reading about Xu's death, we are reading of his re-entering the immortals' land?[37] The narrative of the story and the paradoxical interpretative frameworks set up in the preface discussed before may suggest a yes to all these questions yet guarantee none, making the story truly fantastic and impossible to be resolved on any epistemological plane.

To refuse resolution in a *zhiguai* story is a modern yet perilous move for Wang, for by departing from the *yimin* myth, Wang has refused the reassurance summoned up by a mythologised history: this is the peril of critical history, yet it is only through this break with the past that a new, different model of the self can be imagined. If Wang's *yimin* stories betray a longing as well as suspicion towards that mythic past, a more poignant critique of the *yimin* discourse and of national history is to be realised through dealing with the spectre of spectres: the female revenants.

Female revenants

The tragic death of Xu pulls the reader away from the utopian island right to the centre of a contemporary trauma: deaths caused by the Taiping Rebellion. While a few *yimin* could survive domestic wars by retreating to an overseas island, more (especially women) died as silent victims and became revenants. Female revenants, as mentioned earlier, are a staple of *zhiguai*; like the foxes, they are marked by their otherworldly beauty and their readiness to comfort a lonely male scholar at night.[38] In his stories Wang follows this human-male-versus-supernatural-female convention, but his female revenants are distinct in that they often appear as a group of victims of some particular historical calamity, be it the tumultuous trans-dynastic wars or the contemporary Taiping Rebellion. Frequently they are alluded to have been wives or daughters of loyalists and have courageously committed suicide while their male relatives vindicated their loyalty in war.[39] Thus staged, these "chaste women" revenants are the netherworld sisters of the ghost Zheng Yiniang, both of whom are the female version of *yimin* with the same nobility yet fewer choices. If *yimin* have made themselves the self-willed ghosts of history, then the female revenants are the "ghost" of those ghosts. For on the one hand, stories of female revenants expose the darker side of the *yimin* discourse: the suffering and suppression of the silenced many who had no choice in dynastic changes, whose virtuous death could not bring them glory, and moreover were used by writers of history to promote the latter's own loyalty ideals. On the other hand, revenants as anachronic entities travelling freely across history become the antithesis of *yimin* who try to escape from history to a static temporality. Revenants return to remind one of the repetitiveness of dynastic history, and onto their eternally suffering bodies is projected contemporary Chinese men's urgent masculinity anxiety engendered by another dynastic fall looming on the horizon.

Dynastic wars were a great trauma for everyone, but more particularly it was often women who suffered the most in these wars, as the possession of their body became the contesting site of males of various sides. Rape was prevalent, and the female relatives of government officials were often encouraged to commit suicide to preserve their chastity and vindicate their loyalty to their men. However, a cruel fact accompanying virtuous women's heroic suicide is that while some had chosen death willingly, some deaths were coerced and even forced by the women's male relatives to accomplish a loyalty ideal.[40] Despite such tragedies and betrayals, chaste women who died tragically in war were a favourite subject for literati during or after dynastic changes, who would meticulously record these deaths in their books as embellishments to the loyalty discourse that they themselves may not be able to participate yet are determined to promote.[41] In a sense, the death of the virtuous women becomes a sacrifice that their male relatives and male historians offer to the altar of loyalty.

Wang's stories of female ghosts participate in this literati tradition of writing "chaste women" in war, yet they also significantly deviate from it. The typical plot of his revenant story goes thus: a man sojourning alone in a forlorn place accidentally overhears the feast of a group of women in a nearby garden at night, and the women's merry chatter turns gradually into a bitter recollection of their tragic death in a past (usually trans-dynastic) war. When the man returns to the same spot the next day, he finds nothing but some weathered tombstones, indicating the talks he overheard the previous night were but the re-animated shadows of history long past.[42] In these stories, the traumas of war and the cruel human suffering within it are re-enacted again and again through the ghosts' nocturnal parties. However merry their feast and however gorgeous their clothes, it still saddens them that they are victims of war and are made into ghosts by some brutal historical events in which they have no say.

By turning the focus of the narrative from the nobility of the women's death to their subsequent eternal sorrow as ghosts, Wang's stories pass subtly a critique on the chastity discourse discussed above. In "Liu Qing", two ghosts engage in a discussion of the merits and defects of ghosthood and personhood, with one lamenting: "I'd rather become a human again than a *jian*" 與其為靈，不如仍復為人 (*SBSH* 3.52).[43] And in stories without such a polemic, the merriment of the ghosts' party always sinks into melancholy once they start retelling their death. The agonies of dynastic change and especially the irretrievable personal losses within it become a trauma they cannot work through, however well the orthodox loyalty discourse may put the virtuous women on a pedestal. Thus, the revenants' nocturnal parties turn into an eternal mourning for their traumatic past, and the revenants themselves become the Freudian melancholic who is forced to re-open the wounds of history again and again and who ritually perform a silenced critique of it: however glorious the *yimin*'s loyalist discourse, suicidal acts cannot be rationalised, and dynastic wars bring only suffering, not glory.[44]

Apart from the critique of the *yimin* discourse, the frequent appearance of female revenants as "chaste victims of war" in Wang's stories may serve another purpose: giving expression to a suppressed yet acutely felt masculinity anxiety among the late-Qing literati. Chinese literati's obsession with the "chaste women" in dynastic wars is founded on the traditional equation between female chastity and male loyalism. For the male literati who are not a *yimin*, to exalt the chaste women is to vicariously promote a loyalism that they themselves aspire.[45] However, as Martin Huang notes, this equation, together with the equation between manhood and nationhood, can also be a source of tremendous masculinity anxiety, especially during the violent Ming-Qing dynastic change.[46] Failing to protect their country from alien invasion is already a sign of Chinese men's impotence, yet what is worse is that many women had passed the loyalty test by committing suicide while their men surrendered to the new regime, making the defeated Han males seem emasculated.[47] In this context, the female revenants in Wang's tales appear to the contemporary Chinese man to rekindle his past guilt of failing to save his country as well as reminding him of a current danger: just like the forced repetition of the ghosts' feast, history may repeat itself too.

In a sense, the late-Qing literati were not only aware that their age seems to be a repetition of the late Ming, they also actively promoted this identification. Both the late Ming and the late Qing were times when the Chinese civilisation was under siege by an alien intruder, and what often interests modern scholars is the conscious or unconscious imitation or re-appropriation by the late-Qing intellectuals of the late-Ming loyalist ideals.[48] Participating in this vogue, Wang too enacts a straightforward parallel between the late Ming and his contemporary late Qing in his female revenant stories, but his focus is not on a nostalgic longing for the romanticised past represented by its heroic men and women, but rather, the violence of history past and present to which the ghost's body bears eternal witness. "Jixian yishi" 乩仙軼事 (The Lost Stories of the Planchette Spirits, *SYML* 4.198) is such a story that juxtaposes the chaotic late-Ming wars with the recent Taiping Rebellion through the bodies of victimised women. The story takes a symmetrical pattern composed of two women's biographies: the late-Ming palace lady Liu Cuiyun who was constantly kidnapped by lustful males after the fall of the Ming court before she could finally commit suicide, and a parallel story of a contemporary girl named Cheng Jiyu who narrowly escaped the Taiping troops yet soon died a rape victim of a Qing soldier. The repetitiveness of the women's suffering is spelt out by the narrator's remark conjoining their biographies: "although two hundred years stand between them, the happenings are similar and the sorrows the same" 前後二百年，事若相類，有同悲焉 (*SYML* 4.200).

Indeed, sorrow is the central tenor of Wang's biographies of the virtuous women, decidedly veering away from a tendency to aestheticise and even extract pleasure from women's deaths often found in literati writing on similar topics.[49] Instead of dwelling on the glory of heroic death, Wang's biographies put the two women's personal suffering at the centre of the story. This square look at death strips the lustre off the loyalist discourse and exposes the brutality of dynastic changes: in such chaos, emperors and soldiers are not so different from servants and bandits; while the interpretation of official history is legitimised by those in power, the individual sufferings indicate the opposite.

As a proclaimed historian of the ghosts, Wang knows well that a sense of truth is a must to give the story its due dignity. To enhance the authenticity of the women's history, Wang makes sure that his account of the virtuous women is devoid of any melodrama and begins both biographies with the formula of historiographic biographies: reporting the woman's name, family, and hometown.[50] There is nothing supernatural in the accounts themselves, yet their ending surprisingly evokes the supernatural to lend historicity to the women's accounts, which, ironically, banishes the women's stories from history irrevocably. We are told that as no one witnessed the women's death, their sacrifices are never known in history; it is only when the women's spirits possessed the planchette in the local literati's gatherings (some elegant poems supposedly composed by the ghosts are also recorded) that their stories are made known and transmitted by sympathetic literati and collected by the equally sympathetic Wang in his *zhiguai* collection. Ironically, this appeal to authorial authenticity confirms the ghost's absolute silence in the construction of her own history—for it is clear that no story can be written about the ghosted women but as spiritual messages solicited by male literati.[51] Sympathetic as Wang is in his careful excavation of silenced ghosts, it is, after all, a man-made "history of the ghosts" to express his anxiety implicated in the historical present, whereas the female ghost herself is still excluded from the making of her own history.[52]

The impossibility to enter the ghost woman's story into history, falsely resolved in "Planchette Spirits", also exposes the sinister side of the noble *yimin* discourse that haunts the late Qing contemporary: the *yimin* discourse, together with the discourses on patriotism and loyalism promoted in official history and consecrated in Xuan's mythic history, establishes a glorious national history which demands sacrifice and the continuity of tradition, but in many cases that ideal notion is untenable and can be a burden to many, even males. In this sense, ghost women as victims of dynastic change serve another purpose for the male scholar who conjures them up: they bear metonymically the man's sense of impotence and give expression to their urgent masculinity anxiety.

If this sense of impotence is only figured precariously through the female ghosts in "Planchette Spirits", then "Yaoniang zaishi" 窅娘再世 (Yaoniang Reincarnated, *SYML* 7.300) spells out the masculinity anxiety. The marvellous woman Yaoniang foregrounded in the title serves to connect the contemporary story with the historical figure Li Yu 李煜 (937–78), the last emperor of the Southern Tang and the accompanying motif of male impotence and the collapse of a nation. Living in a haunted house in the ruins of Nanjing after the fall of the Taipings, the protagonist Zhou Weihuang is one day visited by a beautiful woman named Xianglin, and they soon fall in love. While the two lovers are sailing down the Yangtze River, Zhou is befriended by a charismatic man, who invites him to a feast with a gallery of beautiful ladies. The host reveals himself to be the Southern Tang Emperor Li Yu, and the accompanying women all his favourite royal consorts. What's more, Zhou's mysterious mistress Xianglin is none other than Li Yu's consort Yaoniang. Zhou is embarrassed to face his "cuckolded" host, yet it is the "cuckolded" ex-emperor who finds words to comfort him: "A man [like me] cannot keep intact his state, let alone his concubines! Yaoniang is only yours temporarily, but not for long", 江山尚不能保，況乎妾媵之流哉？屬君不過一時暫耳，非常也 (*SYML* 7.303). Several years later Yaoniang disappears without a trace.

Identified as Li Yu's favourite concubine and implied as a new ghost made during the Taiping Rebellion, Yaoniang's body bears a double inscription of history, and as the shared object of desire between two men, Yaoniang becomes the defining other through which a homosociality is enacted between men of two falling dynasties.[53] Li Yu's explicit equation between his failure to protect his state and his women makes it clear that masculinity again is enacted by objectifying women: one loses control of the state and one loses control of his women, and vice versa. By exchanging concubines with Li Yu, the humiliated emperor and cuckolded husband, the protagonist shares vicariously with Li Yu his impotence and his fear of losing his state.

As shown in this section, the traumas of China's dynastic history are repeatedly conjured up in Wang's stories through encountering the spectres of that history: male *yimin* and female revenants. This evocation of ghosts is not a reliving of past splendour and heroism, but a problematisation of the inherent ideology held in that history. Indeed, for both the chaste women who choose suicide and *yimin* who render themselves the living remains of the past, their heroic act of death vindicates the loyalty discourse but also exposes the irrationality and brutality of it. By writing the spectres of history, Wang gives expression to the particular masculinity anxiety plaguing his generation of Chinese literati. Moreover, by critiquing the cultural values represented by the *yimin* discourse—which is clinging to the past and tradition, Wang also effects a critique of the model masculinity embodied in the *shi* (士) ideal, thus making it possible to envisage other, more open-minded masculinity models which no longer rely on perceiving the self as the eternal centre of the world and are willing to go out and learn from others. Therefore, for Wang, to question Chinese history and its accompanying Sinocentrism, though agonising enough, helps the contemporary Chinese man to step outside of his comfort zone when he sets out to confront the new challenge of his age—the inevitable competition with the West.

Journey to the West and journey to the heart

Compared with a demonised West embodied in the fox woman in Xuan's stories, the West in Wang's travel writing and *zhiguai* stories is much more realistic—his experience of travelling in Europe simply makes it impossible for him to paint the foreign lands in his fiction in distorted and fabulous brushes. The West, for him, is not an undifferentiated idea, but a land composed of distinct countries like Prussia, France, and Britain, each with their own distinct cultures and customs.[54] The traditional "centre–periphery" framework seldom leaves traces in Wang's stories, and the West is portrayed to be a land as civilised as China. However, even if the West no longer possesses only a peripheral position vis-à-vis China in Wang's stories, the gendered imagination of alien cultures pertains: the encounter between China and the West is always garbed in the form of a romantic encounter between a masculine self and a feminised other.

Four of Wang's *zhiguai* stories that involve a romance between a Chinese man and a foreign woman—"Haiwai meiren" 海外美人 (Overseas Beauties, *SYML* 4.193), "Haiwai zhuangyou" 海外壯遊 (A Grand Tour Overseas, *SYML* 8.355), "Haidi qijing" 海底奇境 (Wonderland at the Sea Bottom, *SYML* 8.350), and "Meili xiaozhuan" 媚黎小傳 (A Biography of Mary, *SYML* 7.305)—have been so far the most studied stories of Wang's *zhiguai* oeuvre.[55] While Sheldon H. Lu reads such tales of transnational encounter as a "wish fulfilment about the status of the Chinese citizens in a global arena",[56] Huili Zheng regards these tales as implicating the anxieties of male impotence and a civilisational crisis of Wang's generation.[57] The "Chinese-man-versus-foreign-woman" plot in Wang's encounter stories indeed is full of paradoxes, and I will demonstrate that its author is trying to negotiate with a Sino–Western relationship far more complex than one of domination and submission suggested by previous scholars. I focus on the story "Overseas Beauties", for it not only envisages a potential encounter between China and the West but also enacts a symbolic encounter between China's past and present. The latter is an important undercurrent in both Wang's and Xuan's *zhiguai* writings, for it is where a new cultural identity may be moulded to answer the contemporary challenges. Combining an outgoing journey to explore the West and an inward journey through which the Chinese man re-examines his own cultural and historical inheritance, "Overseas Beauties" in a sense dramatises the circular textual move in its author's preface to *SYML* examined above. As mentioned before, the outward journey to explore the world is one deeply troubled by the spectres of one's own national history, and the journey ends not in the dreamt-of West but in a return to a Chinese home anchored in the fantastic in-between space in *zhiguai*, where multiple layers of realities exist, and no single worldview is to dominate.

As the epitome of contemporary Chinese intellectuals' mental journey to the West, "Overseas Beauties" presents at the beginning an unconventional and open-minded couple as its protagonists: the husband Lu Meifang is heir to a prosperous shipping business and has aspired to sail across the world since he was young; his wife, contrary to the modest and gentle type of Confucian ladies, is a martial arts master and shares her husband's dreams. Declining the suggestion to take a Western ship, Lu builds for his grand tour a ship of his own design according to traditional Chinese astrology—a triumphant execution of Chinese science and technology instead of a Western one. Yet, the ship is lit with electronic bulbs, another Western invention (*SYML* 4.193). The unconventional formation of this Chinese couple and their bizarre invention of the ship make it clear that this is no ordinary journey: from the beginning it is staged as a competition between Chinese civilisation and its Western rival. As a projection of the author's ideal self, the open-minded and outward-looking Lu couple represents the hope of late-Qing China.[58]

The first stop on the couple's overseas journey is some island off the coast of Japan. Wang's visit to Japan in 1879 showed him how this neighbour of China had kept intact much traditional Chinese culture[59] while at the same time had been quickly westernising itself since the Meiji reform. Therefore, Japan becomes the ideal place where a Chinese man may encounter the spectres of Chinese history as well as envisage his future confrontation with the West. The Japanese host tells the Lus that the island has been honoured by the remains of three Chinese Ming-dynasty loyalists, who came there after the Ming army's defeat by the Manchus.[60] Legend has it that these three officers had vowed to recover the land lost to the Manchus, yet failing that, they committed suicide and their bodies immediately turned into giant corpses, miraculously kept intact over the centuries, and receiving due respect from the Japanese islanders. If the *yimin* previously discussed are only fossilised in a metaphorical sense, here the undecomposed corpses of these Ming *yimin* are clearly presented as corporeal spectres of that part of Chinese history. Expectedly, Lu is greatly moved by the nobility and loyalism of his compatriots and asks to pay homage to the remains in person. As Lu gets close to the remains, one of the corpses stirs and makes a gesture of courtesy to Lu just as they vowed to do upon their death—yet Lu flees, the uncanniest of this uncanny encounter with *yimin*.

Lu's unheroic retreat is a cynical attack on the illusions of patriotism and loyalty embedded in the splendid Chinese history. The Ming *yimin*'s undecomposed corpses bear witness to their loyalty to a bygone dynasty and gesture to future sympathetic Chinese descendants, who may take over their duty of reclaiming Chinese glory. Whereas Lu, representing the essence of Chinese culture with an outward-looking orientation, proves to be just that ideal descendant. However, such a perfect reunion of China's past and present ends in Lu's shameful retreat, as if the remains of history are too horrible a sight to bear even for its legitimate heir. Is Lu a coward, or is the loyalty and patriotism discourse inscribed in orthodox history really an uncanny burden, so that no matter what rationalisation of its arbitrariness and cruelty has been made, it scares instead of empowers the descendants? As with the fantastic *yimin* stories discussed above, here again Wang problematises the validity of the *yimin* discourse. If, as Yanchun Qin remarks, the *yimin* identity during dynastic changes is a crystallisation of the traditional *shi* ideal,[61] then Lu's inability to stare *yimin* in the face puts into question the very essence of *shi* and its associated ideal construction of masculinity, moral perfection, and loyalty to the state. To say that Wang totally denies the Confucian ideal of *shi* may be exaggerating the case, yet his own unconventional life path forever exiled from the orthodox centre did enable him to imagine and live out masculinity models deviating from the *shi* ideal yet be beneficial to his country too.[62]

The Lu couple's encounter with the uncanny remains of Chinese history on the Japanese island speaks of a painful break with their ancestors, a further deviation from tradition compared with their bold decision to sail across the world. Could this break from tradition offer the Lus a firmer control of their present when confronted with their Western rivals? The story offers a bleak answer. Promptly, it presents an allegorical battle between China and the West in the Lus' next stop. On a certain Southeast Asian island on the edge of China's cultural influence, the Lu couple runs into a martial arts contest, implied to be organised by Westerners.[63] Over-confidently, Lu's wife jumps into the ring to avenge her Eastern comrade, a Japanese man just defeated by the host, yet both she and the host die by strangling each other. A baby son is delivered prematurely during this process, and a mysterious Taoist priest promptly appears and requests to adopt Lu's son, promising a reunion twenty years later on Luofu Mountain. Without remonstrance, the traumatised Lu lets the Taoist take away his son.

Halfway through his westward journey, Lu has lost both his wife (his military power) and a premature son (his future). If the ambitious Lu couple has started out symbolising the hope of an open-minded China to confront its Western rivals, the lonely husband by now has lost his initial optimism in seeking rewarding adventures in the dreamt Westland. It is here that the Chinese man's agonising inward journey gradually emerges and replaces his initial confident outbound journey to the West. Lu continues his journey to Europe, yet the closer he gets to the West, the closer his mentality journeys homeward to tradition, so that when he finally arrives in Italy, what he sees around is no longer a real West but an uncanny West blending together unfamiliarity with familiar *zhiguai* motifs. Surrounded by foreign music in the Italian seaport of Messina, Lu feels lonely and cannot work out the sorrow of losing his wife. But soon he is befriended by a generous Chinese expatriate anchoring nearby, who tries to cheer him up by offering him two astonishingly beautiful maidens as a gift. What he says about the maidens immediately places the story in familiar fantastic terrain established through heavy intertextuality to classic *zhiguai* stories. The beauty of the two maidens, the expatriate tells Lu, is only an illusion, for they are horrible Yaksha (*yecha* 夜叉) who have paid to have their ugly bodies covered by painted skins. This description of the Yaksha is derived from two familiar *Liaozhai* stories: "The Yaksha Kingdom" 夜叉國 (1:3.348) and "The Painted Skin" 畫皮 (1:1.119). "The Yaksha Kingdom" depicts how a Chinese merchant marries a savage female Yaksha (portrayed as an ugly, semi-human creature) on an overseas island, while "The Painted Skin" tells a cautionary tale about delusive female appearance: a man is seduced and killed by a heinous devil who covers herself with a painted human skin.

With these allusions to *Liaozhai* stories, the practical-minded Lu's journey to the West, reflecting the author's exaltation of Western practicality in his preface to *SYML*, has by now turned almost into a backward journey into *zhiguai* tropes and a retreat to tradition. The story's ambiguous yet deeply unsettling ending, however, problematises this return and leads the journey further into the undefined realm between illusion and reality. Hearing of the horrible secret of the maidens, Lu refuses the present, yet the expatriate retorts: "What a fool you are! What is real in this world? Beauties can turn into skeletons and a Yaksha with painted skin can be a Bodhisattva" 君真愚矣！世間一切事，孰是真者？紅粉變相，即是骷髏，夜叉畫皮，遂成菩薩 (*SYML* 4.197). The expatriate's reply echoes with yet another *Liaozhai* story, "The Painted Wall" 畫壁 (1:1.14) and common Buddhist rhetoric on the illusoriness of life. The narrator Historian of the Strange in "The Painted Wall" concludes: "Illusions are initiated by people's heart—this seems to be a reasonable saying. A licentious heart begets an obscene world; an indecent heart begets a macabre world. The Bodhisattva enlightens the fool with a thousand illusions" 幻由人生，此言類有道者. 人有淫心，是生褻境；人有褻心，是生怖境. 菩薩點化愚蒙，千幻並作 (1:1.17).

Indeed, the loss of his ability to tell illusion from reality seems to be the final reward that Lu obtains from his journey to the West. Having no intention to make any further exploration in Europe, Lu consents to the proposal of the expatriate and promptly takes the two Yaksha women back to China. He has gazed at the women naked in the bath many times and has never found a sign of painted skin, so he begins to doubt the words of the expatriate. The last sentence tells us that Lu has never been to Luofu Mountain, seemingly suggesting that the promised reunion with the son is never realised (*SYML* 4.197). The reader is left as confused as the disillusioned Lu: are the expatriate's words just a joke, or is Lu really deceived by the illusion of beauty? What about the Taoist's promised reunion? What is illusion and what is reality?

This last question, the deliberate effacing of the distinction between illusion and reality, and an insistence on uncertainty at the end of the story, may indicate the only way of salvation that the author suggests a disillusioned Chinese intellectual could seek. Lu does take back from Italy two "overseas beauties" from his westward journey, but the sexual possession of these women by a Chinese man is not simply a "domesticating strategy" against the West as Zheng suggests,[64] as the ending's surprisingly dense allusion to *Liaozhai* points to the Yaksha women's "traditional" instead of Western origin.[65] Borrowed from Hindu mythology, Yaksha has appeared in Chinese literature since the Tang dynasty and has over time become a derogatory term used to designate China's barbaric others beyond the northeast border and in the South Seas in literary imagination.[66] The encounter with the Yaksha women at the end of Lu's journey, therefore, is a return to *zhiguai* tradition instead of something truly Western. By connecting these Yaksha women with a Chinese compatriot and using dense allusion to classic *Liaozhai* stories, the author is deliberately pulling the protagonist, and the reader too, out of the real Western presence that surrounds him into a linguistic web constructed by layers and layers of old *zhiguai* rhetoric. In this symbolic zone constructed through *zhiguai* motifs, what is real and what is illusion, what is inside and what is outside of fiction is deliberately effaced. The journey to the West ends not in the real West but in the heart of darkness of Chinese supernatural tales.[67]

In this sense, Lu's fictional expedition to the West is reflective of Wang's circular argumentative moves in his preface to *SYML* as well as his own life path: the subject first favours a Western, materialistic perception of the world, but when two incompatible worldviews come into fierce competition and drive him to a corner, the only way out is to resort to the traditional *zhiguai* discourse. However, this return to *zhiguai* rhetoric, as prefigured in Wang's preface, is not a return to the same starting point but a renewal, for the traditional supernatural cosmos promoted by *zhiguai* is again doubted and deferred, as the unresolved question of reality and illusion and unrealised reunion with the son at the end of the story insistently point to a land of uncertainty. The final home for a perturbed and disillusioned Chinese intellectual is therefore a linguistically constructed fantastic zone where identities and realities are fluid, so the bitter question facing the besieged Chinese can be deferred. What Wang faced agonisingly in Edinburgh in real life—to be mistaken for a woman by Westerners[68]—is thus evaded in this fantastic tale. In other stories when a final encounter with the West does happen, as in "A Grand Tour Overseas", "A Biography of Mary", and "Wonderland at the Bottom of Sea", the Chinese man occupies firmly the position of the male and is always able to win the love of a Western woman.[69]

The fantastic departure

Oscillating between incompatible worldviews, Wang's *zhiguai* stories discussed in this chapter usher the reader as well as the author into a truly fantastic land in Todorov's sense. Moreover, Wang's fantastic *zhiguai* tale is also what Campany calls a "contra" literature",[70] departing from the premises of a familiar world order yet deviating into an alternative world contra to or countering the known. Traditionally, the anomalous accounts and stories of ghosts offer such a contradiction to Confucian orthodoxy as embodied in official state histories, yet by the late Qing, the Chinese culture as a whole, whether the disenchanted Confucian ideology or the enchanted world of ghosts and foxes, was confronted and challenged by a new reality represented by Westerners and their culture. Wang's fantastic *zhiguai* writing therefore exhibits a departure not only from Confucian orthodoxy (as evidenced in his critique of history and loyalty discourse in the spectre stories) but also a subtle departure from the *zhiguai* tradition and its idealised world of ghosts and foxes. The result of this departure is a circular movement, evidenced in both Wang's paradoxical *zhiguai* preface and *zhiguai* stories framed by that preface: the Chinese man journeys away from his tradition towards a Western view of the world yet ends in a partial return to tradition. This is a deeply troubled journey traversing disparate terrains yet landing in none, and in the process, established concepts like history, cultural identity, and masculinity are contested and remoulded.

More importantly perhaps, is that the notion of reality is made contingent in these tales. To some degree, this is a true reflection of the chaotic and sometimes dreamlike experiences of Wang and his generation of late-Qing intellectuals. In an age of unprecedented ideological instability, they witnessed the melting of traditional boundaries and categories, which generated in them a tremendous identity anxiety, especially a masculinity anxiety. Wang's fantastic *zhiguai* situated halfway between a Western and a Chinese conceptualisation of the world is reflective of this identity crisis, and in a sense suggests a possible strategy to cope with it. Through these tales, the Chinese man's masculinity anxiety can be figured, curbed, and possibly solved—although eventually it is an ineffective solution, for the final confrontation between the Chinese subject and his Western rival is deferred in a fantastic limbo where no definite reality can be acclaimed.

Although the revalorisation of Chinese masculinity in Wang's stories may be not as effective as Xuan's self-mythologisation, it is certainly a more informed one. By exposing the limits of contemporary epistemology, these tales of strange challenge established notions of norms and unleash the potential of the anomalous. They are unsettling and beneficial for their contemporary as well as modern readers, as they have already touched on one of the fundamental problems of human experience: the relativeness of the "reality" we live in.

Notes

1 An earlier version of this chapter has appeared in *Ming Qing Studies 2017* as "Tales of the New Strange: Wang Tao's Zhiguai Writing (1880–1890)", Paolo Santangelo ed., 11–44.
2 Nietzsche, "On the Use and Disadvantages of History for Life" (1874), in *Untimely Mediations* (1997), 57–123.
3 Nietzsche, "Use and Disadvantages", 67–9, 75–7.
4 For this reason, Wang's earlier biographer, Henry McAleavy, calls him "a displaced person": Wang could not fit among the traditional Confucian scholars in bureaucracy, nor could he find his place among Westerners whom he acutely sensed as his "others". See McAleavy, *Wang Tao: The Life and Writing of a Displaced Person* (1953).
5 Tzvetan Todorov, *The Fantastic: A Structural Approach to a Literary Genre* (1975).
6 Wang recorded his excitement of first seeing Shanghai in *Manyou suilu tuji* (2004), 23–5.
7 On Wang's life in Shanghai, see Catherine Vance Yeh, "The Life-Style of Four Wenren in Late Qing Shanghai", *Harvard Journal of Asiatic Studies* 57. 2 (1997): 419–70.
8 On this episode in Wang's life, see Cohen, *Between Tradition and Modernity*, 39–56 and McAleavy, *Wang Tao*, 14–15. Both Cohen and McAleavy believe that Wang did write this letter.
9 For this reason, I use Legge's translation of Confucian classics for my quotations in this book, as the wording and interpretation may to some extent reflect Wang's understanding of these Confucian texts.
10 Wang's essays on reform were mainly collected in his *Taoyuan wenlu waibian* 弢園文錄外編 (1883). His other writings on European history and politics include *Faguo zhilüe* 法國志略 (prefaced 1870), *Pufa zhanji* 普法戰紀 (1886), *Taoyuan chidu* 弢園尺牘 (1880), *Xixue jicun liuzhong* 西學輯存六種 (1890), etc. For a list of Wang's writings, see Ping Xin, *Wang Tao pingzhuan* (1990), 241–50.
11 See Kuang-Che Pan, "Knowledge of the Different Types of Western Political Regimes in Late Qing China: Jiang Dunfu and Wang Tao", *New History* 22.3 (2011): 113–58.
12 Hereafter the three collections are abbreviated as *DKLY*, *SYML*, and *SBSH* respectively.
13 Xiuyun You's *Wang Tao xiaoshuo sanshu yanjiu* (2006) remains to date the only book-length study on Wang's fiction. The recent decade saw a few more articles on Wang's fiction: Sheldon Lu, "Waking to Modernity: The Classical Tale in Late Qing", *New Literary History* 34. 4 (2003): 745–60 and Huili Zheng, "Enchanted Encounter: Gender Politics, Cultural Identity, and Wang Tao's (1828–97) Fictional Sino-Western Romance", *NAN NU—Men, Women & Gender in Early & Imperial China* 16.2 (2014): 274–307 focus on Wang's transnational romance stories; Emma Jinghua Teng, "The West as a 'Kingdom of Women'" discusses what she terms as "Occidentalism" in Wang's short stories and travel writing.
14 This contempt was partly instigated by Lu Xun's comment on late-Qing *zhiguai* as derivative in his *Zhongguo xiaoshuo*, whose influence in Chinese scholarship could not be overstated. The modern nation-state building of China in the twentieth century was closely correlated with an "anti-ghost" discourse, promoted recurrently by the Republican, Nationalist, and Communist governments. See David Der-Wai Wang, *The Monster That is History: History, Violence, and Fictional Writing in Twentieth-Century*

China (2004), 264–6 on the dramatic suppression of supernatural literature since the May Fourth Movement, and Hui Luo, "The Ghost of *Liaozhai*", 204–49 on the rise and fall of Chinese ghost literature in the twentieth century.

15 Todorov, *The Fantastic*, 25.
16 Genette, *Paratexts: Thresholds of Interpretation* (1997), 179. Genette makes a distinction between the authorial preface and the allographic preface. Here he is talking about the authorial preface, and unless otherwise indicated, by preface I also mean the authorial preface. (In the Chinese case, it is a common practice that an author may ask his friends, teachers, or students to write prefaces for his work alongside his own prefaces, so very often a book may carry quite a few prefaces.)
17 Chan, *Discourse on Foxes and Ghosts*, 19–24.
18 Zeitlin, *Historian of the Strange*, 53.
19 On *Liaozhai* as identity-building, and its influence by the cult of *qing*, see Chapter 2.
20 Chan, *Discourse on Foxes and Ghosts*, 20.
21 Ji, *Yuewei*, "[While] knowing that *xiaoshuo baiguan* is not accounted as one's proper writing, the 'street talks', however, may help with persuasion and admonishment of the people". 小說稗官，知無關於著述；街談巷議，或有益與勸懲 (1).
22 Yuan, *Zibuyu* (2010), 1.
23 *Yuewei* contains five originally separate *zhiguai* collections written during 1789–98: *Luanyang Xiaoxia lu* 灤陽消夏錄, *Rushi wowen* 如是我聞, *Huaixi zazhi* 華西雜誌, *Guwang tingzhi* 姑妄聽之, and *Luanyang xulu* 灤陽續錄, with no authorial preface but only a prefatory note before each collection. In 1800 Ji Yun's student Sheng Shiyan compiled the five books under the title *Yuewei caotang biji* and wrote a preface for it
24 Published in 1875 by the Shanghai publishing house *Shenbaoguan* while the author was still exiled in Hong Kong, *DKLY* is mostly composed of stories written in Wang's Hong Kong days and an uncertain portion of it may have been written even before the author's exile (*DKLY* 1, 3); however, for the first time in Chinese history, *SYML* and *SBSH* stories were first serialised in the Shanghai pictorial *Dianshizhai huabao* from 1884 to 1887 (after Wang returned to Shanghai) and later published as *zhiguai* collections in 1887 and 1893 respectively. On the different existing editions of Wang's *zhiguai*, see Zhenguo Zhang, *Wanqing minguo zhiguai chuanqi xiaoshuoji yanjiu*, 176-8.
25 The title "Dunku lanyan" comes from Wang's studio "Dunku" in Hong Kong; it alludes to Wang's persecution by the Qing government in the Taiping episode mentioned earlier and also reveals Wang's sense of shame and frustration.
26 Huili Zheng asserts that Wang was the first Chinese writer to use the West as a frame of cultural reference ("Enchanted Encounter", 280–1). In my knowledge, Wang probably is the only *zhiguai* writer to do so.
27 More on this in Chapter 2.
28 Here Wang is referring to the incident mentioned earlier: his alleged letter to the Taiping leader that led to his exile in Hong Kong.
29 While the "fictitious" quality of literature or fiction is self-evident in the term itself in Western literary discourse (cf. Chloë F Starr, *Red-Light Novels of the Late Qing*, 17 for the transmission of the word "literature" in English), it is a contested issue in traditional Chinese literature. In the Chinese context, beliefs in the supernatural and the narration of the supernatural as fictitious are not so clear-cut in *zhiguai* writing. See the Introduction on the historiographic features of *zhiguai*.
30 Wang's life path mirrors this cyclical journey: starting his career in Shanghai, going out to Hong Kong, Europe, and Japan to encounter a larger world, and finally, at the time he wrote this preface in 1884, returning to Shanghai as an old man with no nominal success.
31 Zhang, *Unexpected Affinities: Reading across Cultures* (2007), 114–16.
32 遺民 is sometimes used interchangeably with its homonym 逸民. Here I adopt the former as the unifying term.

33 On ramifications of the concept of *yimin* in Chinese history, see Bing Zhang, "Yimin yu yimin shi zhi liubian", *Journal of the Northwest Normal University* 38.4 (1998): 7–12; Yong Fang, *Nansong yimin shiren qunti yanjiu* (2000).
34 Wang, "Hou yimin xiezuo": "遺民指向一個與時間脫節的政治主體" (http://www.fgu.edu.tw/~wclrc/drafts/America/wang-de-wei/wang-de-wei_03.htm). The translation is mine.
35 In the late Qing, the Chinese empire's influence upon its once subordinate neighbours (Vietnam for instance) was waning while Western forces were alarmingly intruding. Wang commented on the danger of Western insinuation during his 1867 voyage to Europe via Southeast Asia. See Wang, *Manyou suilu tuji*, 43, 46. On China's border crises in the late nineteenth century, see Mary Backus Rankin, "Alarming Crises and Enticing Possibilities", *Late Imperial China* 29. 1 (2008): 40–63.
36 The wife's immortal parents are alluded to be followers of Zhang Shijie 張世傑 (*SYML* 1.14) who ranked with Wen Tianxiang and Lu Xiufu as the "Three Loyalists of the Late Song".
37 The Taoist concept of *shijie* (屍解)—one way of becoming an immortal through abandoning the useless body—may serve as a possible interpretation here. Such a process appears as a brutal death to the mortal eyes. Stories on mysterious Taoists and their sometimes "faked-death" abound in Wang's collections, making a similar interpretation in this story not unlikely. See *DKLY*, "Shijie" 屍解, 8.174.
38 On the eroticisation of the female ghost in Chinese literature, see Anthony Yu, "Rest, Rest", 429; Zeitlin, *Phantom Heroine*, 16–28 and Huntington, *Alien Kind: Foxes and Late Imperial Chinese Narrative* (2003), 189.
39 For example, in "Li Yan'geng" (*SBSH* 1.8) and "Bai Qiongxian" (*SBSH* 2.29), they are wives and concubines committing suicide (willingly or coerced) to honour their husbands who died (or anticipating death) in wars; in "Feng Peibo" (*SYML* 5.232), they are the chaste women refusing the lustful Taiping leaders.
40 See Yanchun Qin, *Qingmo minchu de wannming xiangxiang* (2008), 280–2.
41 Yanchun Qin points out that the obsession with narratives about "chaste women" in dynastic changes was especially prevalent in the late Qing (*Qingmo minchu*, 222–3). One example is the late-Qing writer Ding Chuanjing's 丁傳靖 (1870–1930) *Jiayi zhiji gongwei lu* 甲乙之際宮闈錄 (Records of Virtuous Women in the Years 1664–5), a history solely dedicated to women's chaste deaths in the tumultuous late Ming, some of which were deaths forced by the women's male relatives. On Qing literati's construction of women in dynastic falls, see also Wai-yee Li, "Women as Emblems of Dynastic Fall in Qing Literature", in David Der-Wai Wang and Wei Shang eds., *Dynastic Crisis and Cultural Innovation* (2005), 93–150.
42 Such a pattern can be found in "Li Yan'geng" 李延庚 (*SBSH* 1.8), "Bai Qiongxian" 白瓊仙 (*SBSH* 2.29), "Liu Qing" 柳青 (*SBSH* 3.51), and "Feng Peibo" 馮佩伯 (*SYML* 5.232).
43 In ghost lore, a ghost is supposed to become a *jian* when it "dies"; see *Liaozhai*, "Zhang Aduan" 章阿端 (2: 5.627) for a story on how a ghost dies.
44 In Freud's original working of mourning and melancholia, mourning is a normal and healthy process of grief at the end of which the subject is able to reinvest its attachment from the lost loved object to some other object, while melancholia is mourning that never ends, as the subject has internalised part of the lost object into its ego; therefore, while the grieving melancholic blames and laments his own deficiencies, he is criticising the internalised loved object in himself. Similarly, while the ghosts are articulating their sorrows again and again, they are symbolically performing a criticism of the violent force that renders them ghosts. See Freud, "Mourning and Melancholia" in *On the History of the Psycho-Analytic Movement and Papers on Metapsychology and Other Works* (1953), 243–58.
45 See Martin Huang, *Negotiating Masculinities*, 72–86.
46 Huang, *Negotiating Masculinities*, 1.

"What Westerners refuse to believe" 75

47 Compared with those who surrendered, the male loyalists who committed suicide or went into exile did not fare much better in the masculinity test, for it is an as impotent, or as Huang remarks, "feminised" act as the women's suicide, betraying utter helplessness in the face of uncontrollable circumstances.
48 On the late-Qing re-appropriation of the late-Ming scholar-courtesan ideals, see for instance Catherine Vance Yeh, "Wenhua jiyi de fudan—wanqing Shanghai wenren dui wanming lixiang de jian'gou", in Pingyuan Chen, David Der-Wai Wang, and Wei Shang eds., *The Late Ming and the Late Qing: Historical Dynamics and Cultural Innovations* (2002), 53–63; Wai-yee Li, "The Late Imperial Courtesan: Invention of a Cultural Ideal", in Ellen Widmer and Kang-i Sun Chang eds., *Writing Women in Late Imperial China* (1997), 46–73; Yanchun Qin, *Qingmo minchu*, 222–88.
49 For instance, the aforementioned Ding Chuanjing in his preface to *Jiayi zhiji* remarks that the heroic deeds of the chaste women he has read in local histories are "too beautiful to be absorbed all at once" 美不勝收 (118).
50 The formulaic phrasing, "someone, of certain name, born of certain family, native of certain place", is the standard beginning of biographies of historical figures and frequently adopted in *Liaozhai* stories, in which such an introduction is given about the male scholar who is going to have a romance with the titular supernatural heroine. It is worth noting that while such stories bear the title of the supernatural heroine, the narrative invariably focalises around the male scholar, indicating clearly that it is the man's perspective that is perceived as the norm of the fictional world while the supernatural woman is the gazed-at other.
51 Wang did experiment with other ways to validate the female victim's narrative through planchette without the mediation of the literati. "Li zhengu xiatan zishu shimo ji" 李貞姑下壇自述始末記 (Story of Li the Chaste Girl as Told by Herself through Planchette, *SBSH* 12.307) is a first-person narrative of the woman's tragedy. On the planchette motif of Wang's stories, see Yuanyue Zhang, "Lun Wang Tao dui *Liaozhai zhiyi* fuji gushi de jicheng yu bianyi", *Study on Pu Songling Quaterly* 1 (2013): 151–60.
52 Contrastingly, the contingencies and manipulation involved in a ghost woman's history appropriated by men (which seem to be a blind spot for Wang) are the primary focus of Vernon Lee's ghost stories and will be explored in Chapter 4. See also Mengxing Fu, "History-Making and Its Gendered Voice in Wang Tao's and Vernon Lee's Ghost Stories", *Neohelicon* 46.2 (2019): 645–61
53 On homosociality between men through their heterosexual desire of the same woman, see Todd W. Reeser, *Masculinities in Theory: An Introduction* (2010), Chapter 9.
54 It does not mean that Wang would not romanticise or fantasise about the West, but his description of Western countries bears more resemblance to real countries in the world.
55 An English translation of "A Biography of Mary" is attached in McAleavy's biography of Wang.
56 Lu, "Waking to Modernity", 757.
57 Zheng, "Enchanted Encounter", 297.
58 The protagonist Lu Meifang in many aspects resembles Wang himself. The Lus' journey to Europe via Japan also corresponds to Wang's own 1867 journey to Europe and later the 1879 journey to Japan, recorded in his two travelogues *Manyou suilu* and *Fusang youji*.
59 Not knowing Japanese, Wang was able to communicate with his Japanese hosts by written Chinese throughout his stay in Japan, as classical Chinese literature was also standard training for Japanese literati. On this journey, see Wang's *Fusang youji*.
60 Wang may have found inspiration for this portrayal from his Japanese travel. In *Fusang youji*, Wang introduces Ming loyalists like Zhu Zhiyu 朱之瑜 (1600–82) whose temples had been honoured by local Japanese (see *Manyou suilu*; *Fusang youji*, 208).
61 Qin, *Qingmo minchu*, 127.
62 His letter to the Taiping leaders and his collaboration with Western missionaries are all behaviours deviating from the expected loyalty of *shi* to his nation and his emperor.

63 The notice above the ring is written in Sanskrit and English (*SYML* 4.195).
64 Huili Zheng, "Enchanted Encounter", 301.
65 The Chinese word *yecha* is a transliteration of the Sanskrit word "yakṣa", which refers to a kind of half-human demon in Hinduism and the demon follower of Vaisravana in Buddhism.
66 On the origin of Yaksha in Chinese literature, see Li Wang and Yu Hu, "*Liaozhai zhiyi* 'Yecha guo' de fojing yuanyuan ji zhongwai minzu ronghe neiyun", *Journal of Dalian University of Techology* 31.1 (2010): 96–101.
67 Messina was Wang's first stop in Europe in his 1867 journey, as recorded in his *Manyou suilu*, whereas ironically in fiction it becomes the final stop in Lu's journey to the West. Perhaps Wang was reconsidering the effect that his European journey had had on him two decades later when he was composing this story around 1884.
68 On this episode of Wang's life, see the Introduction.
69 On these sexualised encounters, see Zheng, "Enchanted Encounter"; Teng, "The West".
70 See Campany, *Strange Writing*, 235–6.

4 Two ways to conjure up a ghost
Vernon Lee's history versus fiction

The previous chapters discuss how the Chinese ghost story, the *zhiguai*, being a genre germane to male literati identity-building, had become in the late Qing literati's hands a tool for reshaping masculinity and rewriting national history. The untold story in the literati's appropriation of the ghost's history, however, is the implicit objectification and silencing of the female ghost. In this chapter I explore Vernon Lee's (Violet Paget, 1856–1935) ghost stories as precisely a reaction towards this gendered blind spot: they expose and problematise the implicit gendered manipulation in man's history-writing and ghost-making. Furthermore, through juxtaposing marvellous and historical narratives,[1] Lee envisions an ideal femininity characterised by its gender fluidity. To discriminate between different ways of conjuring up a ghost—in other words, different ways to reach the past—has a practical significance, as how to tell the ghost's story inevitably informs how one sees the world and perceives the self. This final concern with the ghost's history is dramatised in Lee's last novel as a competition between man's history and woman's fiction. This is a competition with no single winner but rather, I argue, one that gestures towards an in-between zone lying just between history and fiction and facts and fancy, a fantastic space where the ghost can most effectively haunt the text, the reader, and claim its justice.

History and the historian

As "chroniclers of ghosts", writers of *zhiguai* are always, in one way or another, conjurers of the past, and their evocation of the ghost stands diametrically opposed to histories of the state as recorded by official historians. Pu Songling's self-invented literary persona the "Historian of the Strange" in his *Liaozhai* exemplifies *zhiguai* writers' distancing from as well as adherence to historiography. Following Pu, the Chinese male writers examined in the previous chapters have all self-consciously claimed themselves as "historians", albeit of the ghost's history. While this adopted "ghost historian" persona allowed the male writers to enact their revival or critique of Chinese history in what Nietzsche calls either a monumental or critical fashion, there is a limitation in this type of history-making: theirs is a past reconstructed from a male perspective and the male narrator/historian's subjective position in the making of the ghost's history is assumed to be transparent. However,

DOI: 10.4324/9781003188223-4

the literati's history of ghosts is as much a history of its male makers as it is the history of the romanticised revenants, for the process of appropriating history is inevitably a play of power through imagining the (very often female) ghosts as the other of history. Wang's evocation of female victims in dynastic wars examined earlier lays bare the paradox involved in the assumed objectivity of the ghost conjurer: while the authenticity of the women ghosts' narratives relies on the fact that they were conveyed by the ghosts themselves through a planchette, the planchette message has yet to be transcribed by male literati who organised these séances. In other words, there is always a well-educated male historian standing behind every female phantom conjured up, and the version of the ghost's history thus obtained is always already mediated through their gendered lens.

The concern with the gendered blind spot involved in the process of history-making is an important issue underlying Vernon Lee's career as both art historian and writer of ghost stories. Just as writers in late-Qing China were urged by the contemporary national crisis to re-examine the ideology anchored in their national history, nineteenth-century Britain was also an age preoccupied with a zeal for history. The underlying motive for this enthusiasm was the belief that history is the totality of all experience and therefore all knowledge, as Thomas Carlyle asserts confidently in his "On History" (1830): "For, strictly considered, what is all Knowledge too but recorded Experience, and a product of History?"[2] For Victorians like Carlyle, history was not only the sum of the biographies of the "great men" but also generally accepted as rightfully and exclusively the pursuit of men.[3] Nietzsche also inadvertently betrays this bias in his "On the Use and Disadvantages of History" when he sexualises history as the "eternally womanly", which the despised "objective" historians cannot know how to deal with as they are "a race of eunuchs".[4] In such a crudely sexed conceptualisation, historiography is valorised ontologically as a masculine cause and only true males, not eunuchs, are able to penetrate into its truth, let alone women.

It is perhaps this unchallenged notion that history-writing was the exclusive right of men, extant in both Chinese and British cultures, that had led the two Chinese writers I have examined to presume a (deceivingly) transparent position as ghost chroniclers.[5] The nineteenth century in Europe witnessed the rapid institutionalisation and professionalisation of history.[6] Apart from the traditional history of the state, historians now turned their eyes to social, cultural, and aesthetical realms of human experience. It was within this trend aspiring for more inclusiveness that some Victorian women hesitantly dabbled in art history[7]— hesitantly because, as Christa Zorn observes, they were well aware that they were treading on men's territory and therefore "offered their work hesitantly and merely as supplements to historical master narratives".[8]

Vernon Lee was among these aspiring female intellectuals excluded from a college education and an institutional affiliation. Educated by an unconventional mother who intended her daughter to become at the very least another "Madame de Staël",[9] Lee spent her youth in intensive reading. Indeed, the young Violet Paget decided early on to become "Vernon Lee" when she published her first book *Studies of the Eighteenth Century in Italy* (1880) at the age of 24, and as the masculine pen name suggests, her chosen lifestyle was one devoted to intellectual pursuits instead of marriage. Her career as an author spanned from the 1880s to the 1930s and produced more than forty monographs, ranging over topics as varied as art history, aesthetic philosophy, travel writing, fantastic literature, and politics, although for a long time in the twentieth century she was mainly remembered as a writer of ghost stories. It is in emphasising the scope of Lee's career and intellectual influence that Zorn proposes we regard Lee primarily as a public intellectual as she herself had done.[10] As a Victorian female intellectual, Lee's life embraced all the admiration and hostility that may be met by an unconventional Victorian woman aspiring to a role outside of the family. Lee's lifestyle was ostensibly that of the New Woman: economically independent, roaming the Continent, and participating vigorously in all the intellectual issues of the day. Never a good-looking woman herself, Lee nonetheless maintained long and passionate friendships with two women during her life and in her later days always attracted around her a circle of intelligent and admiring younger women.[11] The latter, probably as much as her competition with male intellectuals, often made her the target of men's contempt which can easily slide from an assessment of her intellectual power to a caricature of her sexuality.[12]

Never hesitating to flaunt her erudition in writing, Lee nonetheless was clearly aware early on in her career the contempt and suspicion awaiting women pursuing a "masculine" intellectual life. Her first book, *Studies of the Eighteenth Century in Italy*, at once showed her ambition and tact. Despite the tone of authority she displayed in it, the young author was aware that as a woman she was poaching on men's territory, as she explained in a letter her choice of the masculine pseudonym "Vernon Lee": "I am sure that no one reads a woman's writing on art, history or aesthetics with anything but unmitigated contempt".[13] Her subject matter, Italian art (mainly music) in the eighteenth century, was overshadowed by the Renaissance. As Colby notes, it was "an age of little apparent historical or cultural distinction",[14] but for this same reason it was also relatively neglected by prominent male scholars like John Addington Symonds and Walter Pater (1839–94), leaving Lee fresh on the field.

Both her choice of a masculine pen name and the tactful distance maintained from male masters in her first book show Lee's understanding of the difficulties facing a woman intellectual eager to establish herself as a qualified historian. Like her contemporaries, she had to manoeuvre between gaining visibility as a woman historian and maintaining her uniqueness as a woman writer, two goals contradicting each other in a society suspicious of women professing an authoritative voice. The masculine pseudonym, at least at first, indicates that she compromised by using a "borrowed" position—a man's position.[15]

But at the same time, Lee was also equally eager to defend her own way of doing history as different from her male colleagues, presenting her amateur position as a unique edge instead of a disadvantage. While Lee's first book only initiated her into the field of Italian art, her next book *Euphorion* (1884) launched her directly into the Italian Renaissance, a crowded field already claimed by famous scholars like Symonds and Pater. In the lengthy introduction to *Euphorion*, Lee only nods perfunctorily to the preceding male masters in the field before dethroning the master's methods and arguing for her own unique brand of historiography. Having Symonds's voluminous *Renaissance in Italy* (1877–97) in mind, she asserts:

> But besides such marvels of historic mapping as I have described, ... there are yet other kinds of work which may be done. For a period in history is like a more or less extended real landscape ..., it may also be seen from different points of view, and under different lights; then, according as you stand, the features of the scene will group themselves ... the scene will possess one or two predominant effects, it will produce also one or, at most, two or three (in which case co-ordinated) impressions. The art which deals with impressions, ... is what you call new-fangled ... Yet it is the only truly realistic art, and it only, by giving you a thing as it appears at a given moment, gives it you as it really ever is; all the rest is the result of cunning abstraction, and representing the scene as it is always, represents it (by striking an average) as it never is at all.[16]

History, like a landscape, is thus essentially a perspective thing to those who had experienced it in different valleys and those who now research it upon different heights. Thus the "marvels of historic mapping", to which the author obligingly gives a salute at the beginning of the paragraph, is dethroned as merely "result of cunning abstraction" and only deceivingly realistic. The past is not an abstract totality but a scene that can yield "one, two, or three" impressions. History viewed as a plurality accords legitimacy to alternative histories such as hers, and moreover, as she has already demonstrated the impossibility of a "scientific representation" (*Euphorion I* 11) of history, her subjective, fragmentary, and impressionistic approach may be the more fruitful one. Lee is aware of the impressionistic feature of her Renaissance studies ("They are mere impressions ... not so much a series of study as a series of impressions", *Euphorion I* 16), yet she defends this "deficiency" rather as her strength, as her understanding of her subject is initiated not from some "abstract and exact" knowledge, but from first-hand life experiences: "I have seen the concrete things, and what I might call the concrete realities of thought and feelings left behind by the Renaissance" (*Euphorion I* 16).

The preference of an impressionistic history over a miraculous historic mapping may be Lee's tactic to carve out a niche in a field already dominated by Symonds who treated history in exactly a comprehensive and schematic fashion.[17] Yet the above quotation from *Euphorion* already contains traces of Lee's insistence on the relativism and perspective-ness of history and a valorisation of the kind of historical understanding gained solely from the "standpoints of personal interest and in the light of personal temper" (*Euphorion I* 8). In other words, what interests her the most is not the "real" past, which is already irretrievable and has never existed as a single unity, but rather the individuals who write history—historians haunted by imaginary ghosts of the past.

This same relativism regarding history has an indelible impact on Lee's ghost story writing. Stories of ghosts as stories of the past are a reconstruction of the past, and the ghost conjurer, like the historian, moulds the ghost according to his/her own interest and temperament. Lee's own experience in contending for the position of a historian acquainted her well with the power manipulation in history-writing and ghost-making. Unlike other women ghost story writers who tend to locate their ghosts in the domestic sphere, Lee's ghost-seers are almost always a contemporary male historian-artist thrown into an environment vibrant with the past, and it is his hitherto unquestioned authority to write the women ghosts' history that her stories make problematic. In this sense, Lee was different from many of her contemporary women writers who wrote directly about women's experiences, but it was probably her position from "without" that better enables her to critique the ideological constructions of women in her time. In her history writing she had to appropriate a man's position largely due to the disciplinary conventions of the day, but in her fantastic literature, she dismantled that position.

In this chapter, I first examine how Lee problematises the gendered, perspectival, and sometimes biased position of the male historian-artist of the female ghost in "Amour Dure" (1887, 1890)[18] and "Oke of Okehurst" (1886, 1890). The contest between history and fiction, facts and fancy, or more narrowly the question of who has access to and control of the past, is another frequent theme of her ghost stories. In "Prince Alberic and the Snake Lady" (1896), Lee juxtaposes a sterile patriarchal court and its "dry historical facts" with a fecund feminine wonderland embedded in a luxuriant fairy-tale.[19] Through the re-valorisation of a fluid femininity represented by the Snake Lady, she celebrates the transformative potentials of an alternative sexuality. In the last section I return to the question of how to write the story of the ghost, which is also the central question in *Louis Norbert: A Two-fold Romance* (1914). The novel stages an escalating contest between history and fiction as two ways to arrive at the secret of the past, enacted as a romance surrounding a "ghosted" figure whose existence can only be located just between facts and fancy and history and fiction, i.e., in the liminal realm of fantasy.

The injustices of man-made history: "Amour Dure" and "Oke of Okehurst"[20]

Scholars have often read the spectral in Victorian women's supernatural fiction as a locale for women writers to articulate their ghostly existence and to critique social problems.[21] Especially towards the end of the nineteenth century, increasing awareness of women's oppression and widespread agitation for women's rights all indicated that the time had come for greater changes, and women writers conjured up ghosts in their writing not only to express the sense of marginalisation and injustice felt by women but also to create space for a reconceptualisation of femininity.

Yet Lee's stories are somehow distinct from this tradition of woman-authored ghost stories in that hers are often not specifically concerned with female experience. In her 1890 supernatural story collection *Hauntings*, all of the four stories have as their first-person narrator a contemporary male figure haunted by sinister traces from the past embodied by some feminine ghost.[22] A close friend of Pater and an important figure in the aesthetic movement, Lee shows in her supernatural stories a distinct streak of aestheticism: the fascination with erotic *femmes fatales*. Yet, still different from those of male aesthetes, Lee's tales dissect the male historian-artist's often self-serving construction of the ghost woman in their fancies. Therefore, although Lee's ghost stories do not offer the reader a promise to tell the ghost woman's true history, it is precisely her focus on the making and maker of the (usually female) ghost instead of the ghost herself that allows Lee a position to deconstruct men's construction of women.

In this section I examine the male historian-artist's construction of the ghost woman in "Amour Dure" and "Oke of Okehurst". The narrator in the former, Spiridion Trepka, is a young historian commissioned to write a history of an old Italian town, while the unnamed narrator in the latter is a portrait painter versed in contemporary aestheticist discourse and takes as objects of artistic study not only paintings but also intriguing personalities. While the attitude of the historian towards his object of study is presumably one of objectivity and indifference, the artist's attitude toward his sitter and painting is one inevitably tinted with personal taste and temperament. Yet Lee's stories artfully disrupt the distinction of the two, exposing the infiltration of desire and ambition in the former's writing of history and the presumption of narrative authority displayed in the latter's construction of character, hence the name "historian-artist" I give to the male narrators of both stories. "Amour Dure" and "Oke of Okehurst", when viewed side by side, show poignantly that both the historian and the artist become a kind of male voyeur in their study of their respective subjects, for it is through fixing or controlling a ghost woman's image in their discourse that their masculinity (exemplified as a triumph over competing males) can be confirmed. The construction of the ghost woman's history in these tales is revealed inherently as a gendered project manipulated by male fancy and possessive desire. However, despite the men's constant endeavour to possess the ghost woman, spectrality in the two stories also offers the ghost woman a power to revolt against that fixing, so that in the end she is able to effect her powerful presence outside of men's history, in the liminal realm of haunting.

"Amour Dure" is related in the form of a diary by the historian Spiridion Trepka, detailing his stay in the Italian town Urbania where he has been sent to research local history. In a sense, Trepka the young historian resembles the young writer Vernon Lee herself: both felt a genuine love for the past, both won acclaim at the young age of 24 with their first book on Italian history and, self-conscious of the high expectation from readers and colleagues, both felt the anxiety of influence, for their next research project entered a field laden with the achievements of previous historians. When Trepka arrives at Urbania, he is already preceded by famous historians whose histories of the town prove to be obstacles that the contemporary historian must somehow surmount to prove his own worthiness.

In this sense, "Amour Dure" could be read as the psychological journey that a latecomer in the field of Urbanian history goes through in dethroning former historians, reminiscent of what Lee did in her self-affirming introduction of *Euphorion* discussed above. However, Trepka's resemblance to Lee stops here, for while Lee establishes her unique brand of historiography through a new approach, the crux of Trepka's competition with former historians is soon revealed to revolve around a woman—the sixteenth-century *femme fatale* Medea da Carpi; or more precisely, it is around excavating and controlling different versions of the ghosted woman's history. While no existing history has been dedicated to this notorious woman, Trepka still tries to put together a sketch of Medea's history from fragmentary mentions in previous histories on Duke Robert of Urbania. Medea, as depicted by these historians, was men's worst nightmares incarnated: her two advantageous marriages that finally landed her as the widowed duchess and de facto ruler of Urbania were strewn with the violent deaths of five lovers, two unsuspecting husbands, and an inconvenient ex-wife. Yet Medea's rule of Urbania was soon ended by the younger brother of the late duke and rightful heir of the duchy (so the historians say) who, being a cardinal, broke his vow and waged war on Medea with the consent of the Pope. For the clemency of Duke Robert, Medea was not immediately put to death but only confined; it was only after surviving an assassination planned by Medea that Robert commanded her to be strangled by two murderesses, thus avoiding seeing the face of Medea throughout his life.

Trepka's major dispute with former historians lies in the interpretation of Medea's history. While preceding histories all exalt the "clement prince" Robert (56) and denounce Medea as a bewitching murderess, Trepka inclines to see Medea as the victim. Determined to find romance in Italy, the male historian despises contemporary women around him but is immediately fascinated by the portraits of the woman of his study. The more he contemplates the portraits of Medea, the more Trepka sympathises with the woman; thus, even before he finds any historical evidence to revise the above sketch of Medea's history, he can already picture in his mind a revisionist version of the woman:

> Yes; I can understand Medea. ... A marriage, let it be noted, between an old soldier of fifty and a girl of sixteen. Reflect what that means: it means that this imperious woman is soon treated like a chattel, made roughly to understand that her business is to give the Duke an heir, not advice; that she must never ask "wherefore this or that?" that she must courtesy before the Duke's counselors, his captains, his mistresses; that, at the least suspicion of rebelliousness, she is subject to his foul words and blows; at the least suspicion of infidelity, to be strangled or starved to death, or thrown down an oubliette. ... Suppose she know that she must strike or be struck? Why, she strikes, or gets some one to strike for her.
>
> (56–7)

The description of the violence that Medea was likely to suffer from her husband is reminiscent of Robert Browning's "My Last Duchess". The pathetic situation of the woman is laid bare: in patriarchal sixteenth-century Italy, even a noble woman had virtually no power of her own apart from her sexual appeal to men, which could easily backfire. So instead of being stricken like Browning's duchess, Medea struck first and used her sexual power to her own advantage. This rehabilitative rendering of Medea's history removes her from the role of the *femme fatale* to that of the victim and connects her to the victimised female ghosts in Xuan and Wang who return to articulate their grievance or have their vengeance. Indeed, Trepka the revisionist historian is just like the counterpart of Wang Tao's narrator persona "The Historian of the Lost" (逸史氏), who sympathises with the victimised and silenced women and purports to bring into light their true history; and just like the ghost-conjuring literati in Wang's stories, Trepka is soon rewarded with the ghost woman's visits.

However, Lee's story about ghost-seeing also offers a gender critique of the male historian's ghost-making which Wang's tales lack. While in Wang's tales the male narrator is presented in a position detached and above his historical subjects, a position suitable to pass authoritative judgements, the legitimacy of Trepka as an objective historian to distribute historical justice is made increasingly problematic in "Amour Dure". Whether the ghost of Medea is real or a product of Trepka's imagination is kept ambivalent throughout the story, but the female ghost's connection with the male historian's sexual desire is unequivocal, as Trepka himself justifies the reality of Medea by the sheer strength of his desire: "Why should there not be ghosts to such as can see them? Why should she not return to the earth, if she knows that it contains a man who thinks only of, desires, only her?" (69). Lee, in her preface to *Hauntings*, defines her "genuine ghost" as "things of the imagination, born there, bred there" (39), and the victimised Medea as imagined by the historian is clearly one such "genuine ghost" created by the haunted. However, if the haunted happens to be a historian, this production of "imagination" ceases to be something innocent; as revealed poignantly in Trepka's case, the desired female ghost gradually becomes indistinguishable from the desired history that the male historian intends to master and possess. Trepka's diary therefore illustrates the mechanism of male historians' (or ghost story writers') making of history by making the story of a ghost woman. It is first the historian's desire to write a history superior to both his predecessors and contemporaries that motivates him to conjure up this Medea from scraps, and then he fleshes up the ghost with a consumptive passion that he deems only he deserves. Thus, Trepka's musings over Medea's history are sprinkled with his ridicule of previous historical portrayals of Duke Robert, revealing that all the time while he is infatuated with Medea, his real targets are the rival historians. The more he believes in his version of Medea, the more glorious a light he sees himself in, as he writes later, "I see it all so well—that crafty, cowardly Duke Robert; that melancholy Duchess Maddalena; that weak, showy, would-be chivalrous Duke Guidafonso; and above all, the splendid figure of Medea. I feel as if I were the *greatest historian* of the age; and, at the same time, as if I were a boy of twelve" (63, italics mine).

If the previous histories in favour of Duke Robert are in service of power, Trepka's revisionist history of Medea is one no less fuelled by desire—the desire to possess the woman and her (and in the sense of it being a creation of the historian, also his) history, the two becoming interchangeable with each other as the story unfolds. The feminist potential of Trepka's sympathetic rewriting of Medea's history has been duly noted by critics,[23] but as Zorn rightly points out, Trepka's sexual obsession distorts his representation of Medea and renders his reconstruction of Medea's history a perpetuation rather than a revision of the *femme fatale* cliché: "He claims to assign to Medea a new historical importance, but unable to think outside conventional gender images, he gives her, first and foremost, a sexual identity".[24] Over his increasing immersion in the fantasy of Medea, Trepka's role is gradually transformed from historian to lover, as is made clear when he is bid by Medea to destroy Duke Robert's statue. The legion of Medea's former lovers met on his way only strengthen the historian's determination to carry out his mistress's command, for what could better prove him as the most deserving lover of Medea than his overriding his rivals? The historian dies, as expected, at Medea's hands, but this only proves his correct interpretation of Medea's love motto: "amour dure—dure amour"—"The love of Medea da Carpi cannot fade, but the lover can die" (57). In death Trepka's ambition to become the greatest historian and the best of Medea's lovers coalesce and consummate each other.

While Trepka's history-making of the ghost woman is shown to be one tinted with his sexual desire and fantasy, it is also revealed as one resulting from his competition with rival males, thus further exposing the masculinity anxiety underlying man's history-making. More precisely, Trepka's masculinity anxiety is engendered by an anxiety with his national identity as a German-born Pole.[25] Throughout his diary, Trepka emphasises his Polish origin, which he sees as elevating him above a prosaic German identity of his colleagues. But, as Peter Christensen points out, the Polish past that he reminisces about is only a blank "place holder" which "has no content at all".[26] Because as a colonised "Pole" he is divested of a genuine Polish past, he has to invent a grandiose past in his study of history, which may vicariously endow him with a past. Thus situated, the historian's yearning for the Italian past gains a new significance: to encounter the Italian past is not only a professional ambition but also a personal necessity sprung from a deeply felt identity crisis. The same identity crisis—a paradoxical faith in and suspicion of one's national pride and history—surfaces in both Wang's and Xuan's history-making and ghost-making discussed before. But Lee's intricate scrutiny of the male historian's ghost-conjuring exposes precisely the exclusion and manipulation of women involved in men's project of salvaging his masculinity: perturbed by an uncertainty with his national identity, the historian seeks to reaffirm his masculinity vicariously by having the final control of another past, which boils down to the writing of a woman's history and substantiating that history with a ghost. The female ghost, bearing man's double desire to possess the woman and history, thus helps the historian to become the man he believes he is: the greatest historian, the supreme lover, and wedded to the past/ghost.

But if Trepka's reconstruction of Medea's history is only a male fancy in service of man's self-aggrandisement, how is the real Medea's history to be written? Or is it even possible to write a woman's history immune from men's manipulation? Lee's relativist view of history explicated in her introduction to *Euphorion* may suggest a negative answer. As history is like a landscape that yields different impressions to people viewing it from different heights, the universal truth of history can never exist and what purports to be the truth is often but cunning abstractions; moreover, as dramatised in Trepka's case, such a history is mediated by the historian's personal obsessions. A more fruitful historical approach, as proposed in Lee's introduction, is to resort to the currents of thoughts and feelings in one's mind. This can be mistaken as an opportune apology to legitimise a historical reading energised purely by personal interest that fits well with what Trepka does with Medea: writing a history of Medea tailored to his own desire and ambition. However, this is not Lee's true intention. Trepka's fault is that he tries to counter the bias of one version (Duke Robert's) of history by another equally biased one while claiming historical objectivity for his own version. As Nietzsche argues, real justice in historical study is a rare quality and too often what purports to be objectivity has nothing to do with justice but vanity and possessiveness of the historian. The truly just historian, according to him, contemplates history as an artist in his "strongest and most spontaneous moment of creation", "the outcome of which may be an artistically true painting but cannot be a historically true one".[27]

And that artistic justice of the past, in Lee's model, is to write a fantasy of the past which dwells between facts and fancy instead of a history of the past which purports to be pure facts but can only be otherwise. Lee's historian, Trepka, is torn between two compelling forces—the historical method required by his profession and his fantasy of Medea fuelled by his passion. Through his passion and desire for the woman he can sympathise with Medea, and yet in attempting to substantiate his desire through a historical discourse, he ends up, as Zorn remarks, "repeating precisely the patriarchal tradition".[28] Reviewing Lee's career as both art historian and fiction writer, Zorn comments that for Lee, "art can create a more immediate contact with the past than can historical scholarship".[29] Therefore to give justice to Medea, a melody, a drama, a fantasy—in essence, a fiction—may better serve its purpose than Trepka's history, and that is just what Lee did in writing the story "Amour Dure". It is true that no definite version of Medea's history is ascertained in the story, and even the existence of the ghost is questionable, but through a narrative permeated by the woman's haunting, a due amount of justice is already accorded to this ephemeral phantom. For, instead of putting to rest the woman's memory by establishing an authoritative history of her, the interpretational gap opened up by Medea's haunting is always there, constantly casting doubts on structures of power and assurances that what is seen and recorded is really there. In the sense of haunting as a ceaseless retelling of the ghost's story in the present, it proves a better way to empower those marginalised figures in society than history does.

While "Amour Dure" dramatises a passion-bond historian as a conjurer of ghosts to substantiate his history, "Oke of Okehurst" presents another story about man's construction of woman—a contemporary Paterian portraitist's efforts in constructing an ideal *femme fatale* in his sitter Mrs Alice Oke first through painting, and when that fails, through the narration of the woman's story three years after her death. As with the case of the infatuated historian, the male artist's narration of the woman's story is also shown to be refracted by the man's self-perception. On the one hand, the artist's impulse to regulate the woman's story betrays his unconscious desire to absolve himself from the Okes' tragic death for which he is partly responsible, effecting Lee's subtle critique of the ethical perils of the contemporary aesthetic discourse.[30] On the other hand, to possess the woman's narrative also means for the male artist a denial of the ghost woman's haunting and a reaffirmation of his own authoritative position as the creator of the woman's image. But at the same time, this masculinist regulation of a woman's image meets with constant revolts from the aesthetic object, the eccentric Alice Oke, who effectively enlists on her side the power of ghosts when alive and after death, unleashing the unsettling power of an "unwomanly" femininity. In this sense, Lee's story provides an instance of a narration of the ghost woman's story which fails to fix the woman, but instead becomes a testament to the spectral power that a ghostly position can afford women.

Many critics have remarked on the story's heavy allusion to the contemporary aesthetic movement, especially through the unnamed male narrator who is presented almost as an incarnation of Pater's ideal aesthetic critic, taking as subjects of his artistic analysis not only beautiful art objects but also "artistic accomplished forms of human life", and the "engaging personality in life or in a book".[31] Through encouraging the contemporary Alice's morbid obsession with her seventeenth-century ancestor and her murdered lover, the portraitist enjoys the pleasure of studying peculiar character as an art object at the cost of the Oke couple's tragedy. Yet what I want to emphasise here is the portraitist's analogous position with the historian in his Pygmalion-project of creating an ideal woman: he not only endeavours to discover a truth and depth in his aesthetic object that may elude his peers and qualify him as the best artist, but also tries to instil that truth into the real woman Alice Oke. Expectedly, Lee's story shows us how this aestheticist tampering with women's character backfires: the male artist's aesthetic gaze kills the woman rather than revives the statue. And apart from this direct confrontation with the misogynist tendency of aestheticism, "Oke of Okehurst" also explores how the woman gazes back at the artist and utilises the position of the ghost to resist the artist's construction of her as an aesthetic object. In a sense, this is a reversed Pygmalion story in which the ghost of Galatea haunts and collapses the creator status of the Pygmalion.[32]

That the portraitist is presented as analogous to Trepka is evident in his desire toward his sitter Mrs Alice Oke. Interestingly, like the historian, the artist feels the need to maintain a position indifferent and above his aesthetic object and actively denies any personal interest involved in his engagement with Mrs Oke: "I became interested in Mrs Oke as if I had been in love with her; and I was not the least in love" (117) and "I did not want Mrs Oke to think me interesting, I merely wished to go on studying her" (118). Yet his subsequent indulgence in Alice's obsession with the scandalous love affair and crime performed by her and her husband's seventeenth-century ancestors effectively estranges Mrs Oke from her husband and secures for him her sole attention, revealing how the portraitist's involvement with his object of study is self-serving.

If the artist has defended his "playing" with Alice's character ("I required to put her into play" 122) as an irreproachable way to grasp the "real character of the woman" (122)—prerequisite in the portraitist's peculiar trade—this motivation to serve art is also gradually exposed as questionable, as what he is fascinated by seems to be not the real Alice but a desirable eccentric image of the woman he tries to impose on her. He confesses that "I derive a morbid and exquisite pleasure" in drawing out the fancies of Alice Oke and exclaims that her eccentricity "completed her personality so perfectly" (129). The portraitist is already picturing in his mind such a personality instilled into the portrait which is even larger than the real sitter: "Mrs Oke even might resent it ... No matter. That picture should be painted, if merely for the sake of having painted it; for I felt ... that it would be far away my best work" (129). The artist's ambition to create the best portrait regardless of the subject of the portrait resembles the historian Trepka's zeal to write the best history even at the expense of rousing the ghost. In both cases, the male historian-artist sees his success lying in the making of a dangerous woman, as if by successfully taming the woman whom no other man has tamed, his authority as the creator is securely enshrined.

However, the dangerous woman Alice Oke proves to be untameable. As Sondeep Kandola points out, throughout the story the husband and the artist have tried continuously to fix Alice in a list of "contemporary categories of aberrant female behaviours (the hysteric, the flirt, the barren woman, and the *femme fatale*)",[33] but by cross-dressing and enlisting ghosts on her side, Alice creates a self that goes beyond these conventional models of femininity. The artist first takes pride in his ability as an aesthetic critic to appreciate the morbidity of Alice's personality, which after all is attributable to her childlessness and the frivolity common to idle women of her class.[34] Yet, soon the woman outstrips even that residue of conventional femininity by her escalating "unwomanly" acts. She first takes the painter to the very spot where her ancestors murdered Alice's lover Lovelock, and then dresses herself as a groom with the very clothes that the seventeenth-century Alice wore in her act of murder in a masquerade ball. This aggressive display of murderous masculinity by the woman finally exasperates the artist, who now resorts to a conventional regulation of femininity—a reference to madness: "It seemed to me horrible, vulgar, abominable, as if I had got inside a madhouse" (139).

In her study on cross-dressing, Marjorie Garber makes the bold argument that cross-dressing engenders a "category crisis" more than just a crisis of gender.[35] In Alice Oke's case, cross-dressing is a bodily revolt against the linguistic net that her husband and the artist cast on her. For although the men control the language about the woman, the woman remains the sovereign of her body and confounds their defining categories through a performance of her body. Whether the secret that this coded performance reveals is a lesbian energy or a revolt against a domestic wife's role,[36] the result is a divorce between appearance and essence, the living Alice resisting the penetrating gaze of the male artist under the garments of a dead woman, so that her real personality "would slip through my fingers like a snake" (149) as the artist later is to admit.

Dressing in the masculine attire of the dead Alice confounds for the living Alice the categories of life and death and makes her into a ghost, which indeed is the woman's self-willed existence for it offers her the only position from which to resist men's definition of her. Taking up the role of the dead Alice and absorbing herself in the love affair with the ghost of Lovelock, Alice in the nineteenth century frees herself from the loveless arranged marriage by remaining childless and denying the wifely duties. Ghosts haunt the Okes' marriage but emancipate the otherwise invisible and immobile wife. Therefore, in the end when the largely impotent husband finally rises to eliminate the danger that Alice poses to categories of gender, ironically he is also helping the woman to fulfil her own wish of becoming a ghost: believing he is shooting Alice's lover, he shoots Alice instead.

If Alice's death three years earlier marks the failure of the artist's Pygmalion project of creating the ideal *femme fatale* (it "kills" the sitter and his would-be best painting), his narration of Alice's story to the anonymous interlocutor can be seen as a renewed attempt in fixing the woman in language. However, the portraitist's narrative is full of paradox and inconsistencies. While he is eager to claim to the interlocutor his authority in telling her story—"I doubt whether anyone ever understood Alice Oke besides myself" (107), he constantly fails to fix her in words and the narrative is filled with the man's frustration and anxiety with his power over language: "I wish, alas!—I wish, I wish, I have wished a hundred thousand times—I could paint her ... But where is the use of talking about her?" (114) and "Something—and the very essence—always escapes" (115). A telling detail reveals the haunting power that Alice exerts on the portraitist even in the present. Just before he is about to tell the interlocutor Alice's story, he enjoins: "Wait; I must turn *her* face to the wall" (107, italics mine), referring to the unfinished portrait of Alice which the narrative alludes to have just been shown to the interlocuter by removing piles of other pictures "away from the wall" (106). Throughout the artist's one-sided narrative, the portrait of Alice occupies a ghostly existence, never explicitly named as such yet seeming to exert an uncanny prohibition on the portraitist so that he even dares not tell "her" story in front of it, as if in awe of its silent watch. In this sense, the portraitist's narration of Alice is haunted from both within and without, with the narrator and reader both realising perfectly that the present interlocutors are being silently gazed at by the ghost of Alice. As in "Amour Dure", the ghost woman of Vernon Lee haunts outside of men's narrative of her and effectively wills out through her haunting an identity that silently counters the one the historian-artist assigns her.

The theme of the aesthetic artist's failed Pygmalion project and the revolting Galatea's transgression of conventional femininity also underlies Lee's first full-length novel *Miss Brown* (1884), published two years before "Oke of Okehurst". The heroine Anne Brown is praised enthusiastically by the narrator for her gender indeterminacy: "Masculine women, mere men in disguise, they are not ... they are, and can only be, true women; but women without woman's instincts and wants, sexless—women made not for man but for humankind. Anne Brown was one of these".[37] Although *Miss Brown* was met with general ridicule and had dampened Lee's interest in novel writing for thirty years,[38] Lee's vision of an unwomanly woman like Anne Brown, "sent into the world ... to be Joans of Arc" to cleanse the world of its ills did find resonance in her fantastic tales.[39] If Anne Brown's homosexuality or "sexlessness" is a form of anomaly in a heterosexual economy,[40] then ghosts and demons in a fantastic setting certainly provide a more hospitable space for envisioning transgressive modes of sexuality and the positive work that they can do for the world, as is shown in "Prince Alberic and the Snake Lady".

Fantasy usurping history: an initiation into the cult of the Snake Lady

"Prince Alberic and the Snake Lady" was first published in July 1896 in *The Yellow Book*, the only of Lee's fantastic tales published in the periodical closely associated with aestheticism; and befitting the taste of *The Yellow Book*, the story is full of sensuous imagery surrounding a woman of abnormal sexuality: the fairy Oriana with a snake tail. Particularly, the story overwrites a popular contemporary misogynist motif—the serpentine *femme fatale*—into an icon of ideal femininity combining both maternal and phallic traits. Like Lee's earlier heroine Anne Brown, the Snake Lady represents for Lee the ideal marvellous woman sent to cleanse the corrupt patriarchal world, and her tutoring of the young Prince Alberic envisions the possibility of the young generation's initiation into her cult of sexual fluidity. The story displays a practice often performed in Lee's writing, the blurring of genre categories as it embeds a lush fairy tale within a dry historical mode. But this time the juxtaposition of narrative modes serves a thematic purpose as well, as each narrative mode exhibits one position towards the Snake Lady's story: the patriarchal court and the church orthodoxy which seek to exorcise the woman from history and the oral and folk narratives which keep her memory alive. Although the Snake Lady's final decapitation may show that Lee was less confident of society's tolerance of marvellous yet sexually "abnormal" women like Oriana, the story's juxtaposition of narrative modes does witness the woman's perseverance in the fantastic realm.

From the beginning of the story the alterity of the Snake Lady is shown to hinge on her snake tail, an anomaly that repulses the world yet fascinates Prince Alberic. Having been isolated in a room in the Red Palace by his grandfather Duke Balthasar Maria for years, the boy Alberic learns to love the old tapestry depicting the Snake Lady and a knight from an early age, as its embroidery of animals and plants offers him the only way to know about nature. Later, as the boy is nearing puberty, his nurse removes the crucifix barring the lower part of the tapestry from view, revealing the snake tail of the woman for Alberic for the first time. This discovery of the snake tail is his first lesson on sexuality from the Snake Lady, for on that snake tail hangs the whole weight of her sexual anomaly—in what is normally the place of the female genitalia, there is not to be found a hole but a protruding snake's tail, a strange blend of gentle femininity and phallic aggressiveness. It is no wonder, therefore, that previously the lower part of her body has been covered by the crucifix, a token of orthodox Christianity, for it is precisely the woman's troublesome sexuality that has excluded her from a society regulated by a patriarchal heterosexual normality, and the crucifix offers a proper suppression of that part which it deems dangerous. As the boy is later to know of the Snake Lady's tragic story, Oriana is a fairy condemned to a snake's body "for no faults", yet it is precisely her snake tail that is viewed by society as "her sins" (210)—her abnormal homosexuality as interpreted by Margaret Stetz[41]—and leads to her tragic betrayal and persecution by previous patriarchs of the House of Luna.

But apart from this biographical reading, I argue that what Lee achieves in this tale is overwriting forcefully the usual misogynist snake motif connected with women's sexuality into a positive symbol of ideal femininity. From the Greek Medusa, the Christian Lilith, the Romantic Lamia, to the little mermaid, the snake tail has marked woman's sexual potency and her power to transform beyond the docile, but it is also regarded as a sign of her bestiality in patriarchal imagination, the revolutionary part of a woman that must be mutilated and suppressed to recuperate her desirability. The stereotype of the venomous snake woman gained new currency with the late Victorian Decadent artists; for them, she was the model of feminine cruelty, epitomised by Algernon Charles Swinburne's (1837–1909) verbal sketch: "Lamia re-transformed, invested now with a fuller beauty, but divested of all feminine attributes not native to the snake".[42] The influence of the contemporary snake trope popularised by Swinburne can also be traced in Lee's stories in the 1880s, as in "Amour Dure" and "Oke of Okehurst" she represents a Medea with lips that "could bite or suck" (52) and an Alice whose figure slips like a snake from one's fingers. Yet in "Snake Lady", Oriana's tail as seen by the young prince free from any preconceived notions of sexual normality, becomes an appealing trait that complements rather than condemns the woman. The boy loves the Snake Lady "only the more because she ended off in the long twisting body of a snake. And that, no doubt, was why the knight was so very good to her" (188). The Snake Lady's sexual anomaly—her snake-ness, her body combining both feminine and phallic traits, is therefore transformed into a positive transgressive sexuality in the boy's eyes.

If the snake tail marks a phallic aggressiveness in the Snake Lady, then the story shows that there is more in Lee's ideal "unwomanly" woman endowed with transformative powers. Alberic's love for the Snake Lady leads to his first rebellion against his grandfather, which ends in his exile in the ruins of the Castle of Sparkling Waters. Yet this only proves to be the next step of his initiation into the Snake Lady's cult, for he soon meets there his beautiful godmother who gives him a humanistic education and a grass snake who becomes his companion. The Sparkling Waters itself is depicted as a veritable utopia—a fertile feminine space full of wild lives in nature in contrast to the barren and heavily surveillanced Red Palace presided over by Duke Balthasar.[43] Moreover, unlike the strict hierarchy of the Red Palace, in Sparkling Waters the low and the high, the humble and the magnanimous live in equality and respect for each other. If the Red Palace, as Alberic intuitively senses, is a personification of his grandfather and a place full of vanity, treachery, and exploitation, the Sparkling Waters then is the incarnation of the Snake Lady, representing all the positive values nurtured by the Snake Lady: sympathy, simplicity, love, and loyalty. Alberic's later discovery that the godmother and the grass snake are but different forms of the fairy Oriana further completes the Snake Lady's ideal image: her unconventional femininity now consists of a maternal abundance, a masculine determination, and even a childlike simplicity. In this analysis, the sensuous Snake Lady resembles another of Lee's androgynous heroines, the "sexless" Anne Brown mentioned previously: both are ideal women who are born "not to have been women", "women made not for man but for humankind".[44] These are the archetypes of Lee's marvellous women who make trouble not only with gender categories but also with the societies they are sent in: they bear the mission of reforming the world.

Yet "Snake Lady" also foretells the tragic fate that the mission taken by representatives of gender fluidity may meet in an intolerant, menacing world, as both practitioners of this cult, Prince Alberic and the fairy Oriana, die of Duke Balthasar's cruelty. Yet if "Snake Lady", more than "Amour Dure" and "Oke of Okehurst", tries to excavate a history of the ghosted woman, the historical justice given to the ghost comes more from the way of presenting her story than what the story is itself. The juxtaposition of the historical mode and the fairy-tale mode in "Snake Lady" presents that subtle struggle over the control of the woman's history rehearsed in the two stories discussed before, and it is shown here more forcefully that it is precisely in the gaps of different narratives that an alternative history of the Snake Lady can be imagined.

"Snake Lady" begins with the dry historical prologue: "In the year 1701, the Duchy of Luna became united to the Italian dominions of the Holy Roman Empire" (182) and then proceeds into the fairy-tale in which Prince Alberic is initiated into Oriana's cult; at the end of the tale, with the death of Oriana and Alberic, the narrative returns cyclically to the historical prologue—"Be this as it may, history records as certain that the house of Luna became extinct in 1701, the duchy lapsing to the Empire" (227). But the text does not end here, instead it proceeds to tell, in the same matter-of-fact tone, that travellers can still find rags of the tapestry "having represented the story of Alberic the Blond and the Snake Lady" (228). The story therefore virtually ends with the words "Snake Lady", forming a rhythmic echo to the title and the extraordinary tale in the centre that the concluding "history" has just suppressed. Although the story purports to begin and end in "dry historical fact", the richly imaginative fairy-tale in the core outshines and threatens to break away from its historical container, with the lingering echo of the spell-like "Snake Lady" in the last sentence serving as a sign of its perseverance.

This mingling of the historical with the fictional, as critics have noted, is a recurrent feature of Lee's writing.[45] In Lee's "A Seeker of Pagan Perfection", a piece that problematises the usual distinction between fiction and non-fiction,[46] the narrative begins with the author speaking directly to her reader: "I give to the reader rather as historical fact than as fiction the study which I have always called to myself: *Pictor Sacrilegus*".[47] But this authorial command is accompanied with an acknowledgement that the story's origin is purely in the historian's mind: "Twenty years have passed since first I was aware of its presence ... It is presumably a piece of my inventing, for I have neither read it nor heard it related".[48] Such an admission might totally disqualify the proceeding narrative as history, but what Lee the historian (as she claims herself to be) demands from her reader is precisely to reconsider the distinction of history and fiction. If the personal and perspectival historical method she proposes in her introduction to *Euphorion* is only mildly remonstrating a historiography aimed at universal truth, here she goes even further to suggest that, if history is people's construction of the past, then a picture of the past originating from the historian's mind is no less "true" to the past than one extracted from external sources. The result of this conflation of genres is an invitation for the reader to rethink the boundary between history and fiction and an experimentation with ways in which one mode of narrative may penetrate and transform into the other.

"Snake Lady" continues this interpenetration of history and fiction, and through the dramatisation of the conflict between the House of Luna and Lady Oriana, it stages how a barren historical record that tries to suppress the anomaly posed by the Snake Lady could be countered by a para-history of the anomalous woman thriving in folk and oral traditions. The historical mode that begins and ends the story tries to confirm what is written is reality, yet it can only tell us that in the year 1701 the House of Luna became extinct; moreover, the fairy-tale contained within this frame reveals that what is written is far from reality and leaves much space for Lady Oriana and Prince Alberic's story to develop. The more the reader gets to know of the history of the Snake Lady, the more fertile and fantastic a landscape the story enters, until in the very centre of the architecture of the whole story, part six of the 13 parts of the story, we are presented with a minstrel's song about how Alberic the Blond, the first prince of the House of Luna, encounters the Snake Lady and pledges to her his loyalty.

The minstrel's song, spatially occupying the core of the story, is by far the closest to the Snake Lady's secret and most sympathetic of her plight. Interestingly, this sympathetic rendering of Oriana's past is partly confirmed and partly condemned in the following part seven where Alberic, shocked to delirium in his sickbed, seeks to verify the story with a neighbour priest. The priest, believing the prince to be possessed by an evil spirit, tries to pacify him by relating how Alberic the Blond and a second Marquis Alberic both failed Oriana. His source is the folk poem he has heard as a boy but representing as he is the orthodoxy of the church, he denounces the poem as "foolish", "in very poor style", of "a very inferior composition" and appeals only to "the uneducated" (211). Thus, already in the oral tradition of Oriana's story there is side by side a commoner's celebration of the fairy and the church's suppression of her as a witch. If parts six and seven at the centre of the story function to establish the snake woman's past, we see two forces competing for the control of that past, dramatised comically in the manner in which the priest recounts the Snake Lady's story to Prince Alberic as a foil to exorcise her. It is the paradox involved in the priest's act of suppression and silencing that testifies precisely to the power of para-history represented by the snake woman: to exorcise her is to speak of her, yet linguistically she will never die but will thrive on in folklore.

This irony rebounding on official history's suppression is also evidenced in the ending of the story. Duke Balthasar succeeds in doing what all former princes of Luna fail to do: he cuts off the head of the grass snake, thereby killing Oriana for good; yet the same brutality also leads to Prince Alberic's suicide, thus terminating the line of the House of Luna. In the end, what we get from the story is a terse historical frame barely containing its fantastic contents, and implicit in this arrangement of different narrative modes is a yearning to break away from history towards fantasy, a yearning that frequently surfaces in Lee's fiction.

Conjurers of the past: *Louis Norbert: A Two-fold Romance*

Nowhere is the conflict between history and fiction more dramatised than in Lee's novel *Louis Norbert: A Two-fold Romance* (1914), where two modern characters, an unnamed archaeologist (another synonym for the historian) and a middle-aged aristocratic Lady Venetia collaborate in historical research on a seventeenth-century French orphan, Louis Norbert, who had been adopted by Venetia's ancestors. The historical research unearths not only the real identity of Louis Norbert but also his ill-fated romance with the poetess Artemisia which is paralleled between the characters of the twentieth century, hence the subtitle "a two-fold romance". The eponymous hero, Louis Norbert, is nicknamed "the ghost" of "the Ghost's Room" in Lady Venetia's ancestral home. This "ghost" of Louis Norbert to be sure is not a ghost verifiable by the Society for Psychical Research, but in haunting Lady Venetia's youthful memories and in being purged from historical records by the French court so that only fragmentary traces of him remain, Louis Norbert is a ghosted figure, a "genuine ghost" in Lee's term, summoned only from imagination yet purged out of history, just like the many who died silent victims of national history and returned as ghosts in the Chinese *zhiguai*. The story focuses on the process of piecing together the lost story of the ghosted; in other words, it is about unearthing the truth of the past. As I mentioned at the beginning of this chapter, unearthing the story of the ghost is one way of conjuring up the past while writing history is another, therefore as a novel that self-consciously contests the different discourses on the construction of the past—history versus fiction—as well as the implicit gendered dimension involved in this construction, *Louis Norbert* is a meta-ghost story about the writing of the ghost's story.

The novel uses a technique now popular with neo-Victorian novels: a parallel narrative of the past and the present. In keeping with the "two-fold" in the subtitle, each character is presented in dialectical relation with other characters both in the seventeenth century and the twentieth century by a logic of desire and identification: not only does the would-be romance between the archaeologist and Lady Venetia mirror that of Artemisia and Louis Norbert, but the modern characters also each form a personal bond with the historical character of the opposite gender. Thus triangulated, desire travels both between man and woman and across time, creating a multi-layered net in which every knot can sympathise with and even personify the others. But even more important than the cross-pairing of characters is a pair of related concepts, corresponding to the methodology used by the archaeologist and Lady Venetia respectively—"to discover" or "to invent". While the historian and the woman's dispute over the two terms seems to be a linguistic question in the beginning, gradually it is revealed to be a vital question in their construction of the ghost's past and in each gender's construction of the other.

The dispute of "to invent" or "to discover" is first spurned by the archaeologist's chivalric suggestion towards Venetia when the latter is frustrated with her fruitless hunt of Louis Norbert in her family's archives. To soothe her, the archaeologist writes to encourage her to "invent" something about her "ghost": "Do you remember writing to me that if I could find out nothing I was to 'make it up'? Well, I venture to say the same to you—*invent*! It is but another form of the Latin word which means to *discover*!"[49] He then proceeds to recollect how one evening in their first acquaintance, Venetia had entertained a group of friends by telling them a sentimental love story of a German couple, revealing only at the end that all these people were products of her imagination. Such, the archaeologist assures, is the woman's genius for "inventing". However, this seemingly complimentary letter meets only with the woman's indignation, who reproaches the archaeologist in her next letter and insists that in the matter of Louis Norbert she refuses absolutely to be associated with the concept of inventing.

Lady Venetia's strong dislike of the archaeologist's seemingly well-meant suggestion seems at first confusing, until later she reveals how this association of women with "invent" veils a sinister bias against women's intellectual capacity, and it is this crude typecasting of women by men that she objects to. Early on, Venetia admits in a letter to the archaeologist her perception of the latter's opinion of women: "I remember you said at Pisa ... that frivolous people ... like me divide the world's contents into things they like and things that bore them, and never suspect there may be any other order in the universe" (227). This description of an aristocratic idle woman immersed in her own fancy of a ghost is reminiscent of the self-absorbed and over-imaginative Alice Oke. Indeed, the middle-aged Venetia might well be a mature Alice if the latter had survived her first loveless marriage from the heyday of aestheticism of the 1880s. At the same time, the amateur woman embarking on historical research with an intuitive method likely to be frowned upon by male professionals also reflects to some extent Lee's self-perception. In this sense, the outspoken Venetia becomes the spokesperson for all of Lee's female characters suffering under male voyeurism and prejudice. While Alice Oke only retreats to a state of indifference to men's ceaseless scrutiny of her, the mature Venetia is ever alert to men's tendency of imposing on women their fancies and is determined to take control of her own image whenever she senses traces of distortion and prejudice.

But the indignant woman is soon appeased, for the archaeologist in his next humble-toned letter assures Venetia of his total respect for the method of inventing, "For a hypothesis is a scientific *invention*" (256). The researchers' first round of disputes over which is the proper method of excavating the ghost's story seems to be solved by the archaeologist's concession that invention has its due place in scientific research. From then on, the archaeologist and the woman seem to have exchanged their positions regarding invention and discovery. While Venetia shuns from "invention" and urges the archaeologist to "formulate historical hypothesis" (258), the latter insists that "for the present saying 'formulate' to him is exactly the same as saying 'invention' to you" (258), while elsewhere he proudly asserts that "*we* [meaning the archaeologist and another young woman who assists his research] invent, dear Lady Venetia" (261). It is as if now the woman has become the scientific-minded historian while the archaeologist turns into a romantic inventor. Does this mean that the amateur woman's intuitive method has now gained full approval from the historian? Her next bold hypothesis about Louis Norbert's parentage brings them back to the initial dispute over "invent" or "discover".

In a long letter, Venetia announces to the archaeologist her "discovery" of Louis Norbert's origin as the legitimate son of the French King Louis XIV. Moreover, she now agrees with the archaeologist that to say "invent" is the same as "to formulate a theory" and goes one step further to equate her discovery with the very truth as she announces, "I have not invented, unless inventing may mean (by the way, you hinted something to this effect)—may mean *discovering the truth*" (269). Such a bold hypothesis (and insisted as *the truth*) immediately meets with the archaeologist's admonishment and disproval, who now recoils from his former encouragement and resorts to a vocabulary that redraws the difference between him as a professional historian and the amateur woman whom he now complements as "a poet or novelist":

> After all, it is only what would have happened to a poet or novelist; and, as I have already ventured to say, a poet and a novelist are lost (or perhaps gained!) in you, dear Lady Venetia; only I, a poor plodding historian, am bound to protest, in the name of historical documents, against the gratuitous interpretation of your vision of Louis Norbert's birth in the light of a marriage between Louis XIV and the Berenice of our Pisan spies.
>
> (275)

Therefore, when the woman does try to equate "invention" with "discovery", the man clings to the rigid historicist standard of his profession and feels obliged to disqualify her theory as the fancies of the "poet or novelist"; moreover, he reverts to his initial prejudice of Venetia as one of those great ladies "addicted to some form or other of spirit-rapping" (201), for which "poet or novelist" is only a euphemism. The woman, in turn, rightly senses the man's condescension, and in her next letter eloquently spells out men's inclination to impose their fantasy on women, which can be read as a protest on behalf of all Lee's female characters moulded by male desire and ambition (Medea da Carpi and Alice Oke instantly come into mind):

> But there it just is, and all men, historians or not historians, are *exactly* alike in this—once you get a wrong notion into your head at the beginning, no power on earth will ever get it out again or prevent you seeing the most *obvious fact* distorted through it! [...] you have written me down as a foolish woman with a hopeless tendency to romancing about everything, what you call *a born poet or novelist*. Almost the most riling part of it is this amiable attempt (so like a man towards a woman!) to turn an unjustifiable accusation into a compliment—of course that all hang together with your recommending me to *invent* (I was perfectly right in being angry with you, although you afterwards explained it away). And now you think I am inventing, I suppose. And all the time it is you, my poor young, learned friend, who have been inventing, *inventing a me* utterly unlike the reality.
>
> (282, 283)

While Venetia's retorts seem to be stretching a scholarly dispute into a general complaint of men's manipulation of women's image, the dispute over "inventing" or "discovery" from the very beginning is a problem concerning each gender's approach towards the past as a series of images and concepts in the characters' research have been aligned along gendered lines. Lady Venetia, being a woman and an amateur, is believed by the archaeologist to be some form of "table-rapper" or "crystal reader", so it is more commendable to ask her to "invent" instead of "to discover the truth" or "form a historical hypothesis", for her method is that of "a novelist or poet", and her childhood affinity with the Ghost's Room binds her irrevocably with fancy and imagination. On the other hand, the archaeologist/ historian is (and consciously presents himself to be) a scientific pedant, who is equipped with scientific scepticism and relies his research solely on dry historical documents excavated from the Muniment Room and the Pisan Archives. Therefore, if the archaeologist is right in protesting against Venetia's flippant historical deduction, the latter is also justifiable in pointing out the historian's hidden gender biases—her reaction is a protest of men's marginalisation of women into the charming but ephemeral role of intuitive spiritualist mediums or ghost-seekers and a revolt against men's making of women's image.

So far, the joint historical research of the contemporary characters is presented as a competition between each one's method of reaching the past, which in a dramatic sense re-enacts the subtle competition of the two historical discourses I have traced out in Lee's introduction to *Euphorion*: one is men's, scientific, authoritative and that of the historian; the other is women's, intuitive, amateurish, and prone to be discredited as fantasy or "poetic". However, just as the two approaches clash with each other, they are also shown in the story to be complementing and even converging with their opposite as the man and the woman enter a deeper understanding of each other and of the past. The major dichotomies in their historical research—invention versus discovery, facts versus fancy—gradually shift sides so much so that while the above delineated gendered dyads are highlighted, they are also being confounded. The "most obvious facts" in Venetia's complaint quoted above, of course, refer to what she perceives as the historian's prejudice of her, yet in each person's case, fancy is always inseparable from what he or she perceives to be the fact about the other, so the archaeologist suggests: "After all, are not all the persons in whom we take the most vivid interest just, to that extent, creations of our own?" (248). Furthermore, it is increasingly difficult to tell who is inventing. Venetia rightly accuses the archaeologist of inventing a "she" who never exists; however, is she not also inventing a pedantic historian in her self-defence, and inventing a Louis Norbert whose tragic death fits her own perception of romance?

Although the archaeologist disapproves of Venetia's intuitive method, gradually more evidence emerges in their research to support her claims. It seems that the novelist's approach is gaining the upper hand, yet a newly discovered record of Louis Norbert's death in the Florentine archive shatters all their previous construction of the ghost's story and brings their research to a dead end. The truth surrounding Louis Norbert becomes utterly ungraspable at this point, as the secret story of Louis Norbert they have pieced together from documentary fragments is contradicted by this historical testimony. Now the "ghost" Louis Norbert risks forever remaining a ghost, i.e., little more substantial than a woman's fantasy.

When historical records seem to be denying the ghost's story, it is the archaeologist who saves the ghost from oblivion by presenting in his next letter a vital document: a translation of the memoir of Abbess Artemisia. This document not only explains how Louis Norbert met his death but also chimes perfectly well with Venetia's initial vision of the lovers' romantic tragedy. However, such a critical historical document in the reconstruction of the ghost's history, as the archaeologist admits, is obtained through a "Faustian contract", and the purportedly fantastic origin of the document inevitably problematises the nature of the ghost's history it seeks to confirm:

> I was ready, like Faust and others among my fellow pedants, to sell my soul.
>
> I have done so, and I venture to send you herewith registered, and as a humble Christmas greeting, its price.
>
> These Memoirs of the Abbess of St Veridiana, previously known in the world as Artemisia del Valore, were composed in a language you are not quite familiar with, though (for reasons which I will later explain) I am unable to inform you whether that language is Latin, Greek (which that learned muse possessed fluently) or mere Italian; so what I send you is a translation made to the best of my slight powers.
>
> (333)

The historian's statement is deliberately evasive. Has he really made a Faustian contract, or is it only a euphemism for the forgery he has made to console Lady Venetia? Venetia's exclamation that "I really do not know ... whether I believe you to be a dealer in stolen goods or a poet" (350) may suggest that she suspects it is the latter, but it is clear that by now both agree, after all, only the novelist/poet's method can give a history to Louis Norbert. However, the paradoxical nature of the document as the price of a "Faustian contract" and a translation of an original manuscript places it forever in the liminal space between history and fiction. The word "translation" itself implies both the difference between the translated and the source text and something in common between the two, with the translator or transcriber taking full responsibility for the difference. In this case, the archaeologist's request of Venetia to "desist from all questions concerning the original of this document and its whereabouts, let alone the manner in which it has come into my hands" (333) is a gesture that both veils and reveals the critical part that the translator plays in this final product. Such a claim and disowning resembles exactly what Lee the historian does in her historical-fictional essay "Ravenna and Her Ghosts", where taking full advantage of the potentials promised by "translating", she presents the reader a new translation of a Ravenna ghost story whose manner of acquisition "I am not at liberty to divulge".[50] In their conspiracy to take liberty with a "translation" of the past, the archaeologist, who "after all, was secretly a poet" (206) merges with the historian Lee, and the historian-poet's final solution to arrive at the past is to contract a Faustian compact that blends facts and fancy into an indissoluble "translation" (or in other words, an invention).

The way the historian works as a "translator" of a forbidden language is reminiscent of the ghostly messages obtained through the planchette in Wang Tao's stories mentioned in the beginning of the chapter. The stories of these ghosts are believed to be "transcribed" (another way of translating) by the literati who hold the séances, therefore constituting a genuine trace of the ghosts. What Wang emphasises is the authenticity of the ghosts' "testimony" while downplaying the mediation of the literati transcribers. The inescapable effects of shadowing and covering-up of such a method have been explored above. Lee's romance foregrounds the inventive role of the translator/historian, but still, to obtain a half-historical half-fictional message from the dead seems to be the only possible way to conjure up the ghost. In this sense, every novelist/poet is a conjurer of the past, and every historian is a translator of the unobtainable ghostly message.

The final evocation of a Faustian contract, as analysed in this chapter, blurs the distinction between history and fiction, and the romantic tragedy of Louis Norbert and Artemisia in the seventeenth century, if we trust it did exist, exists only just beyond what historical evidence can verify. The whole romance of the twentieth century, in the form of a historical excavation of a ghost and a constant probation of its own historical method, is a meta-ghost story as it comments on the making of the ghost's story. In form and content, the novel tries to answer the question: how to arrive at the truth of the ghost? And its answer points to the realm of fantasy: the undecided zone between facts and fancy, history and fiction. Therefore, for Lee, to conjure into life a ghosted figure like Louis Norbert, the best strategy may not be reinstating him into history (as Lee's stories analysed in this chapter have shown abundantly its perils) but creating a fantasy which springs from history yet tentatively hinges just beyond the verifiable real.

Like the *zhiguai* stories discussed in previous chapters, Lee's ghost stories are also permeated with a sense of the past. But as a female art historian and a lesbian writer, Lee may be more alert to the gendered method of historiography. By exposing the complex gendered manipulation in men's history-making and ghost-making, Lee problematises the seemingly objective position of the male historian/ghost-maker; in this way she frees the ghost woman from the role of a mere spectacle scrutinised and moulded by male desires. Moreover, as with all writers of the ghost's story, Lee is aware of the powerful and subverting potential of spectrality and haunting. Terry Castle summarises well the persistent power of the ghost: "The ghost, in other words, is a paradox. Though non-existent, it nonetheless appears. Indeed, so vividly does it appear—if only in the 'mind's eye'— one feels unable to get away from it".[51] Castle, of course, is using the ghost as a metaphor for the phantomised lesbian identity in Western culture, of which Lee as a lesbian writer must have felt poignantly. But not only lesbians can make up their identity through the figure of the ghost; indeed, a ghost is such a potent being that a variety of people who could not enter "history" for various reasons can now come back as ghosts. Lee's ghost stories show her suspicion towards history-making, and instead of legitimising the ghost's history, she proposes haunting as a more efficient returning of ghosts. As the deconstructionist Julian Wolfreys argues in his *Victorian Hauntings*, haunting in a broader sense is not only the visitation of ghosts from the past, but a process that "puts into play a disruptive structure", or, as Wolfreys quotes Rodelphe Casche's remark of the phantom, "the phantasmatic is the space in which representation is fragmented".[52] To accept the state of haunting, as Lee's stories suggest, is to refuse to put an end to the ghost's story by either locating that story in authoritative history or mere fancy but to allow it to persist in the liminal realm of fantasy, between facts and fancy, fiction and history, yet always a part of reality. Haunting also points to the fragmentation in representation, the fissures in interpretation, the incomprehensibility of life, and the alterity within. This revolt against interpretation and textual closure, as Chapter 5 will show, will also surface in E. Nesbit's Gothic ghost stories.

Notes

1 Here I use the word "marvellous" in Todorov's sense: texts where the existence of the supernatural is taken for granted.
2 Carlyle, "On History", in *A Carlyle Reader* (1984), 56.
3 Christina Crosby argues that "In the nineteenth century 'history' is produced as man's truth, the truth of a necessarily historical Humanity, which in turn requires that 'women' be outside history". See Crosby, *The Ends of History: Victorians and "the Woman Question"* (1991), 10, passim.
4 Nietzsche, "On the Uses and Disadvantages of History for Life", in *Untimely Meditation* (1997), 86. Nietzsche of course immediately warns that he actually regards history as the "eternally manly" rather than the "eternally womanly" (87), but the sexed metaphor nevertheless indicates the assumed important correlation between history and the historian's sex.
5 See Joan W. Scott, "Gender: A Useful Category of Historical Analysis", *The American Historical Review* 91. 5 (1986): 1053–75. Scott argues that history has been gendered

as a masculinist discourse, and the masculine subject it evokes is disguised as neutral and universal.
6 On the institutionalisation of history as a discipline, see Bonnie G. Smith, *The Gender of History: Men, Women, and Historical Practice* (1998).
7 See Hilary Fraser, "Women and the Ends of Art History: Vision and Corporeality in Nineteenth-Century Critical Discourse", *Victorian Studies* 42.1 (1998), 90–3.
8 Zorn, *Vernon Lee: Aesthetics, History, and the Victorian Female Intellectual* (2003), 27.
9 Vineta Colby, *Victorian Literature and Culture: Vernon Lee, a Literary Biography* (2003), 6.
10 Zorn, *Vernon Lee*, Introduction, xv.
11 Lee had enjoyed intimate friendships with Mary Robinson (Mary Duclaux) and later Clementina Ansthuther-Thompson, two women who have been recognised by Lee's biographers as her lovers. Lee is termed by her biographer Burdett Gardner as a "failed lesbian", for her contemporaries seemed to agree that none of her relations came to a physical level. On Lee's sexuality, see Sally Newman, "Archival Traces of Desire: Vernon Lee's Failed Sexuality and the Interpretation of Letters in Lesbian History", *Journal of the History of Sexuality* 14.1 (2005): 51–75.
12 See for instance Max Beerbohm's and John Addington Symonds's sarcastic remark on Lee's intellectual power in Colby, *Vernon Lee*, 270, 51.
13 Colby, *Vernon Lee*, 2.
14 Colby, *Vernon Lee*, 30.
15 Shortly after her first book, the real gender of the author was no longer a secret, yet Lee kept the masculine pen name all her life and used it in most of her private correspondence, showing that "Vernon Lee" by this stage was no longer a borrowed man's position but a re-invented identity for a woman conscious of her unconventional gender-positioning. See also Zorn, *Vernon Lee*, Chapter 4 on the androgynous subjectivity adopted in Lee's philosophical writings.
16 Lee, *Euphorion: Being Studies of the Antique and the Mediæval in the Renaissance* (1884), vol. 1, 9–10.
17 See Hilary Fraser, *The Victorians and Renaissance Italy* (1992), 217–20 and "Women and the Ends" for a comparison of Lee's art history with those of Symonds and Pater. Fraser argues that in methodology, Lee is more a disciple of Pater and situates herself as the opposite of Symonds. In fact, Lee admits in the bibliography of *Euphorion II* that she had deliberately avoided reading the parts of Symonds' *Renaissance In Italy* that deal with Renaissance literature, "from fear that finding myself doubtless forestalled by him in various appreciations, I might deprive my essays of what I feel to be their principal merit, namely, the spontaneity and wholeness of personal impression" (quoted in Colby, *Vernon Lee*, 67). This deliberate distancing of her work from Symonds's certainly was felt (and perhaps meant) less as a compliment than a disavowal.
18 "Amour Dure" was originally published in *Murrey's Magazine* in 1887 and "Oke of Okehurst" was first published as a novella titled "A Phantom Lover" by William Blackwood in 1886 before the two were collected in *Hauntings and Other Fantastic Stories* in 1890.
19 Lee, *Hauntings and Other Fantastic Tales* (2006), 183. If not otherwise indicated, quotations of Lee's ghost stories all refer to this edition.
20 An earlier version of parts of this section has appeared in the article "History-making and Its Gendered Voice in Wang Tao's and Vernon Lee's Ghost Stories", *Neohelicon* 47. 2: 645–61.
21 See for instance Dickerson, *Victorian Women*; Makala, *Women's Ghost Literature*; Wallace, *Female Gothic Histories*, and Victoria Margree, *British Women's Short Supernatural Fiction, 1860–1930: Our Own Ghostliness* (2019).
22 Three of the four tales, "Amour Dure", "Oke of Okehurst", and "Dionea" have a ghostly female figure from the past, while the ghost in "A Wicked Voice" is a feminised castrato singer.

23 See for instance Mary Patricia Kane, *Spurious Ghosts: The Fantastic Tales of Vernon Lee* (2004), 28–9, in which Kane contrasts Medea's portrait and Robert's equestrian statue as representing respectively an alternative version of history and the authoritative one; see also Catherine Maxwell, "From Dionysus to Dionea: Vernon Lee's Portraits", *Word and Image* 13.3 (1997), 267.

24 Zorn, *Vernon Lee*, 163. Elsewhere in her book (149–50) Zorn points out the unconscious sexual desire that tints the narrator's portrayal of his protégée Dionea in "Dionea", which makes the male reporter an unreliable narrator. The same can be said to apply to Trepka, an unreliable narrator/historian whose gendered manipulation is invisible to himself yet obvious to the reader.

25 On discussions of Trepka's Polish identity, see Peter Christensen, "The Burden of History in Vernon Lee's Ghost Story 'Amour Dure'", *Studies in the Humanities* 16.1 (1989): 33–43; and Sondeep Kandola, *Vernon Lee* (2010), 43–5.

26 Christensen, "The Burden", 39. Trepka was said to come from Posen, a province of Poland which was taken over by Prussia in 1793 (See *Hauntings*, 42, n1). As Trepka dies in 1885 at the age of 24, it is clear that he must have been brought up as a German and the memory of a Polish past is largely constructed from imagination.

27 Nietzsche, "On the Uses and Disadvantages of History for Life", 91.

28 Zorn, *Vernon Lee*, 163.

29 Zorn, *Vernon Lee*, 147.

30 On "Oke of Okehurst" as Lee's response to aestheticism, see for instance Stefano Evangelista, "Vernon Lee and the Gender of Aestheticism", in Catherine Maxwell and Patricia Pulham eds., *Vernon Lee: Decadence, Ethics, Aesthetics* (2006), 91–111; Kandola, *Vernon Lee*, 25–6.

31 Walter Pater, qtd. in Evangelista, "Vernon Lee", 95.

32 On "Oke" as an inverted Pygmalion myth, see Mengxing Fu, "The Subversion of the Ghost Narrative: The Pygmalion Myth in Vernon Lee's Oke of the Okehurst", *English and American Literary Studies* 30 (2019):121–37.

33 Kandola, *Vernon Lee*, 27.

34 Lee is especially sympathetic for the plight of upper-class women constrained to a life of compulsory idleness and frivolity. She explores this subject in her short story "A Worldly Woman" (1892) which portrays sympathetically the awakening of such a "worldly" woman and an unsympathetic male artist who fails to free her from this condition. Lee's sympathy for women's forced idleness was later transformed into a more systematic feminism in her "The Economic Parasitism of Women" in *Gospels of Anarchy* (1908).

35 Garber, *Vested Interests: Cross-Dressing and Cultural Anxiety* (1992), 16–17.

36 For instance, Pulham reads in Alice's cross-dressing a lesbian sexuality, and the coded language surrounding Lovelock implies that he is a substitute for a woman. See Pulham, *Art and Transitional Object in Vernon Lee's Supernatural Tales* (2008), 128–32.

37 *Miss Brown* (1884), vol. 2, 308–9.

38 On the disastrous reception of *Miss Brown* and its impact on Lee, see Colby, *Vernon Lee*, Chapter 6. Lee's next and only novel after *Miss Brown* is *Louis Norbert: A Twofold Romance* (1914).

39 *Miss Brown* (1884), vol. 2, 308

40 Many critics read in the novel a subtext of lesbian desire. See for instance Pulham, *Art and the Transitional Object*, 81–4; Kathy Psomidades, 1999, "'Still Burning from This Strangling Embrace': Vernon Lee on Desire and Aesthetics", in Richard Dellamora ed., *Victorian Sexual Dissidence* (1999), 21–42; and Martha Vicinus, *Intimate Friends: Women Who Loved Women, 1778–1928* (2004),154–6.

41 Stetz argues that the story's appearance in *The Yellow Book* in 1896 was Lee's implicit support for Oscar Wilde, a fellow sexual minority whose tragic downfall happened just one year earlier. See Stetz, "The Snake Lady and the Bruised Bodley Head: Vernon

Lee and Oscar Wilde in the *Yellow Book*", in Maxwell and Pulham eds., *Vernon Lee: Decadence, Ethics, and Aesthetics* (2006), 112–22.
42 Swinburne, "Notes on Designs of the Old Masters at Florence", excerpted in Lee, *Hauntings* (2006), 280. See also Nina Auerbach, *Woman and the Demon: The Life of a Victorian Myth* (1982), on the many manifestations of the serpent-woman in Victorian literature.
43 The twelve plaster Caesars, one presiding over each window of the Red Palace which Alberic always found uncanny, as Kane observes, resemble one model of Foucault's panopticon; see Kane, *Spurious Ghosts*, 54.
44 *Miss Brown*, vol.2, 308–9.
45 See for instance Zorn, *Vernon Lee*, 55–6 and Colby, *Vernon Lee*, 247–8. Apart from "Prince Alberic and the Snake Lady" and the following example, Lee's "The Wedding Chest" (in *Pope Jacynth and and Other Fantastic Tales*, 1904) is also a fantastic tale contained in a historical frame, and her "Ravenna and Her Ghosts: A Medieval Legend" (in *The Collected Supernatural and Weird Fiction of Vernon Lee* vol.2) is an essay that digresses into fiction.
46 The piece was first published in 1891 in *The Contemporary Review* and included in Lee's essay collection *Renaissance Fancies and Studies* (1895), but later it was treated as a fantastic tale and often anthologised in Lee's supernatural story collections, for instance in *The Snake Lady and Other Stories* by Grove Press in 1954 and *The Collected Supernatural and Weird Fiction of Vernon Lee*, by Leonaur in 2011.
47 *The Collected Supernatural and Weird Fiction of Vernon Lee*, vol. 1, 132.
48 *The Collected Supernatural and Weird Fiction of Vernon Lee*, vol. 1, 132.
49 *The Collected Supernatural and Weird Fiction of Vernon Lee*, vol. 2, 247, italics original. Later in-text quotations from *Louis Norbert* all refer to this edition.
50 *The Collected Supernatural and Weird Fiction of Vernon Lee*, vol. 2, 188.
51 Castle, *The Apparitional Lesbian: Female Homosexuality and Modern Culture* (1993), 46.
52 Wolfreys, *Victorian Hauntings: Spectrality, Gothic, the Uncanny, and Literature* (2002), 6.

5 The dead woman returning
E. Nesbit's Female Gothic myth

In her long narrative poem "The Moat House" (1886),[1] Edith Nesbit (1858–1924) relates the story of an innocent nun seduced and abandoned by her noble lover for an advantageous marriage. Pregnant with the man's child, the rejected woman's only method of revenge is to throw herself under the wheel of her former lover's wedding carriage. The wedding continues, but the guilt-stricken man is forever haunted by ghosts: "And at night he wakes and shivers with unvanquishable dread/ At the ghosts that press each other for a place beside his bed/ And he shudders to remember all the dearness that is dead".[2] The poem's dramatisation of a woman betrayed and abandoned by her lover, as Nesbit's biographer Julia Briggs remarks, might contain traces of the author's suppressed resentment for her own unfaithful husband.[3] Yet the same narrative pattern—the fall of the wronged woman and her return as a ghost to her human lover—is to surface again and again in Nesbit's ghost stories in the 1890s. This chapter explores the various reincarnations of the dead woman in Nesbit's tales and how her resurrection as a ghost converges and clashes with popular Victorian myths of women and death to weave new Female Gothic myths.

In Chapter 4, I trace how Vernon Lee's ghost stories expose the manipulation and distortion in man-made histories of the ghost woman. The idea of history is important to women writers in the *fin-de-siècle* because knowledge about the past provides a starting point for rethinking women's status in the present and interrogating current social establishments. While not all women writers had the insight of a historian such as Vernon Lee, another way to probe the construction of gender through fiction was to appropriate existing myths. As metahistorical and metafictional narrative patterns that are pertaining to the way we make sense of everyday life, myth has always already informed the construction of history, literature, and philosophy. In Laurence Coupe's conceptualisation, "myth shapes history, and therefore it shapes culture. The religious beliefs, social customs and linguistic commonplaces of each age are reaffirmations of, and elaborations upon, primitive mythic pattern".[4] In this sense, the literary texts that are informed by primary mythic patterns can be seen as both mythography—offering interpretations to existing mythic paradigms, and mythopoeia—functioning as a new myth. This is especially true in a genre like the Gothic that is saturated with conventions, for conventions in other words imply a discernible literary lineage

DOI: 10.4324/9781003188223-5

and repetition of powerful plots that are pertaining to myth. In this chapter, I explore E. Nesbit's Gothic ghost stories as both mythography and mythopoeia. Specifically, I argue that these stories, while working with an awareness and adaptation of the existing Female Gothic literary tradition, satirise existing myths about femininity and weave new ones for the Gothic heroine, with the returning female ghost functioning as the pivotal figure.

Two aspects of Nesbit's ghost stories constitute my focus: their Gothic opacity and their convergence with myths about the dead woman. Nesbit's Gothic stories capitalise on textual irresoluteness and often refuse a linear, coherent explanation, which not only disrupts the signification process but also reflects the contradictions experienced in the lives of contemporary Victorian women. These features strengthen the unsettling power and gender critique of the stories, for anti-resolution means refusing to moralise, which points to an epistemological uncertainty instead of a reaffirmation of order. The thematic concern of these stories—the dead woman rising and returning—in a sense are all variants of the prototype in "The Moat House", yet they are complicated with new interpretations and convergence with other narrative traditions. The idea of ghostly justice is no longer equated with the grip that the ghost asserts on her human lover as implicated in "The Moat House", but instead it relies on the unending haunting effects that the text creates; in other words, the ghost of the returning woman aims not at revenge but to upset, expose, and parody. In "The Ebony Frame" (1893),[5] the ghost woman's return to her human lover is dramatised as a clash between the past and the present, the result of which is not a triumph of the ghost over the present but the melancholic effect that her haunting creates, thus ensuring the ghost's eternal presence; in "The Shadow" (1905?),[6] the ghost figure becomes an emblem for inexplicableness and anti-interpretation, yet it is this anti-linear logic that offers an occasion for female characters to build mutual understanding. In "From the Dead", the journey taken by the heroine merges with two contemporary myths about women—the ideal dead woman and the fallen woman, but the story deconstructs these myths from within. Finally, in the concluding section I analyse Nesbit's creative myth-making in "The House of Silence" (1906), which rewrites the familiar Female Gothic plot into a gender allegory, stripping bare the romanticisation involved in the plot of female death and itself an empowering myth for the Gothic heroine.

An ambiguous life

Since Ellen Moers coined the phrase "Female Gothic" in 1978, the notion has evolved much from Moers's original stipulation. Yet although different definitions pertain, critics using the term can generally discern a distinct tradition of Gothic fiction originating with Ann Radcliffe, which focuses on the persecution, imprisonment, escape, and spiritual growth of an innocent Gothic heroine, favours the sublimated terror over the violent horror, and employs ghostly elements to indicate past injustices which more often can be explained away or set to rest once family secrets are revealed and the villain's threats are eliminated.[7] In exploring the suffering and sense of persecution that female characters feel in society, home, and marriage, Nesbit's ghost stories certainly touch upon the central themes of Female Gothic. The Gothic heroine, constantly in danger in a menacing environment, is reincarnated in various forms in the stories by Nesbit which I am to discuss in this chapter, some familiarly recognisable while some ironically transformed. However, the other common features of Female Gothic—resolution and realisation of justice—are rarely found in Nesbit's stories, with the bleak ending of her most famous "Man-size in Marble" (1893) just one such example. Ambiguity and the deliberate refusal of closure are an important trademark of Nesbit's stories, and they open fissures in the seemingly coherent social structures and unleash a more powerful critique of existing moral orders than what are called by Nesbit "artistically rounded-off" stories.[8] In this sense, Nesbit's stories about a heroine's sufferings and fears that cannot be explained unequivocally capture vividly the often tumultuous experiences of Victorian women in a fast-changing society and can be regarded as a variation of Female Gothic.

However, to re-evaluate Nesbit's ghost stories as Female Gothic has its own difficulties. On the one hand, Nesbit's ghost stories are often neglected even by her biographers and were never considered an important part of her oeuvre, as the author has long been typecast as a writer of children's literature.[9] Unlike her popular children's fiction, her horror story collections, *Grim Tales* (1893), *Something Wrong* (1893), and *Fear* (1910) have long been out of print, and it is only recently with the publication of two anthologies of her stories, *The Power of Darkness* (2006) and *Horror Stories* (2016), that many of her ghost stories are made more accessible.[10] On the other hand, for those who want to recuperate Nesbit's ghost stories from a feminist perspective, they have to confront the "feminist-or-not" question. Yet it is here that the problem arises: for Nesbit, while sometimes challenging the limits that society allowed for her gender, is otherwise difficult to categorise as a feminist as she conspicuously distanced herself from the political activism struggling for women's rights. Yet if her adult novels, as Amelia Rutledge argues, are a domestication of the New Woman character,[11] her ghost stories, as some critics show and as I will demonstrate in this chapter, apparently allow her more freedom to interrogate the unequal gender relations of her time.[12]

Nesbit, in her biographer Briggs's words, is a woman "who presented a mass of contradictions, and whose various roles, whether imposed or willingly assumed, were often difficult to reconcile".[13] Being one of the founding members of the socialist Fabian Society, a prolific writer who for a long time was the chief breadwinner of her large family, and somewhat an experimenter of open marriage with her husband Hubert Bland, Nesbit's bohemian lifestyle embraced that of the New Woman in many aspects. Yet at the same time she was resolutely reticent about women's suffrage even when her Fabian friend Charlotte Wilson (1854–1944) enlisted her in the cause. Briggs in her biography mentioned that when invited to read a paper on "Motherhood and Breadwinning" by the Fabian Women's Group, Nesbit changed her topic to "The Natural Disabilities of Women" which shocked her audience and spurred a series of rebuttals.[14] Nesbit attributed her reluctance to support women's suffrage to her worries that it may endanger the socialist cause, yet as Briggs shows, this is at best a tactical excuse while the real reason might be a mixture of the influence of Nesbit's more conservative husband Hubert Bland, who believed women's rightful place to be in the domestic sphere (an ironic opposite of the real situation in his marriage), and Nesbit's own idealisation of romantic love.[15] Nesbit in her own political stance, therefore, could not be easily reclaimed as pro-feminist.

However, whatever Nesbit's political stance towards the suffrage movement, her fiction may or may not voice the same set of ideas. The fantastic mode, as many critics have noticed, often allows women writers more freedom to express ideas or sentiments that may otherwise be censored in more "serious" genres.[16] Therefore, I agree with Margree in her recent re-evaluation of the feminist orientation in Nesbit's ghost stories. Margree argues that the special form of Gothic supernaturalism releases possibilities for critiquing social hegemonies, especially the unequal Victorian gender relations.[17] Nesbit's writing as a whole may be heterogeneous, incoherent, and swinging between conservative or radical moves, as her life choices were; but this, I believe, is the very reflection of the contradictions that featured in many and even the most radical Victorian women's lives in a time riddled with contradiction. The transitional *fin-de-siècle* was characterised by ideological shifts regarding notions of marriage and sexuality and witnessed radical changes in gender relations and women's roles in society. Perhaps no genre is better than the Gothic ghost story in encapsulating such disruptions and inconsistencies, for it is a genre that destabilises meaning and capitalises on inconsistency and inexplicableness.

Indeed, an important feature of Nesbit's ghost stories as I mentioned above is their Gothic opacity—the ambiguity in language and interpretation, and a refusal to lay the ghost to rest, which, as explored in Chapter 4, is an important feature of texts that haunt. The abrupt violent ending of "Man-size in Marble" in which the guiltless heroine dies as a rape victim of two marble soldiers whose motive is not accounted for, still shocks today and must have done more so in the 1890s when the readers were more familiar with ghost stories in which the comings and goings of ghosts are governed by a logic of retribution. Ghosts in many cultures, as observed, are a marker of guilty conscience or hidden injustice, and the appearance of the ghost itself sets in motion the mechanism for righting wrongs. Nesbit's ghosts indeed are often concerned with past injustices, especially the injustice and persecution suffered by women from the men they love or from a hostile patriarchal community. In this case, the past that returns and the present it disrupts are tinted with gendered tones. In the next section, I explore the conflicts between past and present and between women and men unleashed by the ghost's return. What is most upsetting in this clash is the narrative's refusal or the present's inability to appease the ghost and therefore to set the past to rest. This results in a bleak ending in which the wound from the past can never heal, and the shattered protagonist turns into the melancholic, awaiting a life of perpetual mourning. In other words, the haunting of the past never ends, and the fissure of normality opened by the ghost is never fixed. The resolute ambiguity and denial of closure in Nesbit's ghost stories showcase the most subversive perspective of Gothic haunting as they attack the unity of meaning and the seeming coherence of reality, exposing the contradiction inhering in Victorian women's lives.

Conflict between past and present: the amorous ghost returning

While Lee's ghost stories often place the ghost seer in an environment vibrant with history and render the encounter with the ghost an encounter with history embodied in a human figure, Nesbit's ghosts often are bounded with the ghost seer's personal history, their returning exposing grievances and guilt of a more personal nature, as the aforementioned poem "The Moat House" shows. Yet "The Ebony Frame" and "Uncle Abraham's Romance" in *Grim Tales* (1893) are exceptions to such rules. In the stories, the male protagonist's ghost lover is indicated to have been a witch and ousted by society to varying degrees in their previous lives. Such a history of being a "witch" immediately summons up scenes of persecution that might be suffered by the woman, which, although not occupying the contemporary setting, serve as a backstory for the ghost's interaction with her modern male lover. The ghost woman's past identity as "witch" also make her analogous to the female victims of war depicted in Wang Tao's stories. For both groups of victims, their ghostly status recalls injustices suffered by women on a structural level. In this sense, the romance between the living man and the ghost woman becomes symbolically a convergence or conflict between the present and the past, with the Victorian man's comfortable conscience upset by a sense of guilt from the past. However, Nesbit's stories refuse to resolve this conflict or offer a textual closure; instead, in their deliberate departure from a logic of moral retribution, the past is never put to rest and allowed to upset the peace of the present forever.

"The Ebony Frame" centres on a modern man's fascination with an ancient portrait of a beautiful woman. As if in answering his desire, the portrait woman steps down from the painting and tells the man that they have been predestined for each other, and that the doomed love in their previous life had left the woman in the cursed state of the undead. Curiously, this story in 1893 reads almost like a sequel to Lee's "Prince Alberic and the Snake Lady" (1896) relocated in the modern time. The climax of both stories concerns the male protagonist's encounter with a deadly beautiful woman in a portrait, and both writers rewrite their *femme fatale* into a victim of their respective tyrannical society—while the Snake Lady is persecuted by the House of Luna for her abnormal sexuality, the lady in the ebony frame is burnt as a witch simply because of her above-average intelligence. While the seventeenth-century Prince Alberic fails to keep the promise with the Snake Lady, will the lady in the ebony frame fare better this time with her lover's modern incarnation in the heart of nineteenth-century London?

In the beginning, the story shows a sentiment quite different from Lee's nostalgic fairy-tale; instead of beckoning towards the past, the reader is plunged directly into the prosaic concerns of the modern male narrator: the hard-up-ness of struggling in London as an unsuccessful journalist, the exuberance of suddenly becoming rich by inheritance, and the conceit of possessing a furnished house in Chelsea and the love of a pretty girl. All these are the very down-to-earth concerns of a modern man, but perhaps a little too down-to-earth, so that the reader might sense in the man's self-congratulatory narrative a subtle sarcasm from the author. The man's desire for wealth is so dominant that he feels "life had nothing left to offer except immediate possession of the legacy", and his urge for gratification even outweighs his feelings for his hitherto sweetheart Mildred (143). The courtship between the narrator and this mediocre Mildred is revealed to be lacking in sincerity and even secretly mocked by the narrator. Like Lee's historian Trepka, the man in Nesbit's story aspires to romance of a grander style, but his narrative also inadvertently reveals his pettiness of mind, which throws doubt on whether he is worthy of such a romance. Nevertheless, the narrator soon finds in the new house a portrait that promises a remarkable romance: in an ebony frame two portraits are nailed together face to face, one apparently of the narrator himself in cavalier dress, the other a woman in a black gown of the type of beauty admired by the Pre-Raphaelite artists—a sure trait of a *femme fatale*.

The discovery of a magic painting in supernatural literature is crucial, as the painting often marks the crossable boundary between normality and anomaly. Once the protagonist steps into the magic painting world—a heterotopia bound by rules different from the everyday world—the dissolution and rewriting of boundaries ensue. The classic "The Painted Wall" in *Liaozhai*, introduced earlier in this volume, serves as an epitome for such stories: while the man gazes at the object of his desire, the marvellous woman in the painting, he is also absorbed in the woman's gaze, and in a moment of self-abandonment the man finds himself inside the painting world, a world of magic governed by the woman's rules.[18] "Snake Lady" also uses the magic painting motif: it is the young prince's love for the embroidered tapestry that leads him to the wonderland of the Sparkling Waters, restaging the motif of a man entering the world of his desired painting. In both "The Painted Wall" and "Snake Lady", the painting world marks a fantastic space governed by the marvellous woman, a departure from the normality of the world outside, and in entering this alternative painting world, the male lover must relinquish all known rules and let himself be guided by the woman's instructions. Whether this alternative magical realm is considered as an illusion (as in Pu's case) or a utopia (as in Lee's case) is subsequently determined by the author's attitude towards the alterity that is woman.

Therefore, it is significant that in Nesbit's story, it is not the man who enters the woman's painting world, but Pygmalion-like, he wills the woman out of the picture by the sheer strength of his desire. The different term of the encounter determines that Nesbit's tale is decidedly different from Lee's, for instead of exalting a luxuriant past, the past that is represented by the ghost woman is thrown into the midst of a disenchanted and industrialised present. It is this juxtaposition of two languages and two modes of love—one archaic and grand, the other modern and prosaic—that strikes a jarring note to the reunited couple's declaration of love. The painting woman recounts to the narrator the sacrifice she has made in return for their reunion: she has sold her soul to the devil to be kept as a ghost in the ebony frame, waiting for the man's reincarnation in centuries to come. To be reincarnated in the present to become the narrator's wife, the woman asks for his promise to sell his soul too. The overwhelmed narrator responds with a ready promise of love; however, even as he denies his insincerity, the denial reveals a retrospective caution that distances him from the woman's passionate speech:

> "If I sacrifice my soul", I said slowly, with no thought of the imbecility of such talk in our 'so-called' nineteenth century"—"if I sacrifice my soul, I win you? Why, love, it's a contradiction in terms. You *are* my soul".
>
> (149, my emphasis)

The militant advancement of scientific materialism in the nineteenth century had largely exorcised talks of the devil, hell, and soul from people's lives.[19] Especially in this story, the prosaic London setting at the end of the century and the male narrator's previous obsession with wealth and rank render the ghost woman's ecclesiastical terms such as heaven and soul sound comically out of place. Therefore, notwithstanding the man's promise, the incompatibility of such high-sounding language with a mundane setting already foretells the futility of the ghost woman's attempt to re-enter the present. If the returning of a victimised spirit of the past brings with her the opportunity to acknowledge and even rewrite her sad story, such a hope is undermined here, for her modern lover does not even want to enter an empathy for her: "Make me understand. And yet—No, I don't want to understand. It is enough that we are together" (148). In contrast, once initiated, Prince Alberic in Lee's tale sets out to learn of Oriana's past, even if knowing the past means for him a symbolic death and a rebirth. The male narrator in "The Ebony Frame" in the beginning is established in the comfortable position of a bourgeois life (emblematically represented by the "furnished house in Chelsea"); to step into the woman's alternative painting world, or even to allow her full entrance into his world, would be a risky departure from this self-contended norm.

It is thus not difficult to predict the story's bleak ending. Having promised to revive the painting woman the coming midnight, the narrator is forced to roam away from the house the next day to avoid receiving his fiancée Mildred, only to return at midnight to find his house on fire. If running from Mildred offers the narrator a pretext to keep away from the painting woman, his next action only heightens the ambivalence of his motive: he instantly runs into the flame and rescues Mildred while inadvertently witnessing the ebony frame consumed by fire. Unconsciously or intentionally, the man effects a second and final burning of the undead witch/ghost.

The fire thus drastically pulls the narrator back from alterity to normality: on the verge of abandoning Mildred for a reunion with the woman of the past, the fire restores him to an uneventful middle-class marriage. Although the fire is alluded to be an accident, the vagueness surrounding the final scenes suggests implicit schemes and betrayals. It is questionable whether the narrator had not secretly wished for the burning of the witch, for although a life of transgression is titillating enough, to totally abandon his comfortable middle-class life for the ghost woman would be too much of a sacrifice. A telling detail reveals the real stake of the man: as all the inherited furniture is heavily insured, the burning of the house does not affect his financial standing. Therefore, the text, containing the ghost woman's grand speech of immortal love in the middle, still begins and ends with the man's practical monetary concerns. The past intervenes in the present briefly with the ghost woman's visit yet seems to lack the vital power to fully take hold of the "stout and dull and prosperous" present (152).

"Uncle Abraham's Romance" also involves a man's romance with, and inadvertent betrayal of, his ghost lover. Having promised to return to the churchyard on a certain date to meet a beautiful girl with whom he has had a nightly rendezvous, the uncle is sent to delirium after accidentally learning the true identity of the girl (who died in the eighteenth century with the reputation of a witch) and breaks his promise. This ends his one chance for romance in life and the old uncle now can only tell the story to his nephew with regret and nostalgia.

In both stories, the appearance of the ghost woman in front of the mortal man engenders a collision between the past and the present. The past and the ghost woman that embodies it eventually fail to gain recognition and entrance in the man's present world, yet their return is far from ineffectual, for the unresolved ending in Nesbit's stories, here as elsewhere, is less a gesture of compromise than a deliberate refusal of a logic of clear delineation. The stories end without a satisfactory remedy for the ghost's past injuries (their reputation of being a witch and their ghostly status allude to the women's past persecution), but the logic of ghostly retribution at the same time means that once the problem is solved, the ghost will be effectively exorcised, and the text-world will return to its initial state of unquestionable harmony: a world with no ghosts.[20] The ghost's (partial) disappearance in the end, on the other hand, leaves an indelible mark of guilt on the male narrator that is to stay with him for life. The male lover survives the supernatural encounter but is no longer the same man;[21] he becomes the melancholic trauma survivor, bound to keep the lost woman a part of his subjectivity in his retelling of the ghost's story. The traces of the past thus linger on in the present and the ghost woman's haunting memory becomes a loss that the man must learn to internalise and to transmit to the reader. The textual disappearance of the ghost conversely ensures her eternal presence: she is always there and not there.

Christine Berthin argues that Gothic as a haunted writing—haunted by its textually unexplained secrets and undefined shadows and by its own linguistic otherness—must be read as "the literature of melancholy", for "the dead are never dead, and things never totally disappear behind the signifiers that represent them".[22] In Nesbit's stories discussed here, dead women returning as ghosts become a metaphor for an unrelenting past that haunts and penetrates the present, making these texts melancholic literature precisely because of this haunting irresolution they open up. They are truly Gothic for their denial of closure and explanation; they leave a fissure in the text that is neither fully suppressed nor mendable, a constant questioning of the epistemological inconsistency of our seemingly self-sufficient present.

The Gothic, according to Berthin, also embodies an essential fantastic drive for its attack on the smooth chain of signification in language. Building on the framework of fantasy developed by Todorov, Jackson, and Hume, Berthin defines the fantastic as a literary impulse primarily marked by its "untenable position", "born of the impossible stasis between figure and ground, opacity and transparency, depth and surface, inside and outside".[23] The fantastic drive in Gothic disturbs its reader because of its powerful disruption of orders of meaning from within: "it is a force within language which seems to push signification away from mimesis and to undo the sense of objective reality the symbolic system creates".[24] The opacity of meaning and linguistic ambiguity (as for instance manifested in the episode of rescue in "The Ebony Frame") are also important features of Nesbit's ghost stories. Nesbit is skilful at exploiting fear with her sometimes-gruesome representation of death and violence,[25] but the most disturbing horror, as one character in her story "The Shadow" describes it, is the undefinable something that one is "so near to seeing and hearing, just near", but "something one could just not see" (174). "The Shadow" is the exemplary story that capitalises on Gothic opacity. In a self-reflexive manner, it comments on the non-commensurability of ghost stories and perfectly illustrates the powerful critique of gender relations unleashed by this inexplicability.

A shadow haunting love and marriage

Romantic love and marriage are often considered the proper site of interest for women both within and outside of fiction. They are also the familiar themes in Female Gothic, most notably the strand originating with Ann Radcliffe. It is in Female Gothic that family, marriage, and romantic love—the traditional safe havens for women—are exposed to be a site of horror and haunted by ghosts.[26] Nesbit's ghost stories offer many bleak and even macabre representations of marriage (although her adult romances invest much in the opposite). But here I want to stress that it is not merely the representation of horror within marriage that lends her ghost stories the force to upset, but more importantly the lack of textual closure and ontological certainty. Hayden White observes that narrative in general "has to do with the topics of law, legality, legitimacy, or more generally, authority";[27] moreover, a "fully realised story"—a story with a sequence of events endowed with the significance of causes and effects— is also predicated with "the impulse to moralise reality, to identify it with the social system that is the source of any morality that we can imagine".[28] "The Shadow" epitomises ambiguity and difficulty with interpretation. Things in marriage do not go right and a sense of uneasiness prevails, yet as the narrator observes, "there seems to be no reason why any of it should have happened" (169). In White's formulation then it is a not fully realised story for its refusal to pin down causes and effects—to name the origin of horror and then to exorcise it—therefore it fails to moralise the reality in marriage or accord with any existing authority, and this is what makes it an upsetting critique of contemporary women's condition.

In the late Victorian age gender relations were undergoing radical changes, making marriage and women's role in it an uncanny site, permeated with familiarity and strangeness. On the one hand, women were conceptualised as the "Angel in the House" and guardian of the Victorian home, itself sanctified as a protective temple for virtue, nurturing, and reverent love against the corruption and lust outside of the home; on the other hand, until the Married Woman's Property Act in 1882, women's property rights within marriage were barely protected and marriage very much constituted as a civil, and sometimes even literal, death for women, the very opposite of the ideal notion of marriage as the destiny of romantic love. In such a tumultuous time, women's real experience of love and marriage may be as contradictory, multi-layered, and undefinable as the ambiguities evoked in Nesbit's stories.

Nesbit's own unconventional marriage with Hubert Bland was the very opposite of idyllic and peaceful and may offer the psychological origin for her portrayal of troubled marriages. Bland in his acquaintances' description was a womaniser, who not only made Edith pregnant seven months before their marriage but also fathered two children with Edith's close friend Alice Hoatson.[29] However well Nesbit managed to maintain her open marriage with Hubert and Alice, a suppressed feeling of injury and resentment occasionally surfaces in her poetry and fiction.[30] Her favourite plot, as noted by critics, is a love triangle where two women (usually cousins or best friends) fall in love with the same man or two men are rivals over the same woman.[31] Jealousy, resentment, and even wicked schemes thus ensue. Especially when the plot is used in her ghost stories, the lightness of romantic rivalry can easily turn into scenes of violence and death. Both Lowell T. Frye and Victoria Margree note the often-pessimistic portrayal of marriage in Nesbit's ghost stories: what appears in the beginning as promising conjugal bliss often deteriorates rapidly into one or both spouses' death.[32] In Frye's words, the bleak portrayal of marriage serves as a caution that "marriage is truly the end of life for the woman, the loss of self the price of wifehood".[33]

"The Shadow" is framed as a somewhat meta-ghost story for its self-reflexive critique of the genre, and its remark that the "real ghost story" is a story with no logical explanation foregrounds the Gothic inexplicableness. Somewhat singular in Nesbit's ghost stories, the story is told by two women narrators (one narrator's story framed in another's) in an exclusively all-female setting.[34] It is Christmas night in a manor house, and three young girls, after their exhausting dances, retreat to their bedroom to tell each other ghost stories. The Christmas season, the old manor house, the well-lit mantelpiece in contrast to a bitterly cold winter night outside, and even the small female community are all typical ingredients of the genre. The story begins directly with the young narrator—one of the three girls—commenting on the story to be told which reads like the author's comment of the genre: "This is not an artistically rounded-off ghost story, and nothing is explained in it, and there seems to be no reason why any of it should have happened" (169). But presently the narrator assures that, nevertheless, real ghost stories, or in other words the best of the kind, are precisely like this one— "no explanation, no logical coherence" (169). The proceeding story is true to this claim: so much is felt in the ambience it creates, but nothing can be pinned down, and the incoherence creates a haunting trace even after the story ends (or does it ever end?).

After the first young narrator sets up the familiar milieu of ghost storytelling (with vague references to classic stories of the genre), the second narrator, Miss Eastwich, the gloomy housekeeper, enters the ghost storytelling community almost as a ghost herself. The initial foreboding that the young narrator feels towards the elderly woman gradually melts down as the latter softens with the girls' warm welcome and reveals a suppressed self through her storytelling, but this initial confusion of the housekeeper with a ghostly intruder presages her ambiguous position in the story she is to tell. The story happened some 20 years earlier when Miss Eastwich's two best friends married each other. The young narrator, posing herself as one more capable of sophisticated understanding than the other girls, hints at what is left unsaid in the elderly woman's narrative: that she had loved the man too and he knew it but rejected her for her friend. A year after their marriage, Eastwich was invited by the man to nurse his now sick pregnant wife Mabel, but she soon found that it was not Mabel who needed her care but the seemingly perturbed husband. There was something vicious about their villa, a disturbing presence that the haunted inhabitants were just about to hear and see but just could not, and it seemed to disturb only Eastwich and her uncomfortable ex-lover the husband. This exacerbating feeling of being followed by something undefinable almost drove the nurse mad, until one night she saw the always "almost-there" thing finally there. The paragraph that describes this first sighting of "the thing" is poignantly unnerving precisely because of its vagueness, the language itself strained to its limits to show what is perhaps intrinsically un-representable:

> The thing was grey at first, and then it was black. And when I whispered, "Mabel", it seemed to sink down till it lay like a pool of ink on the floor, and then its edges drew in, and it seemed to flow, like ink when you tilt up the paper you have split it on, and it flowed into the cupboard till it was all gathered into the shadow there.
>
> (175)

Afterwards, this shapeless moveable thing was named "the shadow", because to the nurse's horror she found the thing tended to draw itself into a shadow that was nearest, and very often that was her own shadow. Horribly still, the shadow seemed not to be bound by the haunted house rule to attack only a particular spot and time; it could appear at any time, always in the borderline state between the visible and invisible ("It seemed as though I could only just see it, as if my sight, to see it, had to be strained to the uttermost" 175). It is clear that it was not the house that was haunted, for the fashionable villa was newly built and had never been inhabited before;[35] the malicious "thing" was brought about by the inhabitants themselves, as its intriguing trait to merge with its seer's own shadow possibly implies an internal origin of the horror.

In Miss Eastwich's narration, each of the three friends loved the other two dearly, yet the story inevitably becomes darker, as the shadow was increasingly associated with death. After Mabel delivered her baby girl, Eastwich saw the shadow again, this time crouching outside Mabel's door and presently melting inside it. Mabel was found dead; and the next time Eastwich saw the shadow, it crouched between "us"—denoting her and the widowed husband—and Mabel's coffin. Just as the two narrators have warned, this is not an artistically rounded-off story that offers satisfactory explanations; so much seems to be hanging in the air and inviting interpretation, yet nothing can be ascertained. The shadow—the centre of the mystery—becomes a symbol for the dark emotions of everyone involved in the story, but is it guilt, jealousy, or resentment?

Initially, the shadow seems to relate to the husband's past debt to an abandoned lover just like the ghostly shadows haunting the unfaithful lover in "The Moat House". However, even as the guilty husband invited over his potential debtor Eastwich and had obtained her forgiveness, the shadow still could not be exorcised; instead, it seemed to be more and more associated with the nurse and eventually led to the wife's death. Could the shadow then originate from somewhere else? People familiar with Nesbit's biography would be surprised by the similarity between the love triangle represented here and Edith's own entangled relationship with her husband and her friend Alice Hoatson. In 1885, Edith was pregnant with her fourth child, and during February 1886 Alice nursed Edith through her childbirth.[36] Alice was always a good nurse, and her company was a great solace to Edith during her delirium when the child died shortly after birth. However, Briggs' biography shows that it was during this period of nursing that Alice was made pregnant by Hubert Bland. No one could know what happened precisely between Alice and Hubert in those days, just as the pregnant Mabel in the story was excluded throughout from her husband and friend's discussion of the shadow downstairs, even if this exclusion was meant for her well-being. Alice was in the latter months of pregnancy by the autumn, and still not knowing who the father was, Edith in a chivalrous act persuaded Alice to move into her household as a housekeeper and later adopted the daughter as her own, so that her unmarried friend's reputation was saved. The revelation of the affair came years later, and the injured wife somehow managed to forgive both husband and friend, with whatever feelings of jealousy and resentment stifled.[37]

Similarly occupying the position of the nurse and housekeeper in her two friends' marriage, Miss Eastwich in "The Shadow" reads like a fictionalised Alice Hoatson, and her occasional coalescence with the deadly shadow makes her an extremely ambiguous character, for she displays all the familiar characteristics of the innocent and courageous Radcliffean heroine while at the same time seeming to harbour malice.[38] In the housekeeper's narrative she presents herself as the friend who self-denyingly administered to the needs of the married couple; however, it was not peace she brought to their marriage but horror and death. There is a strong implication in the narrative that somehow Mabel's death was brought about by her friend: after seeing the shadow disappearing inside Mabel's door, Eastwich prayed that "Mabel might never know the horror that he and I had known" (175). In this seemingly altruistic wish that spares her friend the ugly knowledge of the "thing", an exclusive intimacy is created between "he and I" that shuts Mabel out. The "thing" that is so horrible and ungraspable thus begins to take on the appearance of desire: a guilty desire that secretly binds the husband and the nurse and shuts the wife out. In a magical manner, it is this exclusion from knowledge that kills Mabel, for somehow the nurse's prayer is answered and Mabel dies in her sleep, never able to learn of the shadow—a miraculous realisation of the nurse's wish which uncannily reveals what is perhaps already hidden in it: the wish to kill Mabel.[39] In the Gothic context, the magically granted wish becomes uncanny because it reveals sinisterly what probably is before language and anti-language: if language is thought to be an intricate system of symbols, then the narrative in which what is meant as metaphor becomes real destroys that system, and together with it the barrier between what is real and what is fictional. The Gothic plot then becomes fantastic writing par excellence for its usurpation of the symbolism of language—meanings run riot and distinctions are nullified.

Nesbit's portrayal of Eastwich is indeed full of contradictions: she seems to be moulded as a conventional innocent Gothic heroine, who now surprisingly becomes the origin of horror, yet her role in her friends' marriage in some respects also resembles Edith's own. Implied as the ex-lover of Mabel's husband, Eastwich was the one who somehow had a longer bonding, and therefore a "prior" right with the man. If, as Briggs argues, the wronged heroine in "The Moat House" reflects Edith's own sense of injury and self-destruction,[40] then a similar case can be argued for Eastwich in "The Shadow" who vicariously embodies Nesbit's self-perception: the earlier and rightful partner of the man who endures the pain of being betrayed by the two people she loves, yet graciously offering them her forgiveness.

As my analysis so far shows, the shadow is utterly undefinable for a deliberate vagueness keeps it so ambiguous that it remains a shapeless horror. The plot so far keeps up with the young narrator's promise of "no explanation, no logical coherence" (169), and in the narrator's view, this is the feature of the only true type of ghost story. However, while Eastwich's story ends with her last seeing the shadow at the husband's funeral, "the ghost story" that the younger narrator promises in the beginning has not ended yet, as the girls soon find their current temporality contaminated by the ghostliness of the past. It turns out that one of the girls who has fainted in the dance is Mabel's baby, and it is seeing her again that stirs up Eastwich's long-buried memory. With this revelation comes the apex of horror: the shadow reappears with the narration of its story outside the door of the fainted girl's room, and everyone in the storytelling community experiences the uneasiness of just almost seeing and hearing it. The ending comes suddenly and unsettlingly: Mabel's baby is found dead inside the room. Although an inherited heart disease from her mother is given by the doctor as the cause of death, the naturalistic interpretation can hardly explain away the tangible reappearance of the "thing" that everyone on site has felt. The threat of the shadow, as it turns out, crosses over not only the narrative boundary of Eastwich's story but also leaves its trace on the reader for its lack of a logically coherent explanation. Beginning with an external comment on the conventions of the genre, the story turns itself into an unending haunted and haunting cycle.

As mentioned earlier, "The Shadow" is a singular case in Nesbit's ghost stories for its all-female narrators and the female-exclusive community established around the act of ghost storytelling; and it is through telling the story of the "ghost"—the shadow—that women's entangled experience and dormant feelings in the intricate case of love and marriage can gain expression. If we situate the story within the Female Gothic tradition, then its deliberate ambiguity explored in this chapter and the exclusively female-controlled narration begin to take on a new significance. While Eastwich's role in her friends' marriage is ambivalent throughout, she, as a character in the younger narrator's story, is also being constantly scrutinised and re-evaluated from perspectives of class and age, thus revealing a totally different realm of the older woman's life which is meant to arouse the reader's sympathy. The housekeeper initially enters the ghost storytelling milieu as a sinister intruder, someone who has "built a wall round her" with "her persistent silence" (170), but her narrative opens the opportunity for the wealthy younger narrator to re-evaluate the serving staff's living conditions, their repressed emotional lives and her own previous lack of understanding of them. The act of ghost storytelling thus operates as a unique way of female socialisation that is both therapeutic (for the teller) and educational (for the listener) and an equalising opportunity for women of different classes and ages to reach over to each other in mutual understanding.

Female exclusivity is important in achieving this mutual understanding. The storytelling happens after the girls' retreat from their Christmas dances, and a sexually suggestive description revealingly indicates how an exclusion from men—metaphorically represented by the scraping "harsh fingers" of cedar branches—is necessary for women to enter a space of confidentiality needed for invoking the ghost:

> the stillness of the manor house, broken only by the whisper of the wind in the cedar branches, and the scraping of their harsh fingers against our window panes, had pricked us to such a luxurious confidence in our surroundings, … that we had dared to talk of ghosts.
>
> (169)

As the story proceeds, voices of men along the corridors are inserted occasionally as a reassuring background noise for the intimate scene happening inside, reassuring precisely because they are safely barred outside just as the "harsh fingers" of the cedar trees are excluded from the warm interior. In Miss Eastwich's story, the man occupying both women's hearts remained a nameless "he", while both Mabel and Miss Eastwich had imposed their presence upon the scene. The revelation of the fainting girl's identity is equally telling—"Mabel's baby" is what everyone calls her. Since the girl is certainly no longer a baby and not only Mabel's daughter but also the husband's, to denominate her as "Mabel's baby" seems to emphasise a distinctive female lineage. Indeed, as the husband has no name in the story, in other words no placeholder, the daughter can only be "Mabel's daughter". Mabel's baby is not the only haunting presence that spills over the narrative; the younger narrator's story also has a lingering trace that goes beyond her narrative: after the death of Mabel's daughter, Eastwich becomes the housekeeper of the "youngest of us all"—the girl who shows the old woman most sympathy and probably would offer her a more comfortable life. The narrative as a whole thus forms an almost complete circle of female reciprocity, which, although lacking a coherent logic demanded by the rule of signification, establishes instead a community of mutual understanding and help among the women characters involved. The feminine circle is almost complete, apart from the narrator's allusion in the end that the heart disease of Mabel's baby might instead be inherited from her father. Although the heart disease explanation does not clear the clouds surrounding the shadow in any way, this tentative beckoning towards the husband does suggest an externalisation of the "pathology" of the story and a subtle reversion of the Gothic trope which tends to attribute the ultimate horror to a monstrous maternity.[41] After all, it may be the father/husband who is the origin of the whole "disease" that traumatised the ex-lover, unconsciously killed the new mother, and passed its cursing trace onto the daughter. The potentially externalised origin of the shadow therefore marks out a safer and healthier feminine space among the women involved.

As with the stories of female ghost examined in the first section, "The Shadow" does not end with a resolution of the ghost's problem or a satisfactory closure of the ghostly narrative. Both the ghost and its effect (the shadow and the "disease" of Mabel's baby) reach out of the older woman's narrative and are barely contained within the younger woman's narrative. The "not artistically rounded-off" story means not only that no explanation is given for the horror, but also that the ghost's story can never end—and that is when the story stops being just a story but also transmits into real women's lives. Nesbit's life as a socialist and a New Woman presents irresolvable contradictions and inconsistencies. Like most women writers of her time, she tended to embrace over time and in varying contexts both extremes of the discourse on women's position in family and society. As Briggs shows, Nesbit at times can be extremely conservative as to deny women's equal abilities to work as men or to work out her sense of injuries in marriage by internalising a wife's subordinate position in her poems,[42] while on the other hand she did not hesitate to enjoy her own sexual freedom or to devote herself to work while delegating the "wifely" duties to others. The inconsistencies in her gender ideologies can be observed in her writing across genres, but the multi-layered-ness of the Gothic lends itself well to accommodate such inconsistencies. Gothic writing intrinsically embraces vagueness and refuses logical consistency; its language at times can be shockingly revealing as well as secretive. "The Shadow", as I have examined, is an exemplary case as such, containing intimate episodes that are almost autobiographical while at the same time remaining ambiguous and full of contradictions. In this sense, the ambiguity and non-resolution of Nesbit's Female Gothic are not only a perturbing exploration of horrors within love and marriage but also a true reflection of the contradictions that characterised many contemporary women's lives in a transitional period.

Fantasy over her dead body: the fallen woman arising

If Nesbit's early poem, "The Moat House", ushers in the figure of the returning ghost as an emblem for men's guilty conscience and a belated justice for the wronged woman, "The Ebony Frame" and "Uncle Abraham's Romance" are all later incarnations of the same ghost woman, though in the Gothic tales the chief power of the ghost lies not in the efficacy of her revenge but in her haunting. The returning ghost woman can also cause trouble for her human lover and expose the hypocrisy of the gender script under which she has suffered when her story as a ghost overwrites contemporary patriarchal myths for women. Stories of the dead woman and the fallen woman are moralising tales for a model womanhood: the woman who deviates from accepted modes of femininity is considered fallen and punished by death; yet death absolves her of her sins, as she is now reduced to the desired state of passivity and therefore can once again be recuperated as an object of male voyeurism and men's ideal goddess. However, if the irresistible charm of the dead woman reflects men's fantasy of a passive feminine ideal, the horror of the dead woman's body suddenly turning active lays bare this self-delusion and mocks its hypocrisy. "From the Dead" reworks precisely this patriarchal myth of an unchaste woman atoning for her sins by death. The most famous variant of this myth is of course the fairy tale "Snow White" which, as explored by feminist critics, chimes perfectly well with the Victorian misogynist myth that "the ideal woman is the dead woman".[43] Gilbert and Guba in their seminal *The Madwoman in the Attic* use the Snow White tale as an allegory for the polarised construction of women in the nineteenth-century cultural imagination: ultimately it is Snow White as a worshipped art object "dead and self-less in her glass coffin" who has triumphed over the Queen and "proven herself to be patriarchy's ideal woman".[44]

"From the Dead" acknowledges this mythical narrative that traces the trajectory of the woman's fall and rise sanctioned by sadistic patriarchal worship of the dead women, but it provides a transformed ironic realisation of this myth that ridicules its illusoriness and impotence. Lawrence Couple draws from the practices of bible interpretation an orthodox typology and a radical typology. "While orthodox typology works in terms of closure, radical typology works in terms of disclosure".[45] Orthodox typology, remarks Coupe, leads to perfectionism and absolutism, which ultimately exorcises the fantastic and closes the narrative, while radical typology perpetuates the process of myth-making. If the original misogynist myth sets the "type" of woman's tale that patriarchy tells women, then Nesbit's reworking, in Coupe's conceptualisation, provides the "anti-type" that creates new ways to tell women's own history, therefore constituting a radical typology of myth-making.

"From the Dead" begins with what is a common plot in Nesbit's stories: love triangles. Ida Helmont is in love with her friend's Elvira's fiancé Arthur Marsh, and by showing Arthur Elvira's love letters to her brother Oscar, she re-aligns the pairing of the four young people. Elvira and Oscar are soon happily married, and Arthur turns his attention to Ida and "loved her as I never loved Elvira" (35). Arthur captures Ida's unconventionality as he pours out praise for his new love:

> There never was anyone like her. She was brave and beautiful, witty and wise, and beyond all measure adorable. She was the only woman in the world. There was a frankness—a largeness of heart—about her that made all other women seem small and contemptible.
>
> (35)

Ida's behaviour in the love triangle shows that she certainly is not the conventional modest Victorian lady; not satisfied with the passive role assigned to women in heterosexual courtship, she openly courts the man she loves. Moreover, she is not hesitant to show her love physically: after showing Arthur the letter, she declares her love by voluntarily kissing his forehead before any reciprocity from the man is guaranteed. In many ways, the woman has strained the limits of acceptable female roles in middle-class courtship, and Arthur declares that he "worshipped her" for these rare qualities (35).

Yet the sincerity of the male narrator's declaration and his tolerance for the woman's transgression are soon to be tested. In their honeymoon, after Arthur declares "Nothing in heaven or earth can come between us now" (35), Ida confesses that the love letter she presented to him was a forgery. It is the man's half-hearted theatrical reaction towards this confession that ruins what could have been a happy marriage. He flings Ida away, reproaches her as a liar and denounces her, even though he knows well he means none of it—it is his injured manly vanity and an imagined manly "nobility" that dictate him to react so. As Margree points out, the contrast between the man's outward indignation and his inward longing for his wife, juxtaposed theatrically in the narrative here, implies a critique of the socially expected gender roles for men and women.[46] Although Arthur has declared his admiration for an unconventional woman like Ida earlier, now he reveals that he is still clinging to a much more conservative gender model as his confession shows:

> I don't know whether I expected her to creep to my knees and implore forgiveness. I think I had some vague idea that I could by-and-by consent with dignity to forgive and forget. I did not mean what I said. No, oh no, no; I did not mean a word of it. While I was saying it, I was longing for her to weep and *fall* at my feet, that I might *raise* her and hold her in my arms again.
> But she did not *fall* at my feet; she *stood* quietly looking at me.
>
> (36, italics mine)

The self-contradictory statements here ("I don't know …" soon contradicted by "I was longing …") reveals that even in reconstructing his memory (the story is narrated five years after the major events) the male narrator is trying to gloss over his true attitude towards his wife. But it is obvious to the reader what the man really wants from the woman: he wants the once goddess-like, worshipped woman to fall at his feet, to acknowledge her subordinate wife's position, to metaphorically kill herself (her self-esteem), so that the husband can once more raise the fallen woman and place her upon his altar.

Elizabeth Bronfen points out insightfully in *Over Her Dead Body* Western culture's aestheticisation of the beautiful dead woman, upon which men transfer their anxiety of their own death and build their immortality. Bronfen's aptly chosen epigraph for her book, a quote from Thomas de Quincey's *Joan of Arc* (1847), summarises well Nesbit's male narrator's mentality: "Yet, sister woman, ... I acknowledge you can do one thing as well as the best of us men ... you can die grandly, and as goddesses would die, were goddesses mortal".[47] It is as a slaughtered and reclaimed goddess—reclaimed, of course, by himself—that Arthur in "From the Dead" desires to redefine his wife's role in marriage. Yet Ida would not fall at his feet and let him raise her up again. Instead, the woman *stands* and *looks* back, asking for a hearing for her explanation and interrogating the man's sincerity. Once again, the deviant woman defies the prescribed gender script by refusing the hysterical and wailing woman's role and usurping the rational "man's role". While she requests a communication between equals, the husband reacts hysterically and constantly aborts the woman's effort to communicate. Denied love and a hearing, Ida manages to maintain her pride by retreating from the man's life quietly. All efforts to find her fail until several months later a brief note from his wife leads Arthur to a gloomy Derbyshire farm, only to be told by Ida's nurse that she is already dead.

The first part of the story ends here, and Part II, through Arthur's conversation with the nurse, reveals Ida's tragic fate after their separation which coincides well with the Victorian myth of the fallen woman. Ida had come to the farm pregnant and let the nurse take her for an unmarried and abandoned woman and later died in childbirth. Ida's death evinces the punishment that society exacts on women who deviate from the respectable womanhood. As Bram Dijkstra demonstrates eloquently in his study of *fin-de-siècle* fascination of feminine evil, one of the prominent misogynist tropes in art and literature of the time was the exaltation of the beautiful dead woman. In Dijkstra's words, death is regarded as "the ideal state of submissive womanhood".[48] A "self-sacrificial sleep death" was encouraged by artists as the model feminine virtue, a Christ-like martyrdom, and any truly loving woman should be contented to die in self-effacement. Similarly, Bronfen theorises the mechanics of power at work in the literary trope of a beautiful female body in death displayed for and gazed at by a male lover. Citing Snow White as an epitome for the aestheticised female death, she points out:

> Finally, as auto-icon, Snow White performs the apotheosis of one of the central positions ascribed to Woman in western culture; namely that the 'surveyed' feminine body is meant to confirm the power of the masculine gaze. In Lemoine-Luccioni's words, Woman doesn't look; she gives herself to be looked at; she is beauty and being beauty, she is also an object of love.[49]

Ida in "From the Dead" is precisely the woman who revolts against this feminine model. Facing her husband's accusation, she does not "fall" at his feet and let herself be surveyed but stands still and *looks* back, and thus she is denounced by the husband. But once she indeed "falls" and lies in a "sleep-death", the dead woman can once again entice the man's desire and be appreciated. Ida's dead body is revealed in the text in what Bronfen calls an aestheticised, or even fetishised manner: as if the dead woman is an art object on display, the nurse draws back the white sheet covering her body and announces: "don't [sic] she look beautiful?" (41). The husband, just like the prince gazing over Snow White's corpse in the glass coffin, cannot help but observe how irresistible the dead woman becomes. While he had shunned physical touch from the woman when she was alive, he now gives her kisses freely in her death:

> It seemed to me, too, that if I kissed her she would awaken, and put her slight hand on my neck, and lay her cheek against mine—and that we should tell each other everything, and weep together, and understand, and be comforted.
> So I stooped and laid my lips to hers as the nurse stole from the room.
> But the red lips were like marbles, and she did not waken. She will not waken now ever any more.
>
> (41–2)

It is important here that the husband affirms repeatedly "she did not" and "will not waken", for although he fantasies about reviving his Snow White with a kiss, he knows perfectly well it is precisely death, which renders the woman in an inaccessible beyond, that removes her disobedience and makes her redeemable. Again, Bronfen's observation of the desired woman's corpse is illuminating here:

> In a superlative manner, she confirms the imaginative power and desire of the mourning lover. This absolutely untouchable dead woman signifies, in Kristeva's words, jouissance as nostalgia, within reach but lost for ever. By turning the feminine into a dead body, phallic idealisation places itself on a pedestal.[50]

The dead Ida is for Arthur the inaccessible nostalgic beyond, upon which he can himself rise in the image of the perfect mourning lover. Early on, when the nurse misunderstands Arthur as never having loved Ida, she reproaches him sarcastically: "p'raps you'd like to see 'er safe under ground afor yer go? I'll bound you'll put a big stone slab on 'er—to make sure she don't rise again" (40). Although the nurse's assumption that Arthur would despise Ida as if she is a vampire is unjustified, the sentences when read retrospectively reveal to be strikingly prophetic and illuminating, for later Ida does "rise again", and Arthur's reaction is no better than putting a stone slab on her, revealing that what leads to the woman's tragedy is essentially her sexual activeness, seen as a dangerous transgression and punished like a vampire by an intolerant society.[51]

So far, the story shows how a non-conforming woman is forced back to the ultimate gender role expected of her, namely death, the "ideal state of submissive womanhood" in Dijkstra's words. However, if Ida refuses the self-effacing compliance required of her, she conforms in an indirect way. Her husband desires her to fall at his feet so he can raise her up again; in a metaphorical sense, she imposes on herself another mode of "falling"—she withdraws from London society, lives invisibly as a social outcast, and lets the nurse assume she is unmarried, a "fallen" woman. All these actions are her self-effected "falling" in a direction other than is expected of her, a rebellion against the society which has failed her. Nina Auerbach in her study of the Victorian myths of women singles out the myth of the "Fallen Woman", which, although it renders the culpable woman a social outcast, also unleashes for her a tremendous transforming power; and death, the most common ending for the fallen woman, becomes the "symbol of her fall's transforming power" which suggests "the simultaneity of her fall and apotheosis".[52] It is worth noting that in Nesbit's story, the identity of a fallen woman is not enforced on Ida but a myth she actively weaves around herself, as if knowing that through her active "falling" she can rise again. Therefore, even when Ida is brought back to a state of model femininity by her death in Part II, her revolt has started well before that. Part II serves as a transition for both husband and wife: the husband initially not believing Ida's death has learned to accept the fact and find peace with the dead woman, while the wife, having fallen so low to death, gathers strength for her rising in Part III.

If so far the story has been a negative manifestation of the misogynist myth that "the ideal woman is the dead woman" examined by Bronfen and Dijkstra, the entrance of the Gothic in the final part adds a new chapter to this myth which rips bare the hypocrisy and male impotence hidden in this gender tale. When lying in bed in the room next to the one where Ida's corpse lies, Arthur realises in darkness a sound coming from the death chamber. Stricken with horror, he struggles to quench his apparent repulsion with a weak declaration of love: "Dead or alive, is she not your darling, your heart's heart? Would you not go near to die of joy, if she came back to you?" (43). However the narrative in this part has already betrayed the man's true attitude towards his dead wife; the dead woman is no longer a person but a thing, the abject reality of mortality that the living man must distance himself from to maintain and reaffirm his subjectivity, so the denominator for Ida since Part III has been changed from "she" to "the dead", "the dead woman", "the corpse", and in the climax of horror when the dead finally enters the room, "it": "It came straight towards the bed, and stood at the bed foot in its white grave-clothes, with the white bandage under its chin. ... Its eyes were wide open, and looked at me with love unspeakable" (43).

The cold-sounding "it" reveals the abject status that Ida now holds in her husband's eyes, but it also denotes a form of being that has transcended the cultural positions allocated to both women and death as in "the dead woman" or "the corpse". Neither dead, nor a living woman, the new status of ghost gives Ida the freedom to transgress walls and men's chambers as well as the newly unleashed power to interrogate, to demand love, and to terrify. Makala in her discussion of women's ghost stories observes the transgressive freedom granted to ghosts: "Apparitions defy categorisation, and therefore defy many of the social limitations placed on the living" and, "Ghosts come back whether they are wanted or not".[53] What Ida's ghost wants from her husband is an opportunity to continue her confession denied her when she was alive. Now as a ghost, standing by the bed of the living man, she can finally explain herself: that although the letter was her forgery, Elvira indeed loved Oscar and there was no deception there. What she says next reveals Ida's distorted compliance with the dead woman plot and Nesbit's parody of the self-delusion involved, for the dead woman asks: "You'll love me again now, won't you, now I am dead. One always forgives dead people" (43). Paralysed by horror, the living man's answer is a weak "yes", yet the ghost wants more—she wants to kiss her husband and moves towards his bed. Ironically, the thrilling scene is a reversal of the climax in Snow White: instead of being gazed at, admired, kissed, and resurrected to life by the prince, the dead woman arises from her exhibition table and makes sexual advances towards the man lying in his bed. This proves to be the final strain that totally "unmans" Arthur, as he shrieks like a hysteric and wraps himself in the bed sheet. The myth that man raises himself up at the altar of the dead goddess is totally exploded, and the dead woman that is conjured up by this fantasy is found dead again outside her death chamber. The narrator in "From the Dead", failing the woman he loves a second time, is doomed to live in remorse and guilt with Ida's child, who has "never spoken and never smiled" (44). As with Nesbit's other stories discussed so far, the ghost's retreat does not mean the end of haunting, as the silent child, taking the place of the ephemeral ghost, stays with the husband as a silent witness for his past cruelties towards the woman he loves.

A new Gothic myth for women

Nesbit's career as a *fin-de-siècle* woman writer is as difficult to categorise as her multi-faceted Gothic ghost stories. A prominent feature of her ghost stories is their ambiguity, contradictions, and refusal to delineate. If Lee's ghost stories are unique among contemporary women writers in their shift of focus from the distinctive women's experiences to the mechanics of men's construction of women, Nesbit's stories are more centrally located in the feminine sphere and prioritise repressed and inexplicable women's sentiments—in a sense, they self-consciously situate themselves as a myth of the ghost woman. Unlike the kind of "social supernatural" that Makala uses to categorise many Victorian women's ghost stories,[54] Nesbit's stories very often start with a self-reflective understanding of woman's writing tradition and proceed to appropriate or remould a myth from it, although a social critique is never lacking as shown in "From the Dead" and "Man-size in Marble". "From the Dead" displays a self-reflective twist of the Victorian myth of the dead and fallen women, and I will illustrate through "The House of Silence" how Nesbit reformulates a common trope into a self-mythologising allegory for men and women.

"The House of Silence" is anthologised in Nesbit's later story collection *Man and Maid* (1906).[55] Perhaps for its unsettling effect, contemporary reviews of the book all singled out this story for praise. An anonymous reviewer for *The Bookman* says the story "has an almost allegorical force",[56] yet what that allegory is is difficult to grasp, for the story, unlike Nesbit's other quick-paced stories, is minimalist in plot and characterisation.[57] In a dreamlike ambience, it follows the thrilling nocturnal adventure of an unnamed thief in an unnamed deserted country house. Throughout the story, the reader is given only the thief's perspective, and as the title suggests, since it is a "house of silence", silence is the only palpable second character, pervading the story with a stifling sense of claustrophobia. The thief, having obtained information that treasures may be found in a long-deserted manor house, skilfully breaks into it and wanders in its endless corridors and empty rooms, until he finds the secret trap door that leads to a chamber full of valuable treasures. The restrained deprecating tone that the text uses to describe the treasures and the overwhelming effects they have on the thief seems to imply a critique of the injustice of class inequality and the pathology of human greediness, a subtle trace of the author's socialist ideology. The unfolding of the story seems to affirm this cautionary tone: the thief, after loading himself with treasures, takes the wrong trap door and immediately discovers that he is now enclosed in a damp vaulted passage whose winding twists and turns give no hope of an outlet and that he must "die like a rat" (230) in this prison of dark passages—a proper punishment for greed.[58]

Yet is this the allegory that *The Bookman*'s reviewer indicates? The climax of horror offers an unexpected turn to this cautionary tale and re-posits retrospectively the whole story as a gender allegory. The thief finally finds a door in the passage, and seizing this opportunity for escape, he hastily passes through the door to enter an enclosed courtyard, where sunlight has yet to arrive and tall weeds grow. In the centre of the weeds, the thief unexpectedly stumbles over a spectacle of horror:

> It was the long, firm, heavy plait of a woman's hair. And just beyond lay the green gown of a woman, and a woman's hands, and her golden head, and her eyes; all about the place where *she* lay was the thick buzzing of flies, and the black swarm of them.
>
> (231, italics added)

The decomposing corpse of a woman as the reward for the thief's escape from the claustrophobic passages, is horrifying for its graphic vividness as well as for the utter inexplicableness of the spectacle. Nesbit's language here showcases the suspended moment of unrepresentability of Gothic horror, when language overstrains and contradicts itself: instead of telling the reader directly it is the corpse of a woman, the language hedges around the "plait of a woman", "the green gown of a woman", "a woman's hands", "golden head", "her eyes", etc., as if the woman has broken down into all parts of a woman all over the place, yet the woman herself is blotted from view, something too terrible to behold, too ungraspable to be named. Yet instead of denaturing the corpse as a repulsive other, as the pronoun "it" used by the male narrator in "From the Dead" does, the text at the same time forces its reader to acknowledge the unrepresentable spectacle, although broken into parts, still as a woman, as the personal pronoun "she" shows. The horror of the dead woman, revealed at the end of the thief's vigil and as the ultimate secret of the imprisoning dark passages, thus is the true allegory of the story. The thief, horrified by the spectacle, hurriedly rushes back to the dark passage, now a lesser horror to him than the corpse of the woman. The story ends with a refrain of the beginning, as the thief finally finds a way out of the passage and returns to the road outside the park. As with Nesbit's other stories, no explanation is given as to why a woman's corpse would appear at the place, and no resolution is reached. But the thief's adventure itself, when viewed retrospectively with the horror of the dead woman as its ending point, becomes precisely an inversion of the Female Gothic plot. As Susanne Becker observes, the house is an iconic metaphor for what she calls "gothic forms of feminine fiction".[59] The house is traditionally gendered as women's space, and more specifically in Female Gothic it evokes the horror of women's confinement; thus the "female figure enclosed" in the most secretive part of the house, remarks Becker, "dramatically signifies women's assigned place of enclosure and constraint; of domestic horror with no escape".[60] "The House of Silence" dramatises precisely that sense of enclosure and horror with no escape, yet it makes the horror suffered not by a woman, but a male villain. The thief's nocturnal adventure in this story retraces the trajectory of the Radcliffean heroine: he enters a dilapidated Gothic house hidden from common eyes, gets lost in its endless corridors, and under its appearance of wealth and splendour, finds himself trapped in a womb-like subterranean inside, absolutely cut off from communication with the outside world and threatened to be imprisoned there for life. The thief experiences all the horror, entrapment, and sense of persecution that a Gothic heroine may encounter, and the silence of the house, which the thief senses alternatively as a companion or a stalker, becomes a palpable metaphor for the entrapped woman in a similar situation. The horrible fate of this persecuted heroine, which previous Female Gothic fiction tends to cover up with a final marriage plot, the story reveals graphically as its centre: the dead woman swamped with flies.

However, the thief as the protagonist of this inverted Gothic plot is in every respect the opposite of the Gothic heroine: he is far from innocent or virtuous, and instead of being driven to the dungeon by villains, he is the villain who penetrates the house of silence with a criminal intent. In making the Gothic villain experience vicariously the sense of persecution and entrapment suffered by the Gothic heroine, the story epitomises the radical mythography conceptualised by Coupe as it turns the old myth of women's persecution in patriarchy into a new one. The silent womb-like house not only takes in the man, but also engulfs and overpowers him, and confronts him at the end of his pilgrimage with what he has always endeavoured to deny or transmit to his other: the very materiality of death, the abjection that he has attributed to women to establish his own ego.[61] In this sense, the story becomes effectively an empowering myth of femininity: it is a house of silence, seemingly passive and long deserted, defenceless to the thief's penetration, yet it has a magic of its own, hiding at its core not only boundless treasures but also the collapse of reason and symbolisation—that which governs the world outside—the unrepresentable dead woman in the courtyard.

Nesbit's ghost stories, as I have demonstrated in this chapter, are full of contradictions and ambiguities as her life was, but it is precisely this opacity, this refusal to resolution and clear delineation that give these stories a power to upset, a valuable quality of fantastic writing that has been given much academic attention. Nesbit's ghost stories, like Vernon Lee's, are distinctive productions of their time that trace the struggles of a newly emergent consciousness of women's roles, sufferings, and capacities. While Lee's stories focalise history and the mechanics of history-making, Nesbit's stories are in themselves a para-history-making, in other words, a myth-making—by appropriating and remoulding various myths about women and femininity, she makes a new myth of her ghost women as inexplicable, anti-interpretation, and powerfully haunting.

Notes

1 Collected in Nesbit's poetry collection *Lays and Legend* (first series, 1886).
2 "The Moat House", in *Lays and Legends*, 7. *Victorian Women Writers Project.* http://webapp1.dlib.indiana.edu/vwwp/view?docId=VAB7091;chunk.id=d1e1999;toc.depth=1;toc.id=d1e1999;brand=vwwp;doc.view=0;query=
3 Briggs, *E. Nesbit: A Woman of Passion* (1987), 119.
4 Coupe, *Myth* (2009), 112.
5 "The Ebony Frame", "Uncle Abraham's Romance", and "From the Dead" are collected in Nesbit's 1893 horror story collection *Grim Tales* after having appeared in periodicals, but I am not able to locate the periodicals where they initially appeared.
6 "The Shadow" is included in the 2006 anthology of Nesbit's horror stories *The Power of Darkness*, with no information for its original publication. The *ISFDB* (Internet Speculative Fiction Database) identifies the story as originally published with the title "The Portent of the Shadow" in the magazine *Black and White*, December 23, 1905, which I am not able to verify (http://www.isfdb.org/cgi-bin/title.cgi?583501). I have found "The Portent of a Shadow" published in *North Otago Times*, May 12, 1906, Supplement, from *Papers Past*, a website of digitalised New Zealand publications (see https://paperspast.natlib.govt.nz/newspapers/NOT19060512.2.36).
7 In Wallace and Smith's words, there is a discernible plot that "centralized the imprisoned and pursued heroine threatened by a tyrannical male figure, it explained the supernatural, and ended in the closure of marriage" (*Female Gothic*, 3).
8 "From the Dead", in Nesbit, *The Power of Darkness: Tales of Terror* (2006), edited by David Davies, 169. If not otherwise indicated, later citations of Nesbit's ghost stories all refer to this edition.
9 Her biographer Doris Langley Moore (*E. Nesbit: A Biography*, 1966) does not explore this part of her work at all, while in Briggs's more recent biography (1987) Nesbit's ghost stories are only mentioned in passing in connection with her suppressed childhood fears (12–14, 20).
10 *Power of Darkness*, Wordsworth Editions, 2006; *Horror Stories*, Penguin, 2016.
11 Rutledge describes several of Nesbit's adult romances as "boomerang" that resorts to the marriage plot to cancel out the transgression of the New Woman character. See Rutledge, "E. Nesbit and the Woman Question", in Nicola Diane Thompson ed., *Victorian Women Writers and the Woman Question* (1999), 223–40.
12 For criticism of Nesbit's ghost stories, see Nick Freeman, "E. Nesbit's New Woman Gothic", *Women's Writing 13.5 Special Issue: Women and the Victorian Occult* (2008): 456–69; Kathleen A. Miller, "The Mysteries of the In-between: Re-Reading Disability in E. Nesbit's Late Victorian Gothic Fiction", *Journal of Literary & Cultural Disability Studies* 6.2 (2012): 143–57; Emma Liggins, "Beyond the Haunted House: Modernist Women's Ghost Stories and the Troubles of Modernity", in *British Women Short Story Writers: The New Woman to Now* (2015), Emma Young and James Bailey eds., 32–49. and Victoria Margree, "The Feminist Orientation in Edith Nesbit's Gothic Short Fiction", *Women's Writing* 21.4 (2014): 425–43 and *British*

Women's Short Supernatural Fiction, 1860–1930: Our Own Ghostliness (2019), 87–101.
13 Briggs, *E. Nesbit*, xvi.
14 Briggs, *E. Nesbit*, 334.
15 Briggs, *E. Nesbit*, 333–5.
16 See for instance Emma Liggins and Daniel Duffy's discussion of the "conservative or radical" function of Victorian popular genres, of which the ghost story is an important one (*Feminist Readings of Victorian Popular Texts: Divergent Femininities*, 2001, xiv–xv).
17 Margree, "Feminist Orientation", 426.
18 "The Painted Wall" is emphatically structured around the motif of the painting world as an illusion begotten by human mind, but as Zeitlin notes, it is also one about the flexible boundary between illusion and reality and ultimately, the painting as the threshold leading to a higher level of enlightenment (*Historian of the Strange*, 183–93). Wai-yee Li comments on the significant role of the woman in the painting in this fantastic transformation: "She [the lady in painting] embodies the fulfilment of desire and at the same time lays down premises of a new order" (*Enchantment and Disenchantment: Love and Illusion in Chinese Literature*, 44). Although Pu's concern in this tale may be primarily a metaphysical debate on illusion and enlightenment, motifs of painting as an alternative realm and the painting woman as the crucial initiator are powerful and enduring. See more discussion on "The Painted Wall" in Chapter 3.
19 On the so-called "crisis of faith" in the nineteenth century, see Robin Gilmour, "The Crisis of Faith" in *The Victorian Period: The Intellectual and Cultural Context, 1830–1890* (1993); Walter Edwards Houghton, *The Victorian Frame of Mind, 1830–1870* (1957), 58–61, 94–6.
20 On the logic of ghostly retribution, see for instance Yuan-ju Liu, "Xingxian yu mingbao: liuchao zhiguai zhong guiguai xushu de fengyu—yige 'daoyi weichang' moshi de kaocha", *Bull. Institute of Chinese Literature and Philosophy, Academia Sinica* 29.2 (2006): 1–45.
21 Such a plot also appears in other Nesbit stories, for instance "Man-size in Marble" and "From the Dead" from *Grim Tales*.
22 Berthin, *Gothic Hauntings: Melancholy Crypts and Textual Ghosts* (2010), 58.
23 Berthin, *Gothic Hauntings*, 59.
24 Berthin, *Gothic Hauntings*, 60.
25 The frequency and vividness of depiction of death (especially female death) in Nesbit is noted by critics. See for instance Victorian Margree, *British Women's Short Supernatural Fiction*, 88.
26 Nickianne Moody argues that it is precisely the concerns of justice and secrets within the home that make the ghost story a gendered genre which allows women writers to "pursue public or private debates concerning women's experience" (78); see Moody, "Visible Margins: Women Writers and the English Ghost Story", in Sarah Sceats and Gail Cunningham eds., *Image and Power: Women in Fiction in the Twentieth Century* (1996), 77–90.
27 White, *The Content of the Form: Narrative Discourse and Historical Representation* (1987), 13.
28 White, *The Content*, 14.
29 Briggs, *E. Nesbit*, 107–27.
30 Briggs discusses the thinly veiled sentiments of jealousy and self-destruction in several of her poems collected in *Lays and Legends* (1886), but she does not mention her fiction (*E. Nesbit*, 118–20).
31 This is a plot used profusely in her story collection *In Homespun* (1896) as well as in her horror stories.
32 See Frye, "The Ghost Story and the Subjection of Women: The Example of Amelia Edwards, M. Braddon, and E. Nesbit", *Victorians Institute Journal* 26 (1998): 167–209

and Margree, "Feminist Orientation". Examples of such portrayal can be found in Nesbit's "John Charrington's Wedding" where the dead bridegroom returns to claim the life of the bride on their wedding, "Hurst of Hurstcote" which ends in husband and wife dying in a grave, and the famous "Man-size in Marble".
33 Frye, "The Ghost Story", 189.
34 Most of the first-person narrators in *The Power of Darkness* (2006) are men.
35 Emma Liggins interprets the horror of the house as the uncanniness of modernity; see Liggins, "Beyond the Haunted House: Modernist Women's Ghost Stories and the Troubles of Modernity", in Emma Young and James Barley eds., *British Women Short Story Writers: The New Woman to Now* (2015), 32–49.
36 Briggs, *E. Nesbit*, 112.
37 Briggs, *E. Nesbit*, 114–17.
38 In Moers's summary, Radcliffe's Gothic heroine is "a young woman who is simultaneously persecuted victim and courageous heroine" ("Female Gothic", 124).
39 Critics have noted how Nesbit tends to use magic as both a means for gratification of desire and a source of horror in her children's fiction, as wishes granted always lead to something unexpected and ugly that turns against the wisher. See for example Gore Vidal, "The Writing of E. Nesbit" in *New York Review of Books*, 3 Dec. 1964 issue.
40 Briggs, *E. Nesbit*, 118–19.
41 For instance, psychoanalytically oriented critic Claire Kahane interprets the Gothic heroine's fear as ultimately the fear of the monstrous mother. See Kahane, "The Gothic Mirror", in *The (M)Other Tongue: Essays in Feminist Psychoanalytic Interpretation* (1985), 334–51, edited by Shirley Nelson, Claire Kahane and Madelon Garner.
42 Briggs analyses a pair of love poems in *Lays and Legends* (1886), "Husband of Today" and "Wife of All Ages" which offer a different treatment of the theme of jealousy and infidelity than the one explored in "The Shadow". The wife in the poem is resentful of the double moral standards for men and women, yet in the end compromises by accepting that a wife is contented with possessing only a part of the husband's heart (*E. Nesbit*, 119–20).
43 Psychologist Bruno Bettelheim first interprets Snow White as a cautionary tale for pubescent girls' premature sexual desire, yet many feminist critics have criticised this interpretation as precisely an endorsement of patriarchy's polarisation of the sexually aggressive woman and the angelic chaste woman. See Bettelheim, *The Uses of Enchantment: The Meaning and Importance of Fairy Tales* (1977), 199–215. For feminist interpretations of Snow White, see for instance Sandra Gilbert and Susan Guber, *The Madwoman in the Attic: The Woman Writer and the Nineteenth-Century Literary Imagination* (1980), 36–42; Susanne Kord, "Bad Blood: The Cost of Sexual Curiosity in Archetypal Tales", *Oxford German Studies* 38.2 (2009): 203–17. On the Victorian exaltation of the beautiful dead woman in art, see Elizabeth Bronfen, *Over Her Dead Body: Death, Femininity and the Aesthetic* (1992); Bram Dijkstra, *Idols of Perversity: Fantasies of Feminine Evil in Fin-de-siècle Culture* (1986).
44 Gilbert and Guba, *The Madwoman*, 42.
45 Coupe, *Myth*, 100. On orthodox and radical typologies, see Coupe, *Myth*, 98–101.
46 Margree, "Feminist Orientation", 430.
47 Thomas De Quincey, excerpt from *Joan of Arc*, quoted. in Bronfen, *Over Her Dead Body*, epigraph.
48 Dijkstra, *Idols*, 60
49 Bronfen, *Over Her Dead Body*, 102.
50 Bronfen, *Over Her Dead Body*, 98.
51 Kord makes a connection between the undead Snow White and the female vampire. See Kord, "Bad Blood", 210–14. Indeed, if we consider the commonly accepted connection between vampirism and excessive sexual appetite, then the rising Ida in this story is distinctively vampiric.
52 Auerbach, *Women and the Demon*, 161, 165.

53 Makala, *Women's Ghost Literature*, 59.
54 Makala, *Women's Ghost Literature*, 7.
55 Nesbit, *Man and Maid*, London: Unwin, 1906, in *The Complete Novels of E. Nesbit*, 2013.
56 *The Bookman*, August 1906, 187, in *The Complete Novels of E. Nesbit*.
57 Critical attention to this story is sparse, apart from Margree's recent reading of the story in *British Women's Short Supernatural Fiction*, 95–100. Margree also agrees on the strangeness of the story and its enigmatic nature, yet her reading is different from mine as she associates the story with the *fin-de-siècle* aestheticism and reads it as a prototype modernist experimentation. The minimalist and enigmatic qualities of this story certainly allow for diverse interpretations.
58 Contrary to my interpretation, Margree reads the thief as an "aesthete" whose covetousness of the treasures of the house is "treated almost sympathetically" by the narrator. See Margree, *British Women's*, 96.
59 Becker, *Gothic Forms of Feminine Fiction*, 1999.
60 Becker, *Gothic*, 10.
61 On the theme of the abject feminine in Nesbit's stories, see Margree, "Feminist Orientations", 428–30.

Conclusion

Ghosts show a disrespect for our usual defining categories, and travel freely over time, between the self and the other and, as this comparative study of ghost stories has shown, across cultures. Longxi Zhang expresses his belief that "cultural encounters will manifest themselves *in* and *as* textual encounters" (original emphasis),[1] and the preceding chapters are intended to demonstrate a commensurability between Chinese and British cultures in their understanding and appropriation of the powerful and liminal ghost figure. I have tried to show that a comparable poetics of the spectral can be traced in ghost stories of the two countries in the late nineteenth century, which an isolated study of either the English ghost story or the Chinese *zhiguai* would fail to reveal. Ghost stories in both countries were appropriated by various marginalised and disadvantaged groups as a ghostly history of their own that enabled an expression of new gender identities and a contestation of existing narratives of orthodoxy: while male literati in China used their history of ghosts to rethink the history of the state, female British writers found in ghost stories a space for formulating a fantastic women's history opposed to men's manipulation of women's history.

That ghost stories can open up a discursive space for rethinking history and gender relies on the ambivalent status of the ghost as perceived in both cultures: it is at once a cultural anomaly and an inevitable product of the orthodox culture, ephemeral yet at times powerful, belonging to the past yet traversing freely across time. It is this liminality of the ghost, especially its disruption of chronology (as indicated in the conception of history) and categorisation (as the conceptual premise in the delineation between the self and the other) that makes it an especially versatile tool for marginalised groups to question established cultural and societal structures and to construct new possibilities for a changing self. Stories of ghosts, as the Introduction has shown, have traditionally appealed to those people who felt themselves alienated from the centre of power. The marginalised groups harnessed the potency of the ghost by using their ghost narratives to confound social normality, to express the tabooed and unsayable, and to visualise alternative models of social rules and gender relations. In the ideologically unstable late nineteenth century, a shared ethos in both China and Britain was a preoccupation with time, whether embedded in the foreboding of the impending dynastic fall in China or the premonition of imminent social changes in Britain.

The ideological uncertainties of the period engendered tremendous anxieties with one's gender identity as well as anxieties with the ideas of history, whether national or personal. Consequently, the book has traced the textual encounters between Chinese and British ghost stories in the intersection of history-writing and subjectivity formation.

A recurrent idea underlying this book is that ghost stories can be conceptualised as a kind of para-history, and ghost story writers, either overtly or implicitly, appropriate the role of the historian in their creation of the literary ghost. History and fiction are both important ways to narrativise human experience, yet the factual status of history has traditionally granted history a superiority over fiction in professing a position of cultural authority. However, with postmodernist philosophers like Hayden White, history is deconstructed as no less a narrative genre governed by the stylistic rules of literature, whose objectivity effect is not a natural given but the result of its narrativisation.[2] If history as a narrativising discourse is involved in implementing the authority of certain cultural subjects through the process of evaluation, selection, and discrimination inherent in the act of storytelling, then fiction writers self-stylised as "historians of the ghost" can also appropriate the authority and discursive power of history by "historicising" the past with a story. Through constructing a fictionalised history of the "ghosted" figures, writers of ghost stories may establish the authority of other groups of cultural subjects who may not have the opportunity to legitimise themselves through history-writing. History-writing is thus intrinsically connected with the affirmation of subjectivity.

Ghost stories, in this sense, come as an apt tool for fiction writers to implement their alternative "history"-writing. In Chapters 2, 3, and 4, I have shown how writers of ghost stories have used their ghost-making as para-history writing. Both Chinese writers Xuan Ding and Wang Tao revisit their national history (especially the critical moments of history like dynastic changes) in their ghost stories and make this "ghost history" serve contemporary men in different ways. Xuan mythologises the unarchived or badly archived parts of national history so that the contemporary self may reunite with his cultural heroes and gain power from his forefathers in preparation for the dangerous encounter with the (often demonised) Western other. Wang, on the contrary, questions the official version of national history by focusing on its spectres so that the contemporary man, freed from the burden of tradition, may better confront his Western rivals. A critique of the process of history-making, implied in some of Wang's tales about history's silenced others, is also the central concern in Lee's ghost stories, but the female writer relocates her focus on women's history manipulated and appropriated in men's grand project of rewriting national history. If for Wang, official state history is an uncanny burden from which the contemporary Chinese man must break away to remake his nation and himself, for Lee, men's history of women mediated by a male desire of possession is what excluded women from their own history, and this is also what her stories of the ghosted women set to critique. The result of this criticism is to create a liminal space between history and fiction where the ghost woman has the power to haunt and perturb the present narrative of history. If these three writers engage with the idea of history in the public realm, E. Nesbit's stories involve history in the private sphere: the ephemeral, suppressed, and often inexplicable experiences in a woman's private history. Nesbit's stories of the ghost are an appropriation of the tradition of the Female Gothic, and for Nesbit to write the ghost woman's history becomes a literary myth-making which parodies or reverts contemporary misogynist myths about women. Both Xuan and Nesbit are in J. R. R. Tolkien's words "philomythus", as they are fully aware of the power of myth-making.[3] Their ghost tales reveal the proximity of history and myth: while the former elevates the national history into a national myth which reinforces what that history promotes, the latter weaves women's experience into a new myth of the ghost woman that breaks away from contemporary restrictive gender scripts for women. The differing roles that the ghost stories play in the reformation of power once again prove that this is a genre with a paradoxical relation with orthodoxy: at times, it can be dissenting or conforming to the orthodox power centre.

Stories of ghosts, at the same time, are also stories about the self and the relation between the self and the other. The female ghost has always been an embodiment of the ideal self and the defining other for the Chinese male literati who wrote about her over centuries, and in the transitional late nineteenth century, ghosts, together with other anomalies like fox and snake spirits, became an apt device to re-organise the relation between the self and the other. I have mentioned Wang's and Xuan's reworking of national history through their literary ghost, but equally important with this looking back was their preoccupation with a contemporary identity crisis exacerbated by the confrontation with an ominous other: the intruding Westerners. The aim for their reconstruction of history is ultimately to offer the contemporary literati conceptual frameworks to envisage a revalorised male self against a feminised (and sometimes demonised) alien other. While the ghost can occupy both the position of the self and the other for the male writers, for British female writers, the ghost's paradoxically powerful and powerless status makes it more appropriately a metaphor for the marginalised self. While Lee's stories focus more on the mechanism of men's construction of women instead of women's experience, her celebration of the anomalous snake lady does represent for us an ideal model of femininity featuring a sexual fluidity. Nesbit's stories of the ghost woman, on the other hand, penetrate directly into the paradoxes and injustices experienced by many Victorian women, foregrounding the inexplicableness and contradictions in this marginalised experience.

So far, I have traced the textual encounters manifested in the Chinese and British ghost stories in the late nineteenth century studied in the book, but more importantly I want to show how a comparative study of ghost stories from different cultures can mobilise an encounter of diverse literary knowledges and what new understanding about the specificity and commensurability of literary practices this encounter can offer. Throughout the study I have used terminologies like the Gothic, the *zhiguai*, and the accounts of anomaly, each term originating from its distinctive cultural and historical milieu, and now I will explain how the

Gothic and the literature of anomaly as literary knowledges can offer insight to both Chinese and British ghost stories.

The Gothic is a theoretical framework that not only applies to British ghost stories but offers insights into Chinese ghost stories as well. While the Gothic is concerned with the tabooed, the suppressed, and the inexplicable in certain historical and cultural settings, to give expression and an ephemeral shape to what is repressed is the central interest of the ghost story in both cultures, as the ghost itself very often embodies that which is buried, suppressed, and relegated into oblivion. Simon Hay's assertions that ghost stories as a genre are concerned with "historical trauma, its remembrance and its lingering consequences",[4] and that they constitute a way of writing history, apply to not only British ghost stories but also find vibrating resonance in the Chinese *zhiguai*. The Chinese *zhiguai* perhaps more ostensibly than the British ghost story has been conceived as a history of the ghosts, positioning itself always in tension with the history of the state and offering much discursive space for contesting the ideologies held in the former.

Yet Hay's method, in isolating British ghost stories set in foreign cultures within an exclusive post-colonial reading, runs the risk of homogenising disparate traditions of the spectral under the single conceptual framework that posits Europe as the perennial centre of significance. Hay concedes that ghosts in post-colonial writing often "represents locality and specificity", yet to him this representation is simply a placeholder whose local content is not important, as he further asserts "what matters is not the particularities but rather a notion of the pre-colonial, the non-modern".[5] If we still take post-colonialism and the Gothic as the sole conceptual frameworks to understand ghost narratives produced outside of the first worlds or in culturally-hybrid zones, we do not do justice to the work. For instance, the Chinese American writer Ken Liu's short story "Good Hunting",[6] set in nineteenth-century colonial Hong Kong, fuses the traditional *zhiguai* discourse on *huli jing* (fox spirit) with a postcolonial cyberpunk urban Gothic narrative, yet the Chinese anomaly discourse surrounding the fox spirit Yan never simply serves as a "notion of the pre-colonial, the non-modern" to set up the trauma of colonial modernity in the latter part of the story. The dynamics of power that flow along the line of norm and anomaly central to *zhiguai* is crucial in understanding the subversiveness exhibited in the hybrid and anomalous heroine (a prostitute-fox-robot) under a British colonial rule. And that is why, as I mentioned in the Introduction, while postcolonial studies and concepts like global Gothic contribute to the encounter of literatures from Western and non-Western cultures, they do not do full justice to the diversity of world literature if critics do not attempt to meet literary knowledges from other cultures halfway.

Here, I propose that a literature of the anomaly, a concept embedded in the tradition of *zhiguai* (the defining element of *zhiguai* being "strangeness", an anomaly), be used as a lens through which to understand ghost stories in a broader context. The ghost story is singularly interested in the anomalous, the often suppressed opposite of the norm and the orthodox; however, while the anomaly is what is expurgated from the norm, the norm is also negatively defined by the anomaly. In a sense, the anomaly, though despised and often of

Conclusion 135

illegitimate status, is also an indispensable part of the whole social structure without which the other side of the hierarchy—normality and orthodoxy—would not be functioning well. That is why, as I mentioned in the Introduction, ghost stories can be both deconstructive and constructive. Ghost stories are concerned with making trouble with regulatory borders; through narrating and investigating the anomaly, the relation between the norm and the anomaly may be redefined, and what is anomalous may also gain the position of the norm, thus unleashing enormous power for writers of anomaly to create new ways of being and thinking (a redefinition of such anomalous entities as ghosts, foxes, and snakes underline the ghost stories I examine in this book). This elasticity of the ghost perhaps is the reason behind its appeal, especially in transitional times and for marginalised groups, as this study has shown.

While I begin the book with an epigraph from Feng Menglong which stresses the prevalence of ghosts in chaotic times, I want to end it with a note of the ghost story's continuing relevance in the twenty-first century by introducing the ghost stories of a contemporary Chinese internet writer Ma Boyong. From 2014 to 2015, Ma wrote a series of stories collected under the title "Xin zhiyi" (New Records of the Strange) for his personal column on Zhihu.com.[7] The stories are written in a quaint style unlike everyday Chinese yet reminiscent of vernacular translations of classical *zhiguai* stories from *Liaozhai zhiyi*. While the form is ostensibly old, the stories deal humorously with distinctively contemporary concerns: youngsters' addiction to mobile phones, women's reluctance to sacrifice their career for marriage, and more poignantly, the censorship and propaganda of the contemporary government—the last of which won these tales an avid readership, yet expectedly also led to their censorship.[8] One of these stories, "Wuda gui" 武大鬼 (Ghosts in Wuhan University) epitomises the ghost's dialectical relation with orthodoxy. Since the eighteenth National Congress of the Communist Party of China in 2012 and the current Chinese president Xi Jinping's presidency, a set of moral values collected under the title "Core Values of Chinese Socialism" has been militantly promoted by the government in all social sectors.[9] At the apex of this "education" campaign in 2014, it was reported that students in Wuhan University had been forced to recite the Core Values by school authorities, which led to a wave of public criticism. "Ghosts in Wuhan University" responds to this contemporary farce. The Taoist exorcist in the story named Bao Shu asks a group of ghosts haunting the library of Wuhan University why they have been causing such trouble for people, and a hilarious answer from the ghost chief ensues:

> Last month a mandate was issued from the heavenly palace to confer honour to leading educational institutions. The magistrate of Wuchang then dreamt of an immortal who bestowed on him twenty-four chapters of "Values to Promote Harmony among the People" and told him that whenever people recite these, splendid memorial arches would spring from the ground, growing higher with each recitation. If all the people in Wuchang recite these values, the arches can eventually reach the heavenly palace and share aura with the Jade Emperor. Consequently, ferocious government officers were

dispatched to force people to recite these values day and night so that morals can be engrained. We are merely wandering ghosts and we have been greatly agitated by the recitation, so we decided to hide in this library. We really did not mean to harm.

Bao Shu then asks: "If so, why did you recite these values too?" The ghost answers: "If people recite these values, ghosts can be exorcised; if ghosts recite these values, people can be exorcised.

上个月天庭下诏，要旌表教首善之邦。 武昌郡的太守梦中蒙仙人传授了《敦民和洽观》二十四篇，诵之便有五彩七宝牌坊拔地而起。每诵一次，牌坊就增长一分。若武昌百姓皆诵此咒，牌坊便可达于天庭，与玉帝同辉。于是悍吏四出，教人日夜诵经，随时抽查，以彰教化之本。我等皆是孤魂野鬼，不堪其扰。于是计议在图书馆暂避，不是有心害人。

宝树又说："既然如此，那你们为何也要诵咒呢？"鬼怪道："人诵此咒，可以驱鬼；鬼诵此咒，可以驱人。"[10]

Here, the ghost, the usual character in *zhiguai* stories that fulfils the function of the troublemaker, turns out in the end to be not the originator of disorder but a victim of it, and ironically, the "values" issued from the authority to dispel ghosts could be re-utilised by what is exorcised as a weapon against the exorcist. Contemporary ghost stories like this one not only revive *zhiguai*'s traditional function of critiquing official state ideology, its reincarnated existence on the internet, ephemeral, fragmentary, yet persistently haunting, also becomes an uncanny "ghost history" of our age, bearing witness to the irrationality of contemporary political power and resistance to it. The political power centre may seek to exorcise ghosts with its militantly enforced standard narrative, yet ghosts, as the story shows, can always disturb the seeming harmony of the present by usurping precisely orthodoxy's own narrative. Not only do times of chaos call for ghosts; ghosts are always already a part of our contemporary reality and can never be suppressed.

Notes

1 Zhang, *Unexpected Affinities*, 7.
2 See White, *Metahistory: The Historical Imagination in Nineteenth-century Europe* (1973) and *The Content of the Form* (1987).
3 See Tolkien, "Mythopoeia", in *Tree and Leaf: Including the Poem Mythopoeia* (2001), 85.
4 Hay, *A History*, 227. To be specific, by "historical traumas" Hay means the traumatic transition from feudalism to capitalism and the transition to modernity under imperialism.
5 Hay, *A History*, 229.
6 Liu, "Good Hunting", *Strange Horizons*, Oct. 2012, http://strangehorizons.com/issue/2012-fund-drive-special/. Liu comments in his own blog that one of his goals in this story is to "turn the misogynist *huli jing* legend upside down"; see Liu, "Story Notes: 'Good Hunting' in Strange Horizons", *Kenliu.name* November 8, 2012, https://kenliu.name/blog/2012/11/08/story-notes-good-hunting-in-strange-horizons/. The story is also adapted into an episode of the same name in the 2019 animation anthology series *Love, Death &*

Robots, directed by Oliver Thomas, in which elements of the Gothic and the erotic are accentuated to overshadow the original dialectic between the norm and anomaly.
7 Zhihu.com is a Chinese social network website similar to Quara.com.
8 Three of these stories, "Xiang zhong Li" 箱中吏 (Government Officers in the Case), "Wuda gui" 武大鬼 (Ghosts in Wuhan University), and "San guan ji" 三觀記 (A Record of the Three Temples) were originally published on the author's column on Zhihu, censored shortly afterwards. The author reposted ten stories including the above three on zhihu.com on June 5, 2017 under the series title "Xin zhiyi", which have remained until today. As with everything on the internet, its existence is precarious and uncertain.
9 These values are condensed into twelve words: "prosperity, democracy, civility, harmony, freedom, equality, justice, the rule of law, patriotism, dedication, integrity, and friendship" (富强, 民主, 文明, 和谐, 自由, 平等, 公正, 法治, 爱国, 敬业, 诚信, 友善). As they contain 24 Chinese characters, they are also referred to as the "24-word core socialist values". For an official interpretation of these values, see for instance, Du Yifei, "24-Core Socialist Values Engraved on People's Mind", *People.cn.*, People's Daily, March 2, 2016, http://en.people.cn/n3/2016/0302/c98649-9023926.html.
10 Ma Boyong, "Ghosts in Wuhan University", https://zhuanlan.zhihu.com/p/27245077.

References

References in English

Auerbach, Nina. *Woman and the Demon: The Life of a Victorian Myth*. Cambridge, MA: Harvard University Press, 1982.

Becker, Susanne. *Gothic Forms of Feminine Fiction*. Manchester, UK: Manchester University Press, 1999.

Beecroft, Alexander. "World Literature without a Hyphen: Towards a Typology of Literary Systems." In: *World Literature in Theory*, 180–91. Edited by David Damrosch. Hoboken, NJ: John Wiley, 2014.

Behdad, Ali, and Dominic Thomas, eds. *A Companion to Comparative Literature*. Malden, MA: Wiley-Blackwell, 2011.

Berthin, Christine. *Gothic Hauntings: Melancholy Crypts and Textual Ghosts*. Houndmills, UK: Palgrave Macmillan, 2010.

Bettelheim, Bruno. *The Uses of Enchantment: The Meaning and Importance of Fairy Tales*. New York, NY: Vintage Books, 1977.

Black, Alison H. "Gender and Cosmology in Chinese Correlative Thinking." In: *Gender and Religion: On the Complexity of Symbols*, 166–95. Edited by Caroline W. Bynum, Stevan Harrell, and Paula Richman. Boston, MA: Beacon, 1986.

Briggs, Julia. *Night Visitors: The Rise and Fall of the English Ghost Story*. London, UK: Faber, 1977.

Briggs, Julia. *A Woman of Passion: The Life of E. Nesbit, 1858–1924*. London, UK: Hutchinson, 1987.

Briggs, Julia. "The Ghost Story." In: *A New Companion to the Gothic*, 176–85. Edited by David Punter. Oxford, UK: Blackwell Publishing, 2012.

Bronfen, Elizabeth. *Over Her Dead Body: Death, Femininity and the Aesthetic*. Manchester, UK: Manchester University Press, 1992.

Buse, Peter, and Andrew Scott. "Introduction: A Future for Haunting In *Ghosts: Deconstruction, Psychoanalysis, History*, 1–20. Edited by Peter Buse and Andrew Scott. London, UK: Macmillan, 1999.

Campany, Robert Ford. *Strange Writing: Anomaly Accounts in Early Medieval China*. Albany, NY: State University of New York Press, 1996.

Carlyle, Thomas. "On History." In: *A Carlyle Reader*, 55–66. Edited by G. B. Tennyson. Cambridge, UK: Cambridge University Press, 1984.

Casanova, Pascale. *The World Republic of Letters*. Translated by M. B. DeBevoise. Cambridge, MA: Harvard University Press, 2004.

Casanova, Pascale. "Literature as a World." *New Left Review* 31 (2005): 71–90.

Castle, Terry. *The Apparitional Lesbian: Female Homosexuality and Modern Culture.* New York, NY: Columbia University Press, 1993.

Chan, Leo Tak-hung. *The Discourse on Foxes and Ghosts: Ji Yun and Eighteenth-Century Literati Storytelling.* Hong Kong, China: The Chinese University of Hong Kong Press, 1998.

Chan, Wing-tsit. *Neo-Confucian Terms Explained: The Pei-hsi tzu-i [Beixi ziyi] by Ch'En Ch'un, 1159–1223.* New York, NY: Columbia University Press, 1986.

Chang, Shelley Hsueh-lun. *History and Legend: Ideas and Images in the Ming Historical Novels.* Ann Arbor, MI: University of Michigan Press, 1990.

Chiang, Sing-chen Lydia. *Collecting the Self: Body and Identity in Strange Tale Collections of Late Imperial China.* Leiden, the Netherlands: Brill, 2005.

Chow, Rey. "The Old/New Question of Comparison in Literary Studies: A Post-European Perspective." *ELH* 71(2) (2004): 289–311.

Christensen, Peter. "The Burden of History in Vernon Lee's Ghost Story 'Amour Dure'." *Studies in the Humanities* 16(1) (1989): 33–43.

Cohen, Paul A. *Between Tradition and Modernity: Wang T'Ao and Reform in Late Ch'ing [Qing] China.* Cambridge, MA: Harvard University Press, 1974.

Cohen, Paul A. *History and Popular Memory: The Power of Story in Moments of Crisis.* New York, NY: Columbia University Press, 2014.

Colby, Vineta. *Victorian Literature and Culture: Vernon Lee, a Literary Biography.* Charlottesville, VA: University of Virginia Press, 2003.

Coupe, Laurence. *Myth.* 2nd ed. London, UK: Routledge, 2009.

Cox, Michael, and R. A. Gilbert. "Introduction." In *The Oxford Book of Victorian Ghost Stories*, ix–xx. Edited by Michael Cox and R. A. Gilbert. Oxford, UK: Oxford University Press, 1991.

Crosby, Christina. *The Ends of History: Victorians and "the Woman Question."* New York, NY: Routledge, 1991.

Damrosch, David. *What Is World Literature?* Princeton, NJ: Princeton University Press, 2003.

Damrosch, David, Natalie Melas, and Mbongiseni Buthelezi eds. *The Princeton Sourcebook in Comparative Literature: From the European Enlightenment to the Global Present.* Princeton, NY: Princeton University Press, 2009.

Dewoskin, Kenneth J. "The Six Dynasties Chih-Kuai [*Zhiguai*] and the Birth of Fiction." In: *Chinese Narrative: Critical and Theoretical Essays*, 21–52. Edited by Andrew H. Plaks. Princeton, NY: Princeton University Press, 1977.

Dickerson, Vanessa. *Victorian Ghosts in the Noontide: Women Writers and the Supernatural.* Columbia, MO: University of Missouri Press, 1996.

Dijkstra, Bram. *Idols of Perversity: Fantasies of Feminine Evil in Fin-De-Siècle Culture.* New York, NY: Oxford University Press, 1986.

Du, Yifei. "24-Word Core Socialist Values Engraved on People's Mind." *People.cn. People's Daily*, March 2, 2016. http://en.people.cn/n3/2016/0302/c98649-9023926.html.

Eliade, Mircea. *The Sacred and the Profane: The Nature of Religion.* Translated by Willard R. Trask. New York, NY: Harcourt, 1959.

Epstein, Maram. *Competing Discourses: Orthodoxy, Authenticity, and Engendered Meanings in Late Imperial Chinese Fiction.* Cambridge, MA: Harvard University Asia Center, 2001.

Evangelista, Stefano. "Vernon Lee and the Gender of Aestheticism." In: *Vernon Lee: Decadence, Ethics, Aesthetics*, 91–111. Edited by Catherine Maxwell and Patricia Pulham. Houndmills, UK: Palgrave Macmillan, 2006.

Fairbank, John King. "A Preliminary Framework." In: *The Chinese World Order: Traditional China's Foreign Relations*, 1–19. Edited by John King Fairbank. Cambridge, MA: Harvard University Press, 1968.

Feng, Menglong, comp. "Yang Siwen Meets an Old Acquaintance in Yanshan." In: *Stories Old and New: A Ming Dynasty Collection*, 430–49. Translated by Shuhui Yang and Yunqin Yang. Seattle, WA: University of Washington Press, 2000.

Feuchtwang, Stephan. "Domestic and Communal Worship in a Taiwan Town." In: *Religion and Ritual in Chinese Society*, 105–30. Edited by Arthur P. Wolf. Stanford, CA: Stanford University Press, 1974.

Feuchtwang, Stephan. *The Anthropology of Religion, Charisma and Ghosts: Chinese Lessons for Adequate Theory*. New York, NY: De Gruyter, 2010.

Fraser, Hilary. *The Victorians and Renaissance Italy*. Oxford, UK: Blackwell, 1992.

Fraser, Hilary. "Women and the Ends of Art History: Vision and Corporeality in Nineteenth-Century Critical Discourse." *Victorian Studies* 42(1) (1998): 77–100.

Freeman, Nick. "E. Nesbit's New Woman Gothic." *Women's Writing* 13.5 Special Issue: *Women and the Victorian Occult* (2008): 456–69.

Freud, Sigmund. "Mourning and Melancholia." In: *On the History of the Psycho-Analytic Movement and Papers on Metapsychology and Other Works*, 243–58. Standard Edition. Vol. 14. Translated by James Strachey. London, UK: Hogarth, 1953.

Freud, Sigmund. "The Uncanny." In: *The Uncanny*, 121–62. Translated by David McLintock. New York, NY: Penguin, 2003.

Frye, Lowell T. "The Ghost Story and the Subjection of Women: The Example of Amelia Edwards, Rhoada Braddon, and E. Nesbit." *Victorians Institute Journal* 26 (1998): 167–209.

Fu, Mengxing. "Tales of the New Strange: Wang Tao's *Zhiguai* Writing (1880–1890)." In: *Ming Qing Studies 2017*, 11–44. Edited by Paolo Santangelo. Rome, Italy: Aracne, 2017.

Fu, Mengxing. "History-Making and Its Gendered Voice in Wang Tao's and Vernon Lee's Ghost Stories." *Neohelicon* 46(2) (2019): 645–61.

Garber, Marjorie. *Vested Interests: Cross-Dressing and Cultural Anxiety*. New York, NY: Routledge, 1992.

Genette, Gérard. *Paratexts: Thresholds of Interpretation*. Cambridge, UK: Cambridge University Press, 1997.

Gilbert, Sandra M., and Susan Gubar. *The Madwoman in the Attic: The Woman Writer and the Nineteenth-Century Literary Imagination*. London, UK: Yale University Press, 1980.

Gilmour, Robin. *The Victorian Period: The Intellectual and Cultural Context, 1830–1890*. London, UK: Longman, 1993.

Gulik, Robert van. *Erotic Colour Prints of the Ming Period, with an Essay on Chinese Sex Life from the Han to the Ch'ing [Qing] Dynasty, B.C.206–A.D.1644*. Vol. 1. 3 vols. Tokyo, Japan: Privately Published, 1951.

Hanan, Patrick. *The Chinese Venacular Story*. Cambridge, MA: Harvard University Press, 1981.

Harrell, C. Stevan. "When a Ghost Becomes a God." In: *Religion and Ritual in Chinese Society*, 193–206. Edited by Arthur P. Wolf. Stanford, CA: Stanford University Press, 1974.

Hay, Simon. *A History of the Modern British Ghost Story*. Houndmills, UK: Palgrave Macmillan, 2011.

Henderson, John B. *The Development and Decline of Chinese Cosmology*. New York, NY: Columbia University Press, 1984.

Houghton, Walter Edwards. *The Victorian Frame of Mind, 1830–1870*. New Haven, CT: Yale University Press, 1957.

Huang, Martin W. "Sentiments of Desire: Thoughts on the Cult of Qing in Ming-Qing Literature." *Chinese Literature: Essays, Articles, Reviews* 20(December)(1998): 153–84.

Huang, Martin W. *Negotiating Masculinities in Late Imperial China*. Honolulu, HI: University of Hawai'i Press, 2006.

Huggan, Gramham. "The Trouble with World Literature." In: *A Companion to Comparative Literature*, 490–506. Edited by Ali Behdad and Dominic Thomas. Malden, MA: Wiley-Blackwell, 2011.

Huntington, Rania. *Alien Kind: Foxes and Late Imperial Chinese Narrative*. Cambridge, MA: Harvard University Asia Center; distributed by Harvard University Press, 2003.

Kahane, Claire. "The Gothic Mirror." In: *The (M)Other Tongue: Essays in Feminist Psychoanalytic Interpretation*, 334–51. Edited by Shirley Nelson, Claire Kahane, and Madelon Garner. Ithaca, NY: Cornell University Press, 1985.

Kandola, Sondeep. *Vernon Lee*. Northcote: Tavistock, UK; British Council, 2010.

Kane, Mary Patricia. *Spurious Ghosts: The Fantastic Tales of Vernon Lee*. Rome, Italy: Carocci, 2004.

Kang, Xiaofei. *The Cult of the Fox: Power, Gender, and Popular Religion in Late Imperial and Modern China*. New York, NY: Columbia University Press, 2006.

Kipling, Rudyard. *The Phantom Rickshaw and Other Tales*. London, UK: Sampson Low, 1890. *Internet Archive*. July 25, 2007. https://archive.org/details/phantomrickshaw00kiplrich/mode/2up.

Kord, Susanne. "Bad Blood: The Cost of Sexual Curiosity in Archetypal Tales." *Oxford German Studies* 38(2) (2009): 203–17.

Krishnaswamy, Revathi. "Towards World Literary Knowledges: Theory in the Age of Globalization." *Comparative Literature* 62(2) (2010): 399–419.

Lee, Vernon. *Euphorion: Being Studies of the Antique and the Mediæval in the Renaissance*. Vol. 1. 2 vols. London, UK: Unwin, 1884. *Internet Archive*. February 9, 2009. https://archive.org/details/euphorionbeings03leegoog.

Lee, Vernon. *Miss. Brown*. Vol. 2. 3 vols. New York, NY: Garland, 1884. *Internet Archive*. June 9, 2008. http://archive.org/details/missbrownanovel01leegoog.

Lee, Vernon. "A Worldly Woman." In: *Vanitas: Polite Stories*. London, UK: Heineman, 1891. *Victorian Women Writers Project*. Indiana University Digital Library Program, n.d. http://purl.dlib.indiana.edu/iudl/vwwp/VAB7188.

Lee, Vernon. "The Wedding Chest." In: *Pope Jacynth and Other Fantastic Tales*, 114–38. London, UK: John Lane, 1904. *Internet Archive*. February 3, 2009. https://archive.org/details/popejacynthothe00leegoog/page/n123/mode/2up.

Lee, Vernon. "The Economic Parasitism of Women." In: *Gospels of Anarchy and Other Contemporary Studies*. London, UK: Unwin, 1908. Victorian Women Writers Project. Indiana University Digital Library Program, n.d. purl.dlib.indiana.edu/iudl/vwwp/VAB7069.

Lee, Vernon. *Hauntings and Other Fantastic Tales*. Edited by Catherine Maxwell and Patricia Pulham. Plymouth, UK: Broadview, 2006.

Lee, Vernon. *The Collected Supernatural and Weird Fiction of Vernon Lee*. 2 vols. Driffield, UK: Leonaur, 2011.

Leed, Eric J. *The Mind of the Traveler: From Gilgamesh to Global Tourism*. New York, NY: Basic Books, 1991.

142 References

Legge, James, trans. *The Sacred Books of China: Texts of Taoism*. 2 vols. New York, NY: Dover, 1962. [Rpt. of Claredon 1891 edition.].

Legge, James. *Confucius: Confucian Analects, the Great Learning & the Doctrine of the Mean*. New York, NY: Dover, 1971. [Rpt. of the 2nd rev. Clarendon 1893 edition.].

Li, Wai-yee. *Enchantment and Disenchantment: Love and Illusion in Chinese Literature*. Princeton, NJ: Princeton University Press, 1993.

Li, Wai-yee. "The Late Imperial Courtesan: Invention of a Cultural Ideal." In: *Writing Women in Late Imperial China*, 46–73. Edited by Ellen Widmer and Kang-i Sun Chang. Stanford, CA: Stanford University Press, 1997.

Li, Wai-yee. "Women as Emblems of Dynastic Fall in Qing Literature." In *Dynastic Crisis and Cultural Innovation*, 93–150. Edited by David Der-wei Wang and Wei Shang. Cambridge, MA: Harvard University Asia Center; Distributed by Harvard University Press, 2005.

Li, Xiaobing. "Taiping Rebellion (1850–1864)." In: *China at War: An Encyclopedia. Gale Virtual Reference Library*, 440–2. Santa Barbara, CA: ABC-CLIO, 2012.

Liggins, Emma. "Beyond the Haunted House: Modernist Women's Ghost Stories and the Troubles of Modernity." In: *British Women Short Story Writers: The New Woman to Now*, 32–49. Edited by Emma Young and James Barley. Edinburgh, UK: Edinburgh University Press, 2015.

Liggins, Emma, and Daniel Duffy, eds. *Feminist Readings of Victorian Popular Texts: Divergent Femininities*. Aldershot, UK: Ashgate, 2001.

Liu, Ken. "Good Hunting." *Strange Horizons*, 2012 Fund Drive Special. http://strangehorizons.com/issue/2012-fund-drive-special/.

Liu, Ken. "Story Notes: 'Good Hunting' in Strange Horizons." *Kenliu.name*, November 8, 2012. https://kenliu.name/blog/2012/11/08/story-notes-good-hunting-in-strange-horizons/.

Liu, Yuan-ju. "Allegorical Narratives in Six Dynasties Anomaly Tales." In: *Rethinking Ghosts in World Religions*, 269–97. Edited by Muzhou Pu. Boston, MA: Brill, 2009.

Louie, Kam. *Theorising Chinese Masculinity: Society and Gender in China*. Cambridge, UK: Cambridge University Press, 2002.

Lu, Sheldon H. "Waking to Modernity: The Classical Tale in Late Qing." *New Literary History* 34(4) (2003): 745–60.

Luo, Hui. "The Ghost of *Liaozhai*: Pu Songling's Ghostlore and Its History of Reception." PhD diss. University of Toronto, 2009.

Makala, Melissa Edmundson. *Women's Ghost Literature in Nineteenth-Century Britain*. Cardiff, UK: University of Wales Press, 2013.

Margree, Victoria. "The Feminist Orientation in Edith Nesbit's Gothic Short Fiction." *Women's Writing* 21(4) (2014): 425–43.

Margree, Victoria. *British Women's Short Supernatural Fiction, 1860–1930: Our Own Ghostiiness*. Cham, Switzerland: Palgrave Macmillan, 2019.

Marx, Karl, and Friedrich Engels. *The Communist Manifesto*. Shanghai, China: Shanghai Yiwen, 2019.

Maxwell, Catherine. "From Dionysus to Dionea: Vernon Lee's Portraits." *Word and Image* 13(3) (1997): 253–69.

Maxwell, Catherine, and Patricia Pulham, eds. *Vernon Lee: Decadence, Ethics, Aesthetics*. Houndmills, UK: Palgrave Macmillan, 2006.

McAleavy, Henry. *Wang Tao: The Life and Writing of a Displaced Person*. London, UK: The China Society, 1953. The China Society Occasional Papers No. 7.

McMahon, Keith. *Polygamy and Sublime Passion: Sexuality in China on the Verge of Modernity*. Honolulu, HI: University of Hawai'i Press, 2010.

Milbank, Alison. *Daughters of the House: Modes of the Gothic in Victorian Fiction*. New York, NY: St. Martin's Press, 1992.

Miller, Kathleen A. "The Mysteries of the in-Between: Re-Reading Disability in E. Nesbit's Late Victorian Gothic Fiction." *Journal of Literary and Cultural Disability Studies* 6(2) (2012): 143–57.

Minford, John. Introduction to *Strange Tales from a Chinese Studio*, xi–xxxvi by Pu Songling. Edited and Translated by John Minford. London, UK: Penguin, 2006.

Moers, Ellen. "Female Gothic." In *Gothic: Critical Concepts in Literary and Cultural Studies*, 123–44. Vol.1. 4 vols. Edited by Fred Botting and Dale Townshend. London, UK: Routledge, 2004.

Moody, Nickianne. "Visible Margins: Women Writers and the English Ghost Story." In: *Image and Power: Women in Fiction in the Twentieth Century*, 77–90. Edited by Sarah Sceats and Gail Cunningham. London, UK: Longman, 1996.

Moore, Doris Langley-Levy. *E. Nesbit; a Biography*. Rev., with new material. Philadelphia, PA: Chilton, 1966.

Moretti, Franco. "'Conjecture on World Literature' (2000) and 'More Conjectures.'" (2003) In *World Literature in Theory*, 159–79. Edited by David Damrosch. Chichester, UK: John Wiley, 2014.

Mufti, Aamir R. "Orientalism and the Institution of World Literatures." In: *World Literature in Theory*, 311–44. Edited by David Damrosch. Chichester, UK: John Wiley, 2014.

Nesbit, Edith. "The Moat House." In: *Lays and Legends* (first series). London, UK: Longmans, 1886. *Victorian Women Writers Project*. Indiana University Digital Library Program, n.d. http://purl.dlib.indiana.edu/iudl/vwwp/VAB7091.

Nesbit, Edith. *In Homespun*. London, UK: John Lane, 1896. *Victorian Women Writers Project*. Indiana University Digital Library Program, n.d. purl.dlib.indiana.edu/iudl/vwwp/VAB7080.

Nesbit, Edith. "The Portent of the Shadow." *North Otago Times*, May 12, 1906. Supplement. Papers Past. n.d. https://paperspast.natlib.govt.nz/newspapers/NOT19060512.2.36.

Nesbit, Edith. *The Power of Darkness: Tales of Terror*. Ware, UK: Wordsworth Editions, 2006.

Nesbit, Edith. *The Complete Novels of E. Nesbit*. Delphi Classics, 2013. Series 4 Book 7. Mobi.

Nesbit, Edith. *Horror Stories*. London, UK: Penguin, 2016.

Newman, Sally. "Archival Traces of Desire: Vernon Lee's Failed Sexuality and the Interpretation of Letters in Lesbian History." *Journal of the History of Sexuality* 14(1) (2005): 51–75.

Nieztsche, Friedrich. "On the Uses and Disadvantages of History for Life." In: *Untimely Meditation*, 57–123, edited by Daniel Breazeale. Translated by R. J. Hollingdale. Cambridge, UK: Cambridge University Press, 1997.

Oppenheim, Janet. *The Other World: Spiritualism and Psychical Research in England, 1850–1914*. Cambridge, UK: Cambridge University Press, 1985.

Owen, Alex. *The Darkened Room: Women, Power and Spiritualism in Late Victorian England*. Chicago, IL: The University of Chicago Press, 1989.

Peeren, Esther. *The Spectral Metaphor: Living Ghosts and the Agency of Invisibility*. Houndmills, UK: Palgrave Macmillan, 2014.

Psomidades, Kathy. "'Still Burning from This Straggling Embrace': Vernon Lee on Desire and Aesthetics." In: *Victorian Sexual Dissidence*, 21–42. Edited by Richard Dellamora. Chicago, IL: University of Chicago Press, 1999.

Pu, Muzhou. "The Culture of the Ghost in the Six Dynasties Period." In: *Rethinking Ghosts in World Religions*, 237–68. Edited by Muzhou Pu. Leiden, Netherlands: Brill, 2009.

Pulham, Patricia. *Art and the Transitional Object in Vernon Lee's Supernatural Tales*. Aldershot, UK: Ashgate, 2008.

Punter, David. *The Literature of Terror*. 2nd ed. 2 vols. London, UK: Longman, 1996.

Punter, David, ed. *A Companion to the Gothic*. Oxford, UK: Blackwell, 2000.

Punter, David, ed. *A New Companion to the Gothic*. Oxford, UK: Wiley-Blackwell, 2012.

Rankin, Mary Backus. "Alarming Crises and Enticing Possibilities." *Late Imperial China* 29(1) (2008): 40–63.

Reeser, Todd W. *Masculinities in Theory: An Introduction*. Chichester, UK: Wiley-Blackwell, 2010.

Rutledge, Amelia A. "E. Nesbit and the Woman Question." In: *Victorian Women Writers and the Woman Question*, 223–40. Edited by Nicola Diane Thompson. Cambridge, UK: Cambridge University Press, 1999.

Santangelo, Paolo. "The Cult of Love in Some Texts of Ming and Qing Literature." *West and East* 50(1/4) (December 2000): 439–99.

Santangelo, Paolo. "An Introduction of *Zibuyu*'s Concepts and Imagery." In: *Zibuyu, or "What the Master Would Not Discuss", According to Yuan Mei (1716–1798): A Collection of Supernatural Stories*, 1–160. Vol. 1. 2 vols. Edited by Paolo Santangelo, in cooperation with Beiwen Yan. Leiden, Netherlands: Brill, 2013.

Saussy, Haun. "Exquisite Cadavers Stitched from Fresh Nightmares: Of Memes, Hives, and Selfish Genes." In: *Comparative Literature in an Age of Globalization*, 3–42. Edited by Haun Saussy. Baltimore, MD: John Hopkins University Press, 2006.

Scott, Joan W. "Gender: A Useful Category of Historical Analysis." *The American Historical Review* 91(5) (1986): 1053–75.

Smith, Andrew. *The Ghost Story, 1840–1920: A Cultural History*. Manchester, UK: Manchester University Press, 2010.

Smith, Bonnie G. *The Gender of History: Men, Women, and Historical Practice*. Cambridge, MA: Harvard University Press, 1998.

Starr, Chloë F. *Red-Light Novels of the Late Qing*. Leiden, Netherlands: Brill, 2007.

Stetz, Margaret. "The Snake Lady and the Bruised Bodley Head: Vernon Lee and Oscar Wilde in the *Yellow Book*." In: *Vernon Lee: Decadence, Ethics, and Aesthetics*, 112–22. Edited by Catherine Maxwell and Patricia Pulham. Houndmills, UK: Palgrave Macmillan, 2006.

Sullivan, Jack. *Elegant Nightmares: The English Ghost Story from le Fanu to Blackwood*. 1978. Athens, OH: Ohio University Press, 1980.

Taylor, Richard. "Voluntarism." In *Encyclopaedia of Philosophy*, 714–17. 2nd ed. Edited by Donald M. Borchert. Vol. 9. Detroit, MI: Macmillan Reference USA, 2006.

Teng, Emma Jinghua. *Taiwan's Imagined Geography: Chinese Colonial Travel Writing and Practices, 1638–1895*. Cambridge, MA: Harvard University Asia Center; Distributed by Harvard University Press, 2004.

Teng, Emma Jinghua. "The West as a 'Kingdom of Women': Woman and Occidentalism in Wang Tao's Tales of Travel." In: *Traditions of East Asian Travel*, 70–96. Edited by Joshua A. Fogel. New York, NY: Berghahm, 2006.

Thornber, Karen. "Rethinking the World in World Literature: East Asia and Literary Contact Nebulae." In: *World Literature in Theory*, 460–79. Edited by David Damrosch. Chichester, UK: John Wiley, 2014.

Todorov, Tzvetan. *The Fantastic: A Structural Approach to a Literary Genre*. Ithaca, NY: Cornell University Press, 1975.

Tolkien, J. R. R. *Tree and Leaf: Including the Poem Mythopoeia*. London, UK: Harper Collins, 2001.
Vicinus, Martha. *Intimate Friends: Women Who Loved Women, 1778–1928*. Chicago, IL: University of Chicago Press, 2004.
Vidal, Gore. "The Writing of E. Nesbit." *nybooks.com*. New York Review of Books. December 3, 1964. http://www.nybooks.com/articles/1964/12/03/the-writing-of-e-nesbit/.
Wang, Ban. "Introduction." In: *Chinese Visions of World Order: Tianxia, Culture and the World Politics*, 1–22. Edited by Ban Wang. Durham, NC and London, UK: Duke University Press, 2017.
Wallace, Diana. "Uncanny Stories: Ghost Story as Female Gothic." *Gothic Studies* 6(1) (2004): 57–68.
Wallace, Diana. *Female Gothic Histories: Gender, History and the Gothic*. Cardiff, UK: University of Wales Press, 2013.
Wallace, Diana, and Andrew Smith. "Introduction: Defining the Female Gothic." In: *Female Gothic: New Directions*, 1–12. Edited by Diana Wallace and Andrew Smith. New York, NY: Palgrave Macmillan, 2009.
Wang, David Der-wai. *The Monster That Is History: History, Violence, and Fictional Writing in Twentieth-Century China*. Berkeley, CA: University of California Press, 2004.
Wellek, René. "The Crisis of Comparative Literature." In: *Concepts of Criticism*, 282–95. New Haven, CT: Yale University Press, 1958.
Wellek, René. "Comparative Literature Today." *Comparative Literature* 16(4) (1965): 325–37.
White, Hayden. *Metahistory: The Historical Imagination in Nineteenth-Century Europe*. Baltimore, MD: Johns Hopkins University Press, 1973.
White, Hayden. *The Content of the Form: Narrative Discourse and Historical Representation*. Baltimore, MD: Johns Hopkins University Press, 1987.
Williams, Anne. *Art of Darkness: A Poetics of Gothic*. Chicago, IL: University of Chicago Press, 1995.
Wilson, A. N. *The Victorians*. New York, NY: Norton, 2003.
Wolf, Arthur P. "Gods, Ghosts, and Ancestors." In *Religion and Ritual in Chinese Society*, 131–82. Edited by Arthur P. Wolf. Stanford, CA: Stanford University Press, 1974.
Wolf, Arthur P., ed. *Religion and Ritual in Chinese Society*. Stanford, CA: Stanford University Press, 1974.
Wolfreys, Julian. *Victorian Hauntings: Spectrality, Gothic, the Uncanny, and Literature*. Houndmills, UK: Palgrave, 2002.
Yeh, Catherine Vance. "The Life-Style of Four *Wenren* in Late Qing Shanghai." *Harvard Journal of Asiatic Studies* 57(2) (1997): 419–70.
Young, Emma, and James Bailey. "Introduction." In: *British Women Short Story Writers: The New Woman to Now*, 1–14. Edited by Emma Young and James Bailey. Edinburgh, UK: Edinburgh University Press, 2015.
Yu, Anthony C. "'Rest, Rest, Perturbed Spirit!': Ghosts in Traditional Chinese Prose Fiction." *Harvard Journal of Asiatic Studies* 47(2) (1987): 397–434.
Zeitlin, Judith. *Historian of the Strange: Pu Songling and the Chinese Classical Tale*. Stanford, CA: Stanford University Press, 1997.
Zeitlin, Judith. *The Phantom Heroine: Ghosts and Gender in Seventeenth-Century Chinese Literature*. Honolulu, HI: University of Hawai'i Press, 2007.
Zhang, Longxi. *Unexpected Affinities: Reading across Cultures*. Toronto, Canada: University of Toronto Press, 2007.

Zheng, Huili. "Enchanted Encounter: Gender Politics, Cultural Identity, and Wang Tao's (1828–97) Fictional Sino-Western Romance." *NAN NU—Men, Women & Gender in Early & Imperial China* 16(2) (2014): 274–307.

Zhong, Xueping. *Masculinity Besieged?: Issues of Modernity and Male Subjectivity in Chinese Literature of the Late Twentieth Century*. Durham, NC: Duke University Press, 2000.

Zorn, Christa. *Vernon Lee: Aesthetics, History, and the Victorian Female Intellectual*. Athens, OH: Ohio University Press, 2003.

References in Chinese

Chang, Hao 张灏. *Chinese Intellectuals in Crisis: Search for Order and Meaning (1890–1911)* 危机中的中国知识分子：寻求秩序与意义. Translated by Like Gao 高立克 and Yue Wang 王跃. Taiyuan: Shanxi People's Press, 1988.

Chen, Chun 陈淳. *Beixi Ziyi* 北溪字義. Beijing: Zhonghua shuju, 1983.

Cheng, Minzheng 程敏政. "Diao Jizhuang ci" 弔稽莊詞. In *Huangdun wenji* 篁墩文集, vol. 60, 16–17. *Online Siku quanshu* (Wenyuange Edition).

Ding, Chuanjing 丁傳靖. *Jiayi zhiji gongwei lu* 甲乙之際宮闈錄. Haikou: Hainan chubanshe, 2001. Gugong zhencang congkan 故宮珍藏叢刊62.

Fairbank, John K. 费正清 and Kwang-Ching Liu 劉廣京 eds. *The Cambridge History of China: Late Qing 1800–1911* 剑桥中国晚清史1800-1911. Vol. 10–11. Translated by Liu Guangjing 刘广京. Beijing: China: Social Science Press, 1985.

Fan, Jinlan 范金蘭. "Baishezhuan gushi xingbian yanjiu." 白蛇傳故事形變研究. MA thesis. National Chengchi University, 1991.

Fan, Zhongyi 范中义 and Tong Xigang 仝晰纲. *Mingdai wokou shilüe* 明代倭寇史略. Beijing: Zhonghua shuju, 2004.

Fang, Yong 方勇. *Nansong yimin shiren qunti yanjiu* 南宋遗民诗人群体研究. Beijing: Renmin chubanshe, 2000.

Feng, Menglong 馮夢龍. *Qingshi* 情史. 2 vols. Changsha: Yuelu Shushe, 1986.

Feng, Menglong 馮夢龍. "Yang Siwen Yanshan feng guren" 楊思文燕山逢故人. In *Yushi mingyan* 喻世明言, 63–78. Shijiazhuang: Hebei: Renmin chubanshe, 1990.

Fu, Chengzhou 傅成洲. "Qingjiao xinjin" 情教新解. *Researches on Ming and Qing Dynasties Novel* 明清小说研究 1 (2003): 40–3.

Fu, Mengxing 符梦醒. "The Subversion of the Ghost Narrative: The Pygmalion Myth in Vernon Lee's 'Oke of the Okehurst'" 幽灵叙事的反叛：佛农·李奥克赫斯庄园的奥克中的皮格马利翁神话. *English and American Literary Studies* 英美文学研究论丛 30 (2019): 121–37.

Huang, Fengxiang 黃鳳翔. "Nanwo" 南倭. In *Jiajing dazheng leibian* 嘉靖大政類編, 748–60. Shanghai: Shanghai guji, 1995. Xuxiu Siku quanshu 續修四庫全書433.

Huang, Zhijuan 黃之雋 and Zhao Hong'en 趙宏恩, comp. "Ming Sun Yiren chongxiu ci ji" 明孫以仁重修祠記. In *Jiangnan tongzhi* 江南通志, 370–1. Siku quanshu edition. Vol. 42. Shanghai: Shanghai guji, 1987. Siku quanshu. 四庫全書 508.

Ji, Yun 紀昀, et al. "*Shanhai jing* tiyao" 山海經提要. In *Shanhai jing*, 1–2. Edited by Guo Pu 郭璞. Shanghai: Shanghai guoji, 1987. Siku quanshu. 四庫全書 1042.

Ji, Yun. 紀昀. *Yuewei caotang biji* 閱微草堂筆記. Hangzhou: Zhejiang Guji, 2010.

Li, Fang 李昉, comp. "Li Huang" 李黃. In *Taiping guangji* 太平廣記. Vol. 485. *Online Siku quanshu* (Wenyuange edition).

Liu, Yongqiang 刘勇强. *Huanxiang de meili* 幻想的魅力. Shanghai: Shanghai wenyi, 1992.

Liu, Yongqiang 刘勇强. "Mingqing xiaoshuo zhong de shewai miaoxie yu yiguo xiangxiang" 明清小说中的涉外描写与异国想象. *Literary Heritage* 文学遗产 4 (2006): 133–43.

Liu, Yuan-ju 劉苑如. "Liuchao *zhiguai* zhong de nüxing yinshen chongbai zhi zhengchanghua celüe chutan" 六朝志怪中的女性陰神崇拜之正當化策略初探. *Thought and Words: Journal of the Humanities and Social Science* 思與言 35.2 (1997): 93–132.

Liu, Yuan-ju 劉苑如. "Xingxian yu mingbao: liuchao *zhiguai* zhong guiguai xushu de fengyu—yige 'daoyi weichang' moshi de kaocha" 形見與冥報：六朝志怪中鬼怪敘述的諷喻——一個「導異為常」模式的考察. *Bull. Institute of Chinese Literature and Philosophy, Academia Sinica* 中國文哲研究集刊 29.2 (2006): 1–45.

Lu, Xun 魯迅. *Zhongguo xiaoshuo shilüe* 中國小說史略. Beijing: Renmin wenxue, 1973.

Ma, Boyong 马伯庸. "Wuda gui." 武大鬼. *Zhuanlan.zhihu.com* 知乎专栏, June 5, 2017. https://zhuanlan.zhihu.com/p/27245077.

Pan, Kuang-Che 潘光哲. "Knowledge of the Different Types of Western Political Regimes in Late Qing China: Jiang Dunfu and Wang Tao" 晚清中國士人與西方政體類型知識"概念工程"的創造與變化——以蔣敦複與王韜為中心. *New History* 新史學 22.3 (2011): 113–58.

Pu, Songling 蒲松齡. *Liaozhai zhiyi huijiao huizhu huiping ben* 聊齋誌異會校會注會評本. 4 vols, 2nd ed. Edited by Youhe Zhang 張友鶴. Shanghai: Shanghai guji, 2011.

Qin, Yanchun 秦燕春. *Qingmo minchu de wannming xiangxiang* 清末民初的晚明想象. Beijing: Beijing daxue chubanshe, 2008.

Shan, Shaojie 单少杰. "Boyi liezhuan zhong de gongzheng linian yu yongheng linian" 伯夷列傳中的公正理念和永恆理念. *Journal of Renmin University of China* 人民大学学报 6 (2005): 129–37.

Shanhai jing 山海經. Edited by Tao Fang 方韜. Beijing: Zhonghua shuju, 2009.

Sima, Qian 司馬遷. *Shiji* 史記. Edited by Binghai Li 李炳海. Changchun: Jilin wenyi, 2003.

Song, Xin 宋鑫. "Preface." In *Zhengxu Yeyu qiudeng lu* 正續夜雨秋燈錄, 1–17. Xuan Ding 宣鼎. Changchun: Shidai wenyi, 1987.

Tang, Xianzu 湯顯祖. *Tang Xianzu shiwen ji* 湯顯祖詩文集. 2 vols. Edited by Shuofang Xu 徐朔方. Shanghai: Shanghai guji, 1982.

Tu, Shan. 塗山, comp. *Mingzheng tong zong* 明政統宗. Wanli Edition. Vol. 27. Beijing: Beijing chubanshe, 2000. Siku jinhuishu congkan; Shibu 四庫禁毀書叢刊; 史部3.

Wang, David Der-Wei 王德威. "Hou yimin xiezuo" 後遺民寫作. In *Fo Guang University World Chinese Literature Research Centre*, n.d. http://www.fgu.edu.tw/~wclrc/drafts/America/wang-de-wei/wang-de-wei_03.htm.

Wang, Li 王立, and Hu Yu 胡瑜. "*Liaozhai zhiyi* 'Yecha guo' de fojing yuanyuan ji zhongwai minzu ronghe neiyun." 聊斋志异夜叉国的佛经渊源及中外民族融合内蕴. *Journal of Dalian University of Techology* 大连理工大学学报 31.1 (2010): 96–101.

Wang, Tao 王韜. *Dunku lanyan* 遁窟讕言. Shijiazhuang: Hebei renmin, 1982.

Wang, Tao 王韜. *Manyou suilu; Fusang youji* 漫遊隨錄；扶桑遊記. Changsha: Hunan People's Press, 1982.

Wang, Tao 王韜. *Songyin manlu* 淞隱漫錄. Beijing: Renmin wenxue, 1983.

Wang, Tao 王韜. *Taoyuan laomin zizhuan* 弢園老民自傳. Compiled by Banghua Sun 孙邦华. Nanjing: Jiangsu renmin, 1999.

Wang, Tao 王韜. *Manyou suilu tuji* 漫遊隨錄圖記. Ji'nan: Shandong huabao, 2004.

Wang, Tao 王韜. *Songbin suohua* 淞濱瑣話. Ji'nan: Qilu shushe, 2004.

Wen, Tianxing 文天祥. *Wenshan ji* 文山集. *Online Siku quanshu* (Wenyuange Edition).
Xin, Ping 忻平. *Wang Tao pingzhuan* 王韬评传. Shanghai: Huadong shifan daxue chubanshe, 1990.
Xuan, Ding 宣鼎. *Zhengxu yeyu qiudeng lu* 正續夜雨秋燈錄 2 vols. Edited by Xin Song 宋鑫. Changchun: Shidai wenyi, 1987.
Xuan, Ding 宣鼎. *Yeyu qiudeng lu* 夜雨秋燈錄. 2 vols. Edited by Chunwen Xiang 项纯文. Hefei: Huangshan Shushe, 1995.
Xue, Hongji 薛洪绩. "Cuotuo bushang lingyunzhi, qieyu baiguan jie huanyuan" 蹉跎不上凌云志，且与稗官结幻缘—宣鼎夜雨秋灯录读解纪要. *Social Science Front* 社会科学战线 3 (1988): 252–60.
Yanxia sanren 煙霞散人. *Zhongkui zhuan: Zhangui zhuan, Pingyao zhuan* 鍾馗傳:斬鬼傳,平妖傳. Wuhan: Changjiang wenyi, 1980.
Yeh, Catherine Vance 葉凱蒂. "Wenhua jiyi de fudan—Wanqing Shanghai wenren dui wanming lixiang de jiangou." 文化記憶的負擔. In *The Late Ming and the Late Qing: Historical Dynamics and Cultural Innovations* 晚明與晚清：歷史傳承與文化創新, 53–63. Edited by Pingyuan Chen 陈平原, David Der-Wai Wang 王德威, and Wei Shang 尚伟. Wuhan: Hubei jiaoyu, 2002.
You, Xiuyun 遊秀雲. *Wang Tao xiaoshuo sanshu yanjiu* 王韜小說三書研究. Taipei: Xiuwei zixun keji, 2006.
Yu, Shihao 于师号. *Xuan Ding yu Yeyu qiudeng lu yanjiu* 宣鼎与夜雨秋灯录研究. MA thesis. Nanjing Normal University, 2005.
Yu, Shihao 于师号. "Xuan Ding jiashi ji shengping shiji xinzheng" 宣鼎家世及生平事迹新证. *The Research on Ming and Qing Dynasties Novels* 明清小说研究 1 (2012): 138–50.
Yuan, Mei 袁枚. *Zibuyu* 子不語. Shanghai: Shanghai guji, 2010.
Zhan, Xiaoyong 占骁勇. *Qingdai zhiguai chuanqi xiaoshuoji yanjiu* 清代志怪传奇小说集研究. Wuhan: Huazhong Keji daxue chubanshe, 2003.
Zhang, Bing 张兵. "Yimin yu yiminshi zhi liubian" 遗民与遗民诗之流变. *Journal of the Northwest Normal University* 西北师大学报 38.4 (1998): 7–12.
Zhang, Shoujie 張守節. *Shiji zhengyi* 史記正義. *Online Siku quanshu* (Wenyuange Edition).
Zhang, Yuanyue 张袁月. "Lun Wang Tao dui *Liaozhai zhiyi* fuji gushi de jicheng yu bianyi." 论王韬对聊斋志异扶乩故事的继承与变异. *Study on Pu Songling Quaterly* 蒲松龄研究 1 (2013): 151–160.
Zhang, Zhenguo 张振国. "Lun Xuan Ding *Yeyu qiudeng lu* dui *Qingshi* de chengxu yu chuangxin" 论宣鼎夜雨秋灯录对情史的继承与创新. *Study on Pu Songling Quaterly* 蒲松龄研究 1 (2009): 149–58.
Zhang, Zhenguo 张振国. "Xuan Ding shengzu nian ji wenxian yicun lüekao" 宣鼎生卒年及文献遗存略考. *Journal of Chuzhou University* 滁州学院学报 11.2 (2009): 5–6.
Zhang, Zhenguo 张振国. *Wanqing minguo zhiguai chuanqi xiaoshuo ji yanjiu* 晚清民国志怪传奇小说集研究. Nanjing: Fenghuang, 2011.
Zhang, Zongtai 張宗泰. *Jiaqing beixiu Tianchang xianzhi gao* 嘉慶備修天長縣志稿. Nanjing: Jiangsu guji; Shanghai: Shanghai shudian; Chengdu: Bashu shushe, 1998. Zhongguo difangzhi jicheng: Anhui fuxianzhi ji 中國地方志集成;安徽府縣志輯 34.
Zheng, Tuyou 郑土友, and Wang Xianmiao 王贤淼. *Zhongguo chenghuang xinyang* 中国城隍信仰. Shanghai: Sanlian, 1994.
Zheng, Zongyi 鄭宗義. "Xingqing yu qingxing: lun mingmo taizhou xuepai de qingyu guan" 情欲明清：逹情篇. In: *Qingyu mingqing: Daqing pian*. 情欲明清：逹情篇, 23–80. Edited by Bingzhen Xiong 熊秉真 and Shou'an Zhang 張壽安. Taibei: Maitian, 2004.

Index

Abraham, Nicolas 6
aestheticism and the aesthetic discourse 82, 87, 90
Alberic, Prince 90–94, 108, 110
"among dark woods and black fortresses" 25, 29, 32, 44, 56
amorous ghosts *see under* ghosts
"Amour Dure" (Lee) 81–84, 86, 89, 91–92
Analects (Confucius) 11, 23n45, 23n47, 47n41
ancestors 33–34, 39
"Angel in the House" 15, 113
anomaly: and ghosts as 131; and homosexuality as 90–91; and literary knowledge 133–135; and narration of 3, 14; and norm 14, 42–44, 72, 109, 134–135; and power 5, 13, 135; and suppression of 90–91, 93; and *zhiguai* 12–14, 42–44, 52
anxieties: and gender identity 132; and history 132; and masculinity 16–18, 43–44, 58, 63–66, 71, 85, 121
archaeologist, unnamed *(Louis Norbert)* (Lee) 94–99
Artemisia *(Louis Norbert)* (Lee) 94–95, 98–99
artist, unnamed ("Oke of Okehurst") (Lee) 82, 86–89
Auerbach, Nina 123

baiguan 稗官 (petty officials) 11
"Bai Laochang" 白老長 (The Old White Snake) (Xuan) 42–44
Balthasar Maria, duke of House Luna ("Prince Alberic") (Lee) 90–92, 94
Ban Gu 班固 11
Bao Shu 135–136
Becker, Susanne 126
"Beiji pilin dao" 北極毗鄰島 (The Island of the Northern Extreme) (Xuan) 41

Berthin, Christine 111–112
"Biography of Boyi" (Boyi liezhuan 伯夷列傳) (Sima) 39
"A Biography of Mary" (Meili xiaozhuan 媚黎小傳) (Wang) 67, 71
Bland, Hubert 106–107, 113, 115
A Brief History of Chinese Fiction (Zhongguo xiaoshuo shilüe) (Lu) 22n40, 25, 72n14
Briggs, Julia 7, 104, 106–107, 115–116, 118
British ghost stories 3, 5–8, 117, 132–134
Bronfen, Elisabeth 121–123
Broughton, Rhoda 7
Brown, Anne *(Miss Brown)* (Lee) 89–90, 92
Browning, Robert 83–84

Campany, Robert Ford 40, 71
Carlyle, Thomas 15, 78
Carpi, Medea da ("Amour Dure") (Lee) 83–86, 91, 97
Casanova, Pascale 4–5
Casche, Rodelphe 100
Castle, Terry 100
Casual Records of My Travels (Manyou suilu 漫遊隨錄) (Wang) 17, 52
The Cave of Retreat ("Dunku") 52, 54
centre-periphery 16, 29, 40–41, 44, 60, 66
Chan, Tak-hung Leo 53
chaste women *see under* women
Chen Chun 陳淳 33
Cheng Jiyu ("Planchette Spirits") (Wang) 64
Chiang, Sing-chen Lydia 13
Christensen, Peter 85
Christianity 42, 90–91
chuanqi 傳奇 (tales of the marvelous) 12–13
City God 38, 47n36; *see also* gods
The Classic of Mountains and Seas (The Classic) (Shanhai jing 山海經) 40–41, 54, 59
Cohen, Paul 34, 50

Colby, Vineta 79
colonialism and postcolonialism 2–5, 134
comparative poetics *see* poetics
Confucian discourse and ideology: and ghosts 28, 32–33; and gods and ancestors 33; and history 71; and "moralising by poetry" 詩教 53; and orthodoxy 12–13, 16, 33; and "rectifying the world" 54; on *shi* 士 12, 66, 68, 75n62; on *xing* and *qing* 26
Confucian scholar 17, 30, 33, 51, 54
Confucius 12, 29, 33, 39
Contagious Disease Acts 15
"contra" literature 71
"Core Values of Chinese Socialism" 135
"cosmic collecting" 40
cosmoses 25–26, 28–29, 32, 53, 57, 70
Coupe, Laurence 104, 119, 126
Cox, Michael 8
crises: of category 88–89, 92, 131; of faith 14–16; of gender 88–89, 92
Crosby, Christina 100n3
cross-dressing 88
Crowe, Catherine 7
"cult of *qing*" 13–14, 26–30, 44, 61

Damrosch, David 21nn7–8
Darwinism 14
dead women: aestheticisation of 82, 87; as the ideal woman 92, 105, 119, 121; myth of 104–105, 119, 124; return to life 1–2, 14, 58, 62–66, 78; *see also* women
death: and anxiety 121; and myths 20, 104–105, 119, 121, 124; and women 1–2, 14, 58, 62–66, 78, 82, 87, 92, 104–105, 119, 121–126
demons 32, 41–43, 48n57, 90; *see also* foxes
demon story 42–43
De Quincey, Thomas 121
Derrida, Jacques 6
desire 84–85, 94–95, 100
Dickens, Charles 7
Dickerson, Vanessa 8, 13–15
didacticism 11, 53, 55
Dijkstra, Bram 121–123
discovery and invention 95–98
Dracula (Stoker) 6
Dr. Jekyll and Mr. Hyde (Stevenson) 6
Du Fu 杜甫 29, 45n2
"Dunku" (The Cave of Retreat) 52, 54
Dunku lanyan 遁窟讕言 (Unverified Words from the Cave of Retreat) (Wang) 52–54

Eastwich, Miss ("The Shadow") (Nesbit) 114–118
"The Ebony Frame" (Nesbit) 105, 108–112, 119
Edward, Amelia B. 7
Elegant Nightmares: The English Ghost Story from Le Fanu to Blackwood (Sullivan) 7
Eliade, Mircea 39
Elvira ("From the Dead") (Nesbit) 119, 124
encounters: centre and periphery as pattern 40–41, 44, 60, 66; with the foreign other 35, 40–44, 67, 132–133; between humans and demons 32, 42–44, 62; masculine and feminine 40, 42–43, 62, 71, 133; between past and present 67–68, 81, 105, 107–111; with the uncanny 60, 68–69; with the West 17–18, 26, 32, 34, 43, 52, 68–69, 71, 133
Engels, Friedrich 5
English ghost stories *see* British ghost stories
Enlightenment 14
E-pang Palace 43
Euphorion (Lee) 79–80, 83, 86, 93, 97
"Europe and..." 4–5
"The Examination of City God" (Kao Chenghuang 考城隍) (Pu) 28
exile 17, 50–52, 68, 91
exorcists 42–43, 135–136
Explanation of Words by Beixi (Beixi ziyi 北溪字義) (Chen) 33

Fabian Society 18, 106
"fairy of butterflies" 30
fairy-tale 81, 90, 92–93, 108, 119
fallen women *see under* women
fantastic literature 51, 79, 81
Fan Xiyan and family ("Bai Laochang") (Xuan) 42–43
Faustian contracts 98–99
Fear (Nesbit) 106
female ghost 2, 13, 27, 29, 58, 65, 77, 82; *see also* women, chaste women
Female Gothic tradition 7–8, 13, 104–106, 112, 117–118, 126, 133; *see also* Gothic tradition
female mediums and spiritualists *see* mediums and spiritualists
female revenants *see* female ghost
femininity: and conventional models of 89, 119; and the demonic 42–44; and fear 42; and feminisation 17, 32; as fluid 81; as idealized 77, 88–92, 119, 133; and

Index   151

ideology 18, 81; and masculinity 15, 28, 46n20; as myth 105, 126–127; and the other 19, 32, 40; and power 87
feminism 102n35, 106–107, 118
femme fatale 44, 83–85, 87–89, 108
Feng Menglong: as author 1–3, 14, 135; and concept of *qing* 26–29; *Qingshi* 情史 (History of Love) 26–27; "Yang Siwen Meets an Old Acquaintance in Yanshan" 1–3
Feuchtwang, Stephen 33, 39
Flowers in a Mirror (Jinghua yuan 鏡花緣) 40
foxes: as anomaly 134; and cult of 8–9; and fox spirit 42; as fox woman 42–43; and ghosts 27–29, 52, 56; and *qing* 27–29; and the relation between self and the other 133; and the West 66, 71; and *zhiguai* writers 52, 56
Freud, Sigmund 6, 74n44
"From the Dead" (Nesbit) 105, 119–125
Frye, Lowell T. 113
Fusang youji 扶桑遊記 (Records of My Travels in Japan) (Wang) 52, 75n59

Galatea 87, 89
Garber, Marjorie 88
Gaskell, Elizabeth 7
gender: and bias 95, 97; and constructions or models 68, 88, 92, 120–123, 133; and cross-dressing 88; and encounters between China and the West 17, 26, 32, 42–44, 66–67, 71; and fluidity 77, 81, 91–92; and gender critiques 84, 105–107, 112, 119–121; and houses 126; and identity 18–20, 131–132; and narration and narratives 2–3, 13, 19, 87, 131; and nationhood 16–17, 64; of the self and the other 40; and travel writing 40–41; and Victorian women 8, 113; and *zhiguai* 14, 42
General Records of the Jiangnan Area (Jiangnan tongzhi 江南通志) 35–36
Genette, Gérard 53
ghost chroniclers *see* "historians of ghosts"
ghost conjurers 65, 77–78, 81, 84, 86, 100
"Ghost-Extinguisher" Zhong Kui 31
ghost lovers 3, 108, 111
ghostly retribution *see* retribution
ghosts: as agents of justice 2, 28, 30, 105–108; as amorous 27–28, 30, 32, 44, 124; construction by men 81–82, 84, 104, 132; and dominant narrations 2; as embodiment 2, 111; and fatherly ghosts 29, 39–40, 44; and female or feminine ghosts 2, 13, 27, 29, 58, 65, 77, 82; as gods or ancestors 33; and historical ghosts 29; and history 3, 82, 104; and the making of one 10, 32–33, 109–110; as metaphor 100; as other 78; and the past 3; and power 8, 87; and *qing* 27; and revenge 2–3, 30; and women 3, 32, 46n17
ghosts and gods 26, 33–34, 38–39, 47n36
"ghost's history" *see* "history of ghosts"
"Ghosts in Wuhan University" (Wuda gui 武大鬼) (Ma) 135–136
The Ghost Story, 1840-1921: A Cultural History (Smith) 7
Gilbert, R. A. 8
Gilbert, Sandra 119
goddesses 31–32, 41, 119, 121, 124
gods 19–20, 26, 33–34, 38–39, 47n36
"Good Hunting" (Liu) 134
Gothic tradition: and affinity with women 7; Female Gothic tradition 7–8, 13, 104–106, 112, 117–118, 126, 133; as genre 6–9, 107, 111–113, 116, 118, 125–126; and ghost story as 7; and global Gothic 134; and Gothic heroines 105–106, 116, 126; as literary knowledge 133–134; and myth 104–105; and opacity 105, 107, 112
"A Grand Tour Overseas" (Haiwai zhuangyou 海外壯遊) (Wang) 67, 71
"The Great Buddha in White" (Mohe gaoyinü zhen fo pusa 摩訶縞衣女真佛菩薩) (Xuan) 41
Grim Tales (Nesbit) 106, 108
Gubar, Susan 119

"Haidi qijing" 海底奇境 (Wonderland at the Sea Bottom) (Wang) 67, 71
"Haiwai meiren" 海外美人 (Overseas Beauties) (Wang) 67–70
"Haiwai zhuangyou" 海外壯遊 (A Grand Tour Overseas) (Wang) 67, 71
Hanan, Patrick 42
Han Chinese 58
Han empire 16
Han Fei 韓非 30
Han Sihou ("Yang Siwen") (Feng) 1–2
hauntings: as disruption 87, 89, 100, 111; and Gothic hauntings 105, 107–108, 112, 116, 124; and identity 89; as liberating 89, 123; and the liminal 82, 84; and memory 94; and persistence or endlessness 105, 107, 124; and power 86, 89, 100, 119
Hauntings (Lee) 81, 84

hauntology and spectres 6
Hay, Simon 21n5, 134
Heading South (Zhinan lu 指南錄) (Wen) 37
Helmont, Ida ("From the Dead") (Nesbit) 119–124
Helmont, Oscar ("From the Dead") (Nesbit) 119, 124
Historian, The Grand *see* Sima Qian 司馬遷
historian-artist *see* artist, unnamed ("Oke of Okehurst") (Lee)
"The Historian of the Lost" 逸史氏 *see* Wang Tao
"Historian of the Strange" *see* Pu Songling 蒲松齡
"historians of ghosts" 39, 65, 77–78, 132
historiography: as gendered 19, 78, 100; and Gothic literature 9; and Vernon Lee 80, 83, 93; and *zhiguai* 11–12, 39, 65, 77–78
history: and antiquarian history 50; and art history 78, 100; and boundaries with fiction 92–94, 99–100, 132; and constructions of 18–20, 30, 32, 65, 84–86, 100, 104, 127, 132; and contingency 39; and critical history 50–51, 62, 77; as gendered 77–79; and ghost stories 3, 6, 9–10, 18; and monumental history 50–51, 58, 77; and myth 34, 36, 39–40, 61–62, 71, 104; as narrative genre 132; and national history 26, 30, 34, 44, 58, 65, 77–78, 94, 132–133; and official history 10–11, 14, 18, 34–37, 39, 44, 50–51, 58, 65, 71, 77, 94, 131; and para-history 93–94, 127, 132; and power 10; and the present 34, 57–58; as relativistic and perspectival 80, 86; and uncanny history 51, 57, 68, 132, 136; and unofficial history 9–11, 18–19, 34, 131; *see also* myths
"history of ghosts": as critical history 50, 131; as ephemeral and haunting 136; and excavating the ghost's history 92, 94–97, 99; as gendered 77–78, 81–82; as negotiation 18; as *zhiguai* 134
History of Love (Qingshi 情史) (Feng) 26–27
Hoatson, Alice 113, 115
homosexuality 88, 90, 100; *see also* sexuality
Horror Stories (Nesbit) 106
"The House of Silence" (Nesbit) 105, 124–126

houses 126
Huang, Martin 64
Huang Wan 黃畹 51
Huggan, Graham 5
huli jing see foxes
Hume, Kathryn 112
Hunt, William Holman 15

identities: and cultural identity 44, 50, 52, 67, 71; and gender identity 18–20, 131–132; and identity-building 12–14, 17, 25–26, 29, 53, 57, 71, 77, 131; and identity crises 71, 85, 133; and identity politics 15; and lesbian identity 100; and masculine identity 15, 19, 26, 46n20, 66; and national identity 19–20, 29, 85
ideologies: and Confucianism 71; and fatherly ghosts 40; and gender 118; and history 39, 78, 134; and instabilities 15–17, 71, 131–132; in narratives 14, 19, 36; and socialism 124; and women 81
"The Immortals' Island" (Xianren dao 仙人島) (Wang) 59, 61
invention and discovery 95–98
"The Island of the Northern Extreme" (Beiji pilin dao 北極毗鄰島) (Xuan) 41

Jackson, Rosemary 112
James, Henry 7
James, M. R. 7
Japan 67–68
Jiajing period 35
Jiangnan tongzhi 江南通志 (General Records of the Jiangnan Area) 35–36
Jinghua yuan 鏡花緣 (Flowers in a Mirror) 40
Ji Song 37–39
"Ji Song after His Death Became the Secretary of Minister Wen Tianxiang" ("Ji Song mo wei wenxinguo gong mingmu" 稽聳歿為文信國公冥幕) (Xuan) 34, 37–39
"Jixian yishi" 乩仙軼事 (The Lost Stories of the Planchette Spirits) (Wang) 64–65, 78, 99
Ji Yun 紀昀 12, 53–54
Ji Zhongxian ("Planchette Spirits") (Wang) 60
Joan of Arc (De Quincey) 121
justice: and demons 43; and expressing injustice 81; and Female Gothic tradition 106; and ghosts 28, 30, 105–108, 133; and hauntings 105, 119;

Index

and historical justice 39, 92; and liminal spaces 77, 86; and a quest for 28, 30, 77; and retribution 107; and revenge 2–3

Kandola, Sondeep 88
Kang Xiaofei 8–9
"Kao Chenghuang" 考城隍 (The Examination of City God) (Pu) 28
"Kingdom of Women" 41
Kipling, Rudyard 2–3, 7
Krishnaswamy, Revathi 4–5

lamias 44, 91
Lee, Vernon: "Amour Dure" 81–84, 86, 89, 91–92; as author 7, 18–20, 44, 77–78, 81–82, 85–87, 89–94, 97, 99, 104, 108–110, 124, 127, 132–133; *Euphorion* 79–80, 83, 86, 93, 97; as historian 19, 79–80, 86, 93, 99–100, 104; as lesbian 100; *Louis Norbert: A Two-fold Romance* 81, 94–99; and masculine pseudonym of 79; *Miss Brown* 89–90; "Oke of Okehurst" 81–82, 86–89, 91–92; personal history 78–79, 82–83, 95; "Prince Alberic and the Snake Lady" 44, 81, 90–93, 108–109; "A Seeker of Pagan Perfection" (Lee) 92–93; *Studies of the Eighteenth Century in Italy* (Lee) 78–79
Leed, Eric J. 40
Le Fanu, Joseph Sheridan 7
Legge, James 17, 52
legitimisation acts 53–54, 132
Lewis, Matthew 6
"Liancheng" 連城 (Pu) 27
"Liansuo" 連瑣 (Pu) 27
"Lianxiang" 蓮香 (Pu) 27
Liaozhai zhiyi 聊齋誌異 (Strange Tales from A Chinese Studio) (Pu) 12, 25–28, 30, 40, 44, 53, 56, 69–70, 77, 109, 135
The Light of the World (Hunt) 15
liminality 82, 84, 92–94, 99–100, 131–132
literary knowledges 3–6, 133–135
literati: and the Chinese male 10, 12–13, 16–17, 19, 58, 64–65, 131, 133; and feminisation of 17; of the late Ming 64; of the late Qing 12, 19, 25, 29, 58, 61, 64, 77; and studios of 30, 42, 54; as writers of *zhiguai* 10, 12–13, 17, 19, 77
literature of the anomaly 3, 134–135; *see also* anomaly
Liu, Ken 134
Liu Cuiyun ("Planchette Spirits") (Wang) 64
"Liu Qing" (Wang) 63
Li Yu 李煜 65–66

London Missionary Press 51
"The Lost Stories of the Planchette Spirits" (Jixian yishi 乩仙軼事) (Wang) 64–65, 78, 99
Louis Norbert: A Two-fold Romance (Lee) 81, 94–99
Louis XIV, king of France 96
Lovelock ("Oke of Okehurst") (Lee) 88–89
Lowe, Louisa 15–16
loyalists *see yimin* 遺民 (loyalists)
loyalty 39, 51, 62–66, 68, 71; *see also yimin* 遺民 (loyalists)
Lu, Sheldon H. 67
Lu Meifang and wife ("Haiwai meiren") (Wang) 67–70
Lunacy Law Act Reform Association 15
Luo Wanxiang ("Spirit Lanterns") (Xuan) 37–39
Lu Xun 25

Mabel ("The Shadow") (Nesbit) 114–117
Ma Boyong 135
The Madwoman in the Attic (Gilbert and Gubar) 119
magic painting *see* paintings
Makala, Melissa Edmundson 7–8, 123–124
Man and Maid (Nesbit) 124
Manchus 58
"Man-size in Marble" (Nesbit) 106–107, 124
Manyou suilu 漫遊隨錄 (Casual Records of My Travels) (Wang) 52
marginalised people: and anomaly 3, 13; and ghost stories 14, 17–18, 81, 131, 133; and power 6, 8–9, 86, 135; and unofficial history 9–10, 18, 131; and women 8, 97
Margree, Victoria 107, 113, 120
marriage 112–113, 117–118, 120–121
Married Women's Property Act (1882) 15, 113
Marsh, Arthur ("From the Dead") (Nesbit) 119–124
Marx, Karl 5
masculinity: and anxiety 16–18, 43–44, 58, 63–66, 71, 85, 121; and challenges to 29, 32, 52; and failure of 2, 66; and identity 15, 19, 26, 46n20; and ideology 15; and impotence 17, 64–67; and literati 13, 19, 58, 64; and the masculine as self 28, 40, 42, 44; and models of 68; and nationhood 16–17, 64; and *qing* 28; and women 82, 85, 87–88

Medhurst, Walter Henry 麥華陀 (son of W. H. Medhurst) 51
Medhurst, W. H. 麥都思 (missionary) 51
mediums and spiritualists 15–16, 97
Meiji reform 67
"Meili xiaozhuan" 媚黎小傳 (A Biography of Mary) (Wang) 67, 71
melancholia 63, 107, 111
memory 10, 34, 36, 39, 86
metaphor see spectral metaphor
Mildred ("The Ebony Frame") (Nesbit) 109–110
Minford, John 30
Ming dynasty 13, 26, 28–29, 34–35, 37–38, 58, 64
Ming-Qing dynastic transition 37–38, 58, 64
"Min Yushu" 閔玉叔 (Scholar Min) (Wang) 59–60
misogyny: and aestheticism 87; and the *femme fatale* 90; and myths and tropes 119, 121, 123, 133; and the snake motif 90–91
Miss Brown (Lee) 89–90
"The Moat House" (Nesbit) 104, 108, 115–116, 119
Moers, Ellen 8, 105
"Mohe gaoyinü zhen fo pusa" 摩訶縞衣女真佛菩薩 (The Great Buddha in White) (Xuan) 41
Mongols 37, 58
Moretti, Franco 4–5
"My Last Duchess" (Browning) 83–84
myths: and appropriating myths 18–20, 124, 127; of death 104–105, 119, 124; and history 26, 32, 34, 36, 58, 65; and identity 26, 30; and myth-making 35–36, 39, 44, 51, 58, 105, 119, 127, 133; and mythography 20, 104–105; and mythopoeia 19–20, 104–105; and self-mythification 25, 29–30, 53; and self-mythologisation 71; and women 104–105, 119, 124; *see also* history

narratives: and colonial historical narratives 2; and narrative modes 90, 94–95; narrative of spectrality 9; narrative of the anomaly 3, 14
Nesbit, E.: as author 20, 100, 104–109, 111–112, 116–118, 121, 123–124, 126–127, 133; "The Ebony Frame" 105, 108–112, 119; as feminist 106–107; "From the Dead" 105, 119–125; "The House of Silence" 105, 124–126; "Man-size in Marble" 106–107, 124; "The Moat House" 104, 108, 115–116, 119; and personal history 18, 106–107, 113, 115–116, 118; "The Shadow" 105, 112–118; "Uncle Abraham's Romance" 108, 111, 119
"New Records of the Strange" (Xin zhiyi) (Ma) 135
the New Woman 18, 79, 106, 118
Nietzsche, Friedrich 50–51, 77–78, 86
Night Visitors: The Rise and Fall of the English Ghost Story (Briggs) 7
Norbert, Louis *(Louis Norbert)* (Lee) 94–96, 98–99

Oke, Alice ("Oke of Okehurst") (Lee) 87–88, 95, 97
"Oke of Okehurst" (Lee) 81–82, 86–89, 91–92
"The Old White Snake" (Bai Laochang 白老長) (Xuan) 42–44
Oliphant, Margaret 7
"On History" (Carlyle) 78
"On the Uses and Disadvantages of History for Life" (Nietzsche) 50, 78
Opium Wars (1839-1942, 1856-1860) 16, 32
Oriana (the Snake Lady) 90–94, 108, 110, 133
orthodox and radical typology 119
orthodoxy: and the anomalous 134–135; and fluidity 33; and ghost fiction 10–14; and history 19, 34, 36–37, 50, 58, 68, 71, 131; and masculinity 16, 44; and power 133, 136; and state history 19, 71
Over Her Dead Body (Bronfen) 121
"Overseas Beauties" (Haiwai meiren 海外美人) (Wang) 67–70
Owen, Alex 16

Paget, Violet *see* Lee, Vernon
"The Painted Skin" 畫皮 (Pu) 69
"The Painted Wall" 畫壁 (Pu) 69–70, 109
paintings 109
Pansay ("The Phantom Rickshaw") (Kipling) 2
Pater, Walter 79, 82, 87
Patmore, Coventry 15
patriarchy: and deviancy 15, 91; and myths 20, 119, 126; and power 83–84; and symptoms 28; and Victorian women 8, 15
Peach Blossom Spring *see* "Record of the Peach Blossom Spring" (Taohuayuan ji 桃花源記) (Tao)
Peach Blossom utopia 59–60
Peeren, Esther 8–9
The Peony Pavilion 牡丹亭 (Tang) 13, 27

"The Phantom Rickshaw" (Kipling) 2–3
"philomythus" 133
The Picture of Dorian Gray (Wilde) 6
poetics: comparative poetics 5; poetics of the spectral 6, 14, 131
portraitist, unnamed ("Oke of Okehurst") (Lee) 82, 86–89
postcolonialism and colonialism 2–5, 134
power: and the female medium 15; and ghosts 8, 87, 123; and hauntings 86, 123; and mythopoeia 19; and orthodoxy 133–135; and sexuality 84; and "spectral agency" 9; and *xiaoshuo* 11; and *zhiguai* 13, 134
The Power of Darkness (Nesbit) 106
"Prince Alberic and the Snake Lady" (Lee) 44, 81, 90–93, 108–109
Punter, David 6, 9
Pu Songling 蒲松齡: as author 12–13, 18, 25–30, 32, 39, 44, 53–56, 61, 77, 109; and the development of the cult of *qing* 26–30, 44; "The Examination of City God" 28; as "Historian of the Strange" 39, 53, 77; *Liaozhai zhiyi* 12, 25–28, 30, 40, 44, 53, 56, 69–70, 77, 109, 135; "The Painted Skin" 畫皮 69; "The Painted Wall" 畫壁 69–70, 109; personal history 12; "Self-Record of *Liaozhai*" 53–54; "The Yaksha Kingdom" 69–70
Pygmalion 87, 89, 109

Qi Jiguang 35
Qin, Yanchun 68
qing: as cultivation 27; and the "cult of *qing*" 13–14, 26–30, 44, 61; and the female ghost as embodiment of 14, 44; and reason 27–28; *see also* Feng Menglong
Qing dynasty: and government 16, 51; as time period 28–29, 32, 34, 37–38, 40–41, 61, 64, 67, 71; and *zhiguai* 12, 25–26
Qingshi 情史 (History of Love) (Feng) 26–27
Qu Yuan 屈原 30

Radcliffe, Ann 6, 105, 112
Radcliffean heroine *see under* Gothic tradition
radical typology and myth-making 119, 126
Random Records by the Song River (Songyin manlu 淞隱漫錄) (Wang) 52, 54–57, 69–70

"Ravenna and Her Ghosts" (Lee) 99
"Record of the Peach Blossom Spring" (Taohuayuan ji 桃花源記) (Tao) 59
Records of My Travels in Japan (Fusang youji 扶桑遊記) (Wang) 52
records of the strange *see zhiguai* 志怪 (records of the strange)
Red Cliff 43
Red Palace 90–92
religion 16, 33
Renaissance in Italy (Symonds) 80
retribution 107; *see also* justice
"The Return of the Soul" *see The Peony Pavilion* 牡丹亭 (Tang)
revenants 1–2, 14, 58, 62–66, 78; *see also* spectres
revenge 2–3, 28, 30; *see also* justice
revenging ghost 28, 30; *see also* ghosts
Riddell, Charlotte 7
Robert of Urbania ("Amour Dure") (Lee) 83–84
Rossetti, Christina 15
Rouge Mountain 31–32
Rutledge, Amelia 106

Santangelo, Paolo 30
"Scholar Min" (Min Yushu 閔玉叔) (Wang) 59–60
"A Seeker of Pagan Perfection" (Lee) 92–93
the self: and forming the self 13–15, 18, 30, 51, 62; and foxes 133; and gender 32, 40; and the masculine 26, 40, 42, 44; and the other 14, 16, 32, 40–44, 67, 132–133; and snakes 133; and uncertainty 61
"Self-Record of *Liaozhai*" 聊齋自志 (Pu) 53–54
A Sequel to Yeyu quideng lu 夜雨秋燈續錄 (Xuan) 30
sexuality: and anomaly 90–91; and conceptions of overseas 41; and fear 8, 42; and fluidity 90, 133; and homosexuality 88, 90, 100; and power 84; as transformative 81; as transgressive 90–91, 122
"The Shadow" (Nesbit) 105, 112–118
Shanhai jing 山海經 (The Classic of Mountains and Seas) 40–41, 54, 59
Shenbaoguan 30
"Shendeng" 神燈 (Spirit Lanterns) (Xuan) 34–37, 39
Shiji (The Book of History) (Sima) 31
Shizong (emperor) 35

shi 士 12, 66, 68, 75n62
Siddal, Elizabeth 15
Sima Qian 司馬遷 30, 39
Sinocentrism 41, 50, 66
"Mr. Situ" (Situ ruyi langjun 司徒如意郎君) (Xuan) 41
Six Dynasties 10, 12
Smith, Andrew 7, 15
"Snake Lady" see "Prince Alberic and the Snake Lady" (Lee)
snakes 42–44, 90–91, 108, 133
"Snow White" 119, 121–122, 124
socialism 106–107, 118, 125, 135
socially marginalised people see marginalised people
solitary indignation 46n24, 56
Something Wrong (Nesbit) 106
Songbin suohua 淞濱瑣話 (Trivial Words by the Song River) (Wang) 52, 54
Song dynasty 1, 34, 59
Songyin manlu 淞隱漫錄 (Random Records by the Song River) (Wang) 52, 54–57, 69–70
Song-Yuan dynastic changes 58
Southern Song dynasty 37, 58
Sparkling Water, Castle of 91–92, 109
"spectral agency" 9
spectral metaphor 8
spectres: and hauntology 6; and history 60–61, 66, 68; and power 9, 87, 100; see also revenants
"Spirit Lanterns" (Shendeng 神燈) (Xuan) 34–37, 39
Spiritualism and spiritualists 15–16, 97
Staël, Madame de 78
Stetz, Margaret 91
Stevenson, Robert Louis 6
Stoker, Bram 6
"The Story of Zhong Xiaomei" (Zhong Xiaomei zhuan 鐘小妹傳) (Xuan) 30–32, 41
Studies of the Eighteenth Century in Italy (Lee) 78–79
"The Studio Visited by the Butterfly Fairy" (仙蝶來館) 30
suffrage movement 15, 106–107
suicide: and men's 68, 75n47, 94; and women's 62–64, 66, 74n39
Sullivan, Jack 7
"A Summer Resort" (Xiaoxia wan 銷夏灣) (Wang) 60
Sun Yiren 35–36, 38
Swinbourne, Algernon Charles 91
Symonds, John Addington 79–80

Taiping Rebellion (1850-1864): as destabilising force 16, 25, 32; and ghosts and revenants 36, 62, 64, 66; and trauma 16, 32, 62; and Wang Tao 24n81, 51; and Xuan Ding 29
Tang dynasty 12–13, 70
Tang Xianzu 湯顯祖 13, 26–28; see also qing
"Taohuayuan ji" 桃花源記 (Record of the Peach Blossom Spring) (Tao) 59
Tao Qian 陶潛 59
thief, unnamed ("The House of Silence") (Nesbit) 125–126
Todorov, Tzvetan 51–52, 71, 112; see also fantastic literature
Tolkien, J. R. R. 133
Török, Maria 6
trauma 1–2, 16, 32, 62–63, 66
travel writing 40–41
Trepka, Spiridion ("Amour Dure") (Lee) 82–88, 109
Trivial Words by the Song River (*Songbin suohua* 淞濱瑣話) (Wang) 52, 54
typology 119

the uncanny: and encounters with 60, 68–69; as history 51, 57, 68, 132, 136; and the repressed 6; and women 113
"Uncle Abraham's Romance" (Nesbit) 108, 111, 119
unofficial history see under history
Unverified Words from the Cave of Retreat (*Dunku lanyan* 遁窟讕言) (Wang) 52–54
utopia 58–59, 91, 109

vampires 42, 122
Venetia, Lady (*Louis Norbert*) (Lee) 94–99
Victorian Ghosts in the Noontide: Women Writers and the Supernatural (Dickerson) 8
Victorian Hauntings (Wolfreys) 100
Victorian women see women
voluntarism 25–26, 28–30, 32, 39

Wallace, Diana 8–10
Walpole, Horace 6
Wang, David Der-Wai 58
Wang Shizhen 王世禎 12
Wang Tao 王韜: as author 17–20, 25–26, 29, 39, 44, 50, 52–71, 77–78, 84–85, 99, 108, 132–133; *Dunku lanyan (DKLY)* 52–54; and his involvement in the Taiping Rebellion 51–52; and his

journey to Europe 52; "Liu Qing" 63; *Manyou suilu* 52; "Overseas Beauties" 67–70; personal history 17–18, 50–52, 56–57, 70–71; and prefaces to his *zhiguai* collections 53–56, 62, 67, 69–71; *Songbin suohua (SBSH)* 52, 54; *Songyin manlu (SYML)* 52, 54–57, 69–70; "A Summer Resort" 60; "The Immortals' Island" 59, 61; "The Lost Stories of the Planchette Spirits" 64–65, 78, 99; "Yaoniang Reincarnated" 65–66
"*wenren*" 52
Wen Tianxiang 文天祥 37–38, 60
Wessington, Mrs. ("The Phantom Rickshaw") (Kipling) 2
Westerners and the West: and demonisation of 32, 42–44, 50, 66, 132–133; and encounters with 17–18, 26, 32, 34, 43, 52, 68–69, 71, 133; and feminisation of 32, 42, 44, 67, 133; and instability 14; intrusion of 16, 20, 29, 42, 44, 57, 133; and literature 5, 29; and masculinity 17, 19, 71; practicality of 55–57, 69; and reality 29, 71; as reference point 54–55; as threat 20, 26, 31–32, 57, 61, 71, 133; and Western women 32, 71
White, Hayden 112, 132
White Snake Lady 43–44
Wilde, Oscar 6
Wilson, Charlotte 106
witches 108, 110–111
wokou (Japanese invaders) 35
Wolf, Arthur 33
Wolfreys, Julian 100
woman, unnamed ("The Ebony Frame") (Nesbit) 109–111
"Woman Question" 15
women: and chaste women 50, 62–64, 66; and controlling or fixing women 82, 85, 87–89, 95, 97; and death 1–2, 14, 58, 62–66, 78, 82, 87, 92, 104–105, 119, 121–126; as excluded and manipulated 85, 132; and fallen women 105, 119, 121–124; and gender identity 17–18; and the Gothic tradition 7–8; and history 9–10, 78, 85–86, 131, 133; and ideal women 92, 105, 119, 121; and marriage 112–113, 117–118, 120–121; and masculine anxiety 65–66; and myths 104–105, 119, 124; as other or outsiders 32, 100n3, 109; and power 87; and revenants 1–2, 14, 58, 62–66, 78, and socialisation 117; and Victorian women 8, 13, 20, 79, 105–108, 113, 117, 120, 133; and war 31, 62–64, 108
"Wonderland at the Sea Bottom" (Haidi qijing 海底奇境) (Wang) 67, 71
world literature *see* literary knowledges
Wo Tian 35–39
"Wuda gui" 武大鬼 (Ghosts in Wuhan University) (Ma) 135–136
Wudi (emperor) 31

Xianglin ("Yaoniang Reincarnated") (Wang) 65–66
"Xianren dao" 仙人島 (The Immortals' Island) (Wang) 59, 61
xiaoshuo 小說 (Chinese fiction) 6, 10–12
"Xiaoxia wan" 銷夏灣 (A Summer Resort) (Wang) 60
"Xin zhiyi" (New Records of the Strange) (Ma) 135
Xiongnu 匈奴 (nomadic people) 31–32
Xuan Ding 宣鼎: as author 18–20, 25–26, 29, 32–34, 37–44, 50, 53, 55, 57–61, 65–67, 71, 84–85, 132–133; and autobiography of 29–30, 51; "Ji Song after His Death Became the Secretary of Minister Wen Tianxiang" ("Ji Song") 34, 37–39; as narrator 31, 36; and self-mythologisation of 71; "Spirit Lanterns" 34–37, 39; "The Story of Zhong Xiaomei" 30–32, 41; "The Island of the Northern Extreme" 41; "The Old White Snake" 42–44; *Yeyu quideng lu (YYQD or YY)* 29–31, 53
Xu Mengtu ("The Immortals' Island") (Wang) 61–62
Xunhuan ribao 循環日報 52

"The Yaksha Kingdom" (Pu) 69–70
"Yang Siwen Meets an Old Acquaintance in Yanshan" (Feng) 1–3
"Yaoniang Reincarnated" (Yaoniang zaishi 窅娘再世) (Wang) 65–66
The Yellow Book 90
yeshi 野史 (wild history) 11
Yeyu quideng lu (Records of Rainy Nights under Autumn Lights) (Xuan) 29–31, 53
yimin 遺民 (loyalists) 38, 50–51, 58–66, 68
Yuan Mei 54
Yuewei (Ji) 53–54

Zeitlin, Judith 25, 53
Zhang, Longxi 57, 131
"Zhang A-duan" 章阿端 (Pu) 27
Zhang Shoujie 32

Zheng, Huili 67, 70
Zheng, Lady (Zheng Yiniang) 1–2, 62
zhiguai 志怪 (records of the strange): and affinities with British ghost stories 5–6; as genre 10–12, 69–70, 136; and legitimisation acts 53–54; and *Liaozhai zhiyi* 12; as literary knowledge 133–134; as literature of the anomaly 3; and prefaces 53, 56; and relationship with *xiaoshuo* 6, 11; and relation with history 10–13, 18–20, 34, 44, 50–51, 58, 65, 77, 131, 134; and subjects of 11–14; *see also specific stories and writers*

Zhinan lu 指南錄 (Heading South) (Wen) 37
Zhongguo xiaoshuo shilüe (A Brief History of Chinese Fiction) (Lu) 25
Zhong Kui "Ghost-Extinguisher" 31
"Zhong Xiaomei zhuan" 鐘小妹傳 (The Story of Zhong Xiaomei) (Xuan) 30–32, 41
Zhou Weihuang ("Yaoniang Reincarnated") (Wang) 65
Zhuangzi 莊子 11
Zibuyu (Yuan) 54
Zong Haifan 31, 47n32
Zorn, Christa 78–79, 85–86